WE THE RAPTORS

30 PLAYERS, 30 STORIES, 30 YEARS

ERIC SMITH AND
ANDREW BRICKER

Published by Simon & Schuster

NEW YORK AMSTERDAM/ANTWERP LONDON
TORONTO SYDNEY/MELBOURNE NEW DELHI

SIMON &
SCHUSTER
CANADA

A Division of Simon & Schuster, LLC
166 King Street East, Suite 300
Toronto, Ontario M5A 1J3

This Simon & Schuster Canada edition November 2025

SIMON & SCHUSTER CANADA and colophon are trademarks of Simon & Schuster, LLC

Simon & Schuster strongly believes in freedom of expression and stands against censorship in all its forms. For more information, visit BooksBelong.com.

For information about special discounts for bulk purchases, please contact Simon & Schuster Special Sales at 1-800-268-3216 or CustomerService@simonandschuster.ca.

Book text designed by Paul Dippolito

Manufactured in the United States of America

1 3 5 7 9 10 8 6 4 2

Online Computer Library Center number: 1492462410

ISBN 978-1-6680-6920-2
ISBN 978-1-6680-6931-8 (ebook)

For Shannon and Jackson.

ES

For Charity.

AB

CONTENTS

FOREWORD

By Kyle Lowry

When I was traded from the Houston Rockets to the Toronto Raptors in the summer of 2012, I didn't know what to expect. I certainly didn't know that I would play for the team for nearly a decade, that I would collect a handful of team records, or that I would win the franchise's only championship—so far—in 2019.

What I did know, or thought I knew, was much simpler. There was Canada: Cold weather. Snow. Hockey. That was about it.

I also didn't know that much about the Raptors, who were informally known as the "EuroLeague" team of the NBA, but at least in Toronto I saw a real opportunity: a chance to win, a chance to lead, and a chance to be trusted.

During my first six years in the NBA, I played for two other teams: Memphis and Houston. I got consistent playing time with the Grizzlies but took advantage of an opportunity to become a bona fide starter—and show that I could lead a team—after being traded to the Rockets. However, over time, things just didn't work out in Houston, and it was clear that a deal had to happen. Enter Toronto.

I played nine seasons with the Raptors—over 600 games—making the All-Star team six straight times between 2015 and 2020. And by my final game as a Raptor, in 2021, I had amassed a number of team records that are still very special to me to this day. None of that would have been possible without this incredible franchise, city, or country and, most importantly, the teammates and coaches I had in Toronto over the years—the foundation of any successful organization or career. I cherish those honors and those relationships more than anyone could ever know. Toronto gave me everything that I had dreamt about, all day, every day, since I was a five-year-old kid in Philadelphia: a chance to play and compete at the highest level in the NBA.

The Raptors, Toronto, and Canada also gave me something larger, something I knew I was looking for: a place to call home in my NBA career. Family has always mattered to me. I even chose to attend Villanova University because it kept me close to home: my mom, Marie Hollaway, my grandmama, Shirley Hollaway (gone but not forgotten), and my brother, Lonnie Lowry. Playing at Nova, I was never far from the Hollaway crib in North Philly and a home-cooked meal (and some clean laundry—thanks, Mom!).

Making a home of a city and a country I didn't know a lot about was a huge surprise. When I first arrived, I was simply there to do a job. I had two years left on a four-year deal, with the fourth year being a team option. I knew I was going to play well enough to get my team option picked up. So that was my whole plan: Play two years in Toronto and I'm out.

Little did I know at the time how much this team, this organization, and all of our fans across Canada would come to mean to me. The Raptors took care of every little thing, making my life in Toronto more comfortable. My family—Ayahna, Karter, and Kameron—was also growing and they, too, were starting to feel at home in Toronto. Then there were the fans, who were crazy passionate, who came out every night, and who supported us no matter how good or bad we were—even in the "Tank for Wiggins" era (IYKYK, hahaha). Suddenly I felt like Toronto was the right place to be. It was an easy choice to *want* to stay and ultimately be given the opportunity *to* stay with the Raptors through all those years.

This book is a chance to celebrate those fans and this organization. We say it all the time as Raptors: You're not playing for just Toronto; you're playing for literally a whole country. You go from

Vancouver and Saskatchewan on one side of the country to Halifax and PEI on the other. There's just one NBA team in Canada, but it's also a team with a diverse fan base from all over the world. It's for all those fans that we won the championship in 2019. I've got an Olympic gold medal and I've got personal awards and accolades, but there are just no words to describe the feeling of bringing home a championship trophy to an entire country. It was the craziest thing I ever did in my basketball career.

This is also an opportunity to highlight all the players who made possible everything this team has accomplished. I wouldn't be Kyle Lowry if it weren't for Dwane Casey or Masai Ujiri or DeMar DeRozan. You have to have humility, and even the stars understand that we won't make it without the other guys. *Period.* Guys like Jonas Valančiūnas or Amir Johnson or Chuck Hayes or Lou Williams. I wouldn't be who I am without them and without them saying, "Yo, we gonna follow you." They knew I would ride or die for them, just like I knew they would ride or die for me.

It's because of all of those players that I often get listed as the "GROAT"—the Greatest Raptor of All Time—alongside the team's most iconic players: Vince and Bosh and DeMar and Kawhi. It's an honor, but it starts with Vince, who put Toronto on the NBA map and made people realize that this place isn't just a hockey town, but a top destination in the league.

I also want to thank and acknowledge DeMar. I've told the story nine thousand times: When DeMar was drafted, he was just another guy on the team, until I realized that he wanted to win at the highest level, no matter what, just like me. We were two guys with a passion for competition. I realized it and he realized it too. He's a true leader and he believed in me. Together, we made sure the team did things the right way and that we won.

I loved my time as a Raptor, and it's always a blessing to come back to Toronto and Canada in general. I never tried to leave and I never wanted to leave. I believed in the city. I believed in the country.

I believed in everything that this team and organization were doing. And, most importantly, I truly believed that this was a place where I could help the team win and where we would win—and win big. Today, so many years later, I still get that feeling: the Raptors, Toronto, and Canada are home.

INTRODUCTION

By Eric Smith

Growing up, I was the weird Canadian kid who never played hockey. It was just too expensive. The endless gear, the league registration fees, the rented ice time (not to mention the horrible 6 a.m. practices). It all added up to too much for a middle-class family with at least one parent bound by the erratic hours of shift work. Plus, with costs needing to be multiplied by two, to include my older brother, Adam, hockey was out.

Not playing Canada's national sport was strange—especially in the 1980s. But perhaps even stranger were my go-to sports: baseball, tennis, and, above all, basketball. For all three, equipment was minimal and access to public courts and parks was easy. But when my dad, Alf, installed a hoop above our carport, that was a game changer. It was also an odd sight in suburban Burlington, Ontario, where I grew up, a forty-minute drive from downtown Toronto. Basketball was far from mainstream.

But there I was, day in, day out, summer and winter, first with my brother and then increasingly with my best friend, Justin. Like me, he was a basketball nut. And like me, he had fallen hard for the "Showtime" Los Angeles Lakers and Magic Johnson. The two of us were increasingly inseparable, the basketball oddballs relentlessly getting up shots in either his driveway or mine, playing pickup at an outdoor court at a nearby high school, watching NBA games on the weekend (whenever we could find a broadcast), and poring over box scores in the newspaper. We were joined at the hip in our mutual obsession, held together like two pieces of basketball parquet.

It was a red-letter day when my mom, Carol, and dad finally upgraded our hoop, a weathered plywood construction that had suffered mightily during those same Canadian winters. I was about twelve years old by then, and the new setup felt like everything cool about '80s basketball: a jet-black rim attached to a Huffy fiberglass backboard, erected on a pole rather than hung above the carport. It was also a welcome upgrade for my dad, who had grown tired of me, Justin, and my brother denting the eaves troughs with errant jumpers and failed trick shots.

As the years went by, my basketball obsession only grew. I remember being transfixed by the Larry Bird–Magic Johnson "Choose your Weapon" Converse campaign, just one of the many NBA posters and pennants I had hung on my bedroom walls (Justin had even more). I was so hooked on the game that I'd shovel snow from the driveway in the winter just to get up shots, wearing long johns under my shorts and gloves with the fingertips cut off so I could still feel the ball.

As a sports-obsessed teenager, I started looking ahead, wondering what I might do with my life. As much as I loved basketball, baseball, and other sports, I wasn't good enough to play at a significant level—and certainly not professionally—but what if I could stay connected to sports through broadcasting? And as luck would have it, in my final year of high school, the NBA announced that Toronto and Vancouver would be awarded new franchises, both set to begin play during the 1995–96 season. I would finally have my own hometown team; I would finally be able to attend NBA games to my heart's content. At that point, I had no idea I would eventually cover the team, as my job, for almost thirty years. But the wheels of my career aspirations were spinning.

After graduating from high school in 1994, I was accepted into the School of Journalism at Humber College (now known as Humber Polytechnic), in the West End of Toronto. In my first year at Humber,

I worked for the school newspaper as a student journalist, covering the men's basketball team, which included traveling to games around Ontario and eventually to the national CCAA championships in Montreal.

I had just finished my first year of the journalism program when the Raptors selected Damon Stoudamire as the first-ever pick for the franchise in the summer of 1995. Justin and I actually attended the NBA Draft, which was held at SkyDome, Toronto's massive stadium where the Blue Jays played and which the Raptors would call home until 1999.

The Dome wasn't an ideal venue for basketball—for the players or fans—with the Raptors court sort of nestled between where home plate and first base would ordinarily be for a Jays game. But it didn't matter; the experience was great. Win or lose, the atmosphere was electric: just one giant party, with the Raptors averaging over 23,000 fans per game in their inaugural season, often young people and kids, with music blaring, lights flashing, and the Dance Pak and the Raptor riling everyone up.

I probably went to half a dozen games that opening season, the only year I spent following the team as a fan rather than covering it as an employee. One game predictably stands out, clear as day even from my perch in the upper deck, way out in right field: when the Raptors eked out a win against Jordan's 72-10 Bulls. I still have that ticket stub. The action, from my vantage point, was microscopic, but the vibe was palpable. That late-season game—which literally came down to the final buzzer—cemented the fact that the Raptors and their fan base weren't just happy to be in the league; they wanted to compete with the best in the world every time they hit the floor. Jordan felt Toronto that night.

Prior to the start of the 1996–97 season, while still at Humber, I started as a student intern at the FAN 590 (today known as Sportsnet 590 the FAN), a sports radio station in Toronto. It was truly Internship 101: grabbing coffees, picking up lunches, editing, researching, and generally doing whatever I was told. At the same time, I was always asking for more: to work any shift or job shadow any host or reporter I could.

My persistence paid off in the fall of 1996 when I had the chance to attend the Raptors' second-ever training camp in Barrie, a little more than an hour north of Toronto. I was by no means leading the coverage, but I could hardly believe that my job actually entailed following the NBA. There I was, standing courtside, as Isiah Thomas, another god of my youth and the Raptors' first executive vice president, walked past me. I also couldn't believe what real NBA players looked like up close: their height, their size, their strength, their speed, their athleticism. It's a shock that has never worn off in all my years on press row, and it has never grown old watching players like Shaquille O'Neal, Yao Ming, Kevin Durant, and, most recently, Victor Wembanyama run, jump, and dunk like oversize ballroom dancers. Then of course there was the thrill of seeing the league's all-time greats—Jordan, Kobe Bryant, LeBron James, Steph Curry—up close and personal, day in and day out.

When the calendar flipped to 1997, prior to the collegiate school year officially finishing, the FAN decided to hire me on full-time. That hiring coincided with the sports media ecosystem in Canada expanding from one network to three in less than two years, with both Headline Sports and Sportsnet bursting onto the scene between 1997 and 1998, joining TSN. With various people leaving the FAN to explore opportunities at these new TV stations and elsewhere, doors suddenly opened for me. I hadn't yet turned twenty-two, but I was ready to start my career, in sports, in Toronto. Though I was hired as a producer at the FAN, I was always desperate for new opportunities and experiences—and, most notably, any chances to work on-air. Those opportunities would come over the next few years, including attending more Raptors games as an official member of the press, doing a little reporting, grabbing postgame sound bites, and occasionally even doing on-air hits. Then, at the end of the Raptors' third season, the team's broadcast rights came up. The FAN signed a deal to become the new home of the Raptors, hiring Chuck Swirsky and Jack Armstrong to call the action.

This is when my career truly began to take shape.

The 1998–99 season, Chuck and Jack's first, didn't begin until February 1999 due to a league-wide lockout. That year the NBA season was shortened to 50 games (rather than the usual 82). I was just shy of my twenty-fourth birthday, still producing a show in the afternoons for former Maple Leafs general manager Gord Stellick, before double-shifting on Raptors games at night as the number two to Barry Davis, who had become the FAN's lead Raptors reporter and the host of the station's pregame, halftime, and postgame shows. As part of my job, I was tasked with going to the visiting team's locker room to pull quotes. I still remember the scrum one night after a game in Toronto: reporters and microphones, four people deep, clamoring for a word from Michael Jordan, the best player in the league. Again, I could hardly believe it. From watching "His Airness" play at the Dome from the 500 level in 1996 to asking him questions just a few years later and a few feet away.

The following season, Barry left the FAN and I was elevated to his suddenly vacant seat. Now I was the Raptors beat guy, sitting courtside, hosting the pregame, halftime, and postgame shows, working with Chuck and Jack and even filling in on the broadcasts when needed. For six seasons, I had the honor of learning from two of the best, before both migrated to the Raptors TV broadcast prior to the start of the 2004–05 campaign. Paul Jones, who had already begun cohosting the postgame show with me from time to time, and with whom I hosted a weekly radio show called *Hoops,* was hired by the FAN to become the new color analyst for radio. Paul Romanuk was brought on as the new play-by-play voice, but opted, after just one season, to decamp to Europe, where his wife had been offered a major career opportunity.

A broadcast chair had suddenly opened up. I was now in my

thirties and I got the call from the FAN's program director, Nelson Millman—a call I had been hoping for for almost a decade at that point. I joined Jonesy at the broadcast table and we've now called twenty Raptors seasons together. Today we're the longest-serving broadcast duo in Raptors history, on radio or on TV, and one of the longest-serving broadcast pairs in all of Canadian sports—past or present.

Along the way, I grew up. I got married to my then-girlfriend Shannon. I became a father to my son, Jackson. I've missed weddings, funerals, birthdays, and holidays—you name it—to cover this team over the past three decades. Yet despite all those missed occasions, and time spent away from my incredibly supportive family during the many years I traveled with the team, this is a job I'm grateful for, every single day. It's a privilege to call Raptors games, to work in the NBA, and to bring the sport of basketball to fans every night.

As I grew up with the game and with this team, I also had the opportunity to watch this organization mature and eventually win a championship. It's been nothing short of a life-changing experience. I love covering the Raptors, but above all, I love the special bonds I've watched emerge between this team and these fans, this city, and eventually this country.

This book is an opportunity to share those connections and to explain how a once down-on-its-luck NBA franchise carved out a space in Canadian sports, becoming champions and a model organization in the league along the way. It's also a chance to explore the special bonds that exist between the fans and the team. Raptors faithful have always loved their stars, from Vince Carter and Chris Bosh to Kyle Lowry, DeMar DeRozan, and Kawhi Leonard—among many more. Those guys shaped the team's destiny, and it's through those players that we have defined the team's many "eras" and this book's various sections.

But it was "the guys behind the guys" that fans fell in love with too. The glue guys. The role players. The hustlers. The bench units.

The fellow starters. The second-rounders. The undrafted. These players, in many cases, are just as popular today as some of those all-time greats.

That's one thing I've seen time and again in my nearly three decades covering the team: this special attachment between Raptors fans and players, big or small. If you show love to Toronto, Toronto will love you back. In interview after interview we conducted with former Raptors players, they said the same thing over and over again: the fans made them feel at home in Toronto. For a lot of those players, too, even to their own surprise, their stints with the Raptors proved the best experience of their NBA careers.

We wanted to capture a taste of those experiences and interactions over the team's first three decades. What better opportunity than the Raptors' thirtieth anniversary? We chatted with thirty beloved Raptors players for this book and wrote a chapter about each, highlighting their time with the team and what they liked best about playing in Toronto. But with only thirty chapters and thirty guys, we didn't have enough space for a few. No, scratch that. We didn't have space for *a lot* of players. This book could have had forty, or fifty, or sixty, or even a hundred chapters.

The guys we did interview and write about were all essential pieces in Raptors history—guys who witnessed and were even part of the changes that made the team the organization that it is today. It's a diverse list that cuts across the entire thirty years of the team and offers a true cross section of the players who lived and made history in Toronto.

That's why this book is called *We the Raptors*. The "we" is the fans. It's the city of Toronto. It's the country of Canada. And it's the people all over the world who call themselves Raptors faithful. But that "we" is also the core of this book: those players who came to Canada, who played their hearts out for those same fans, and who became, in turn, part of the fabric of this very city and country.

PART I

THE EXPANSION ERA, 1995–1999

The "Expansion Era." That's one name for it, but plenty of others might have worked.

Maybe, for instance, we should have called it the Stoudamire Era. Taken seventh overall in the 1995 draft, Damon Stoudamire was the Raptors' first star. Before long, "Mighty Mouse," as the 5'10" point guard came to be known, became a fan favorite and was even named the 1996 Rookie of the Year. Behind Stoudamire, the team outperformed the lowly expectations placed on any expansion franchise. The Raptors only went 21-61 that inaugural season, but gave opposing squads grief the whole way, with signature wins over the two teams that would go to the 1996 NBA Finals: the 64-18 Seattle SuperSonics and Michael Jordan's 72-10 Chicago Bulls, the eventual champions. But the Stoudamire Era would come to a hasty close just three seasons in, when Toronto dealt him to Portland after a rocky 11-39 start.

Maybe, instead, we should have called it the Isiah Thomas Era. The Bad Boy Piston was the team's first executive vice president, who, alongside his number two, Glen Grunwald, had planned out a bold and innovative path for the expansion franchise, one that would anticipate a small-ball future dominated by positionless basketball. But that era would also come to a quick close, when Thomas decided to leave the Raptors in late 1997 over conflicts with the new ownership group and after a failed attempt to buy a controlling interest in the franchise.

So maybe it would have made more sense to call it the Change Era. During the team's first few seasons, ownership swapped hands again and again; the team moved from SkyDome to Air Canada Centre; and the organization cycled through GMs and coaches. But all of those changes were fairly typical for an expansion team working through its initial growing pains.

What truly makes this the Expansion Era is the one thing the Raptors could not change: the team's expansion agreement. That agreement defined every move, and every aspect, of how the Raptors—and their fellow expansion team, the Vancouver Grizzlies, who signed a similar agreement—operated, grew, drafted, and improved during the team's earliest years.

According to the agreement, the Raptors could only spend two-thirds of the league cap during the team's first few seasons, an artificial ceiling that prevented the franchise from bidding competitively on quality free agents and that hampered the team's efforts to retain talent. The agreement also barred the Raptors from winning the NBA Draft lottery during the team's first four seasons, which meant Toronto had to give up the first pick of the 1996 draft, which went to the 76ers, who selected Allen Iverson.

Handcuffed by the provisions of the agreement, the Raptors only truly exited the Expansion Era by the end of the team's fourth season. Like so many other things around Y2K, 1999 was a watershed year for the Raptors. In February 1999, they finally moved into their new home at the ACC. It was also, most clearly, the start of a new era under the team's first future megastar, Vince Carter, who was selected fifth overall in the 1998 draft by the Golden State Warriors and who was immediately acquired by the Raptors. Carter made an instant impact, winning Rookie of the Year. It was the dawn of a new age: Vinsanity.

Before Carter took over the team, though, it was the Expansion Era, a period defined by constant change and continual growth as one of the NBA's newest teams tried to find its feet and figure out just what type of organization the Raptors would become.

1

Tracy Murray (1995–1996, 2001–2002)

Tracy Murray was at a crossroads. It was the fall of 1995, and the twenty-four-year-old wing had suddenly found himself sidelined in his still-young NBA career.

After being selected 18th overall by the San Antonio Spurs in the 1992 draft, Murray had been traded a week later, first to the Bucks and then to the Trail Blazers. Led by Clyde Drexler, Portland had just gone to the 1992 Finals, losing in six games to Michael Jordan's Bulls. For Murray, the Trail Blazers looked like a great opportunity. But the team had big ambitions for the coming season and, unfortunately for the rookie, developing their newest acquisition was not one of them.

From a starter and star during his high school and college years to a bench player rarely called upon, Murray was hit hard by the change in role—and status. As a senior at Glendora High School in California, he had led the nation in scoring, averaging a breathtaking 44.3 points per game. That success translated to the NCAA. As a junior at UCLA, Murray averaged 21.4 points and 7 rebounds while leading the Pac-10 in three-point shooting at a 50 percent clip, helping the Bruins to an Elite Eight appearance. He was also twice named to the Pac-10 All-Conference team. "I went from starting my whole life, even in college, to hardly ever playing at all my first two years in the NBA," he recalled in an interview with us. "I was rotting at the end of Portland's bench."

As a Trail Blazer, he was just another guy, a rookie who was still earning his coach's faith. That part, at least, Murray understood. "Rick Adelman is a Hall of Fame coach. He had just come from thc Finals and he had a core of guys that he believed in and that he trusted. He was going to ride with those horses. There was nothing that I could do or say at twenty years old that was going to change their minds."

Murray saw increased playing time during his second season with the Trail Blazers, in 1993–94, thanks in large measure to injuries to the team's aging vets, including Drexler. His shooting form also returned, offering a glimpse of who he was in college and would later become in his career. Murray led the entire league from three, shooting a blistering 45.9 percent.

Things, unfortunately, did not go so well for the team. With their missing starters, Portland foundered in the playoffs, losing in the first round. In the offseason, the Trail Blazers decided to pivot. Adelman and general manager Geoff Petrie were let go; in their stead, P. J. Carlesimo and Bob Whitsitt were installed. The roster also got a makeover. Just before the 1995 trade deadline, the face of the team, Drexler, was sent to the Rockets along with Murray.

Houston had just won the 1994 championship, led by Hakeem Olajuwon and coach Rudy Tomjanovich. The team repeated, winning the 1995 championship, but Murray played only 8 minutes per game. It was as if the third-year player were a rookie all over again. "I was never getting consistent minutes. Most of those minutes were garbage-time minutes or fill-in minutes when somebody got their breather."

Unsurprisingly, Murray once again found it hard to maintain his confidence. "Every kid dreams about being an NBA All-Star, the guy that they're always showing on TV, but everybody can't be that. The hardest thing for a lot of us to do is to settle into a role. Mine was not playing at all. I wasn't in the best shape in the world, not physically or mentally. I did not really understand that as a young person. All I knew was, 'I'm going out here, I feel like I'm doing well, and I'm not playing.' There was a lot I was dealing with, and I didn't know how to handle it."

When the 1994–95 season ended, his third in the league, Murray hit his crossroads.

He was technically a free agent, but all signs pointed to the back-to-back champs re-signing him. Houston even protected Murray during the 1995 expansion draft, meaning neither the Raptors nor the Grizzlies could poach him. "They were going to re-sign me, but then they changed directions on what they wanted to do with the team." Houston was simply eager to keep winning, not developing future rotation players, and even traded for Charles Barkley. The result? "Bye-bye, young guys."

Murray suddenly found himself between a rock and hard place. "They protected me during the expansion draft, so I wasn't able to go to either team. Now they're not going to re-sign me. Now, *no one's* knocking on my door. I was sitting there, hurt, confused, angry. There were a lot of built-up emotions." That crossroads also entailed a long look in the mirror. "I was only twenty-four, but my career was over," Murray thought. "If I went overseas, I probably wouldn't have come back."

It was just one more challenge in a short career that had been inching forward, only to take a step back. But it was also something he could handle, having faced such hurdles pretty much since day one. "I've had ups and downs," Murray told us. "I've always had to fight. I was a chubby kid, with a bad hip and big feet. I wasn't supposed to be in the NBA. At fourteen years old, I had surgery on my left hip and they told me I'd never play again. They killed my dreams at fourteen years old. My parents and I went and got second, third, fourth, and fifth opinions. Finally we found someone would put me back together and said I would be fine. But at fourteen years old—that was tough."

Murray's parents, Bob and Candy, had also prepared him for the obstacles that mark the life of a pro. "I doubted who I was sometimes. When I was down-and-out, and I needed that uplifting, my dad would do the uplift. Dad jumps on a plane. We go in the gym and shoot. We watch old videotapes. 'This is where you can be better. This is where you can get your shot. *That's* who you are.' It was tough love and 'Get your butt back in the game.' I've always had that rock with me. My dad would always take care of the basketball side. My mom would take care of the academic side and help me with the business side. She was also an athlete, so I would be getting cosigns from mom. If I was on the speakerphone with my dad, she would say, 'Yeah, he's right! You need to listen to this!'"

With no one knocking for his services in the summer of 1995, Murray went back to Los Angeles. "I'm at home killing myself, making sure I'm in the best shape, so if I'm blessed enough to get in a situation, I'm going to come in there and hit the ground running."

While he was in LA, the two new expansion franchises were holding off-season workouts. He decided to reach out to Isiah Thomas, who was by then the executive vice president of the Raptors. Murray had met Thomas while still playing for Portland, when the Trail Blazers had faced Detroit. At the time, Thomas could tell that Murray had promise but couldn't make sense of his role in Portland. "What are they doing with you over there?" Thomas asked.

"Nothing," Murray scoffed. "Come get me."

Thomas, the savvy vet, thought Detroit could use the shooter. The Pistons never traded for him, but Thomas filed it away. "He ended up coming to get me years later when he was an executive in Toronto," Murray remembers. "We had some honest conversations, but my agent kept wanting to get more money. I said, 'Give me Isiah's number. Let me talk to him.' Isiah told me the situation. I said, 'Look, it's not about money for me right now. It's about reestablishing myself and getting an opportunity. Send me a plane ticket, and I'm coming.'"

Thomas agreed, signing Murray to a one-year, minimum contract on November 1, 1995. Two days later, the Raptors had their first-ever NBA matchup, against the New Jersey Nets, at SkyDome. Unbelievably, they won that game, 94–79. Murray played 19 minutes off the bench—a blessing, given his struggles to find regular court time in Portland and Houston—scoring 9 points with 3 rebounds, 2 steals, and an assist. That opening-day performance boded well. Murray, in fact, played all 82 games that season, eventually earning a spot in the starting lineup in late February. That first year with the Raptors turned Murray's career—and mindset—around. "I was very thankful for the opportunity in Toronto. It was somewhat like being a rookie again. It was a rebirth of my attitude."

With the Raptors, Murray had finally found an NBA support network. "Isiah became a big brother to me. He'd see me in practice get a little feisty or hit some buckets. Everybody's talking trash, everybody's competitive. Isiah would walk by, and he would look at you with that smile and say, 'I see you. I see it.' See what? 'You a gangster. I know it.' I'm sitting there, wondering what he's talking about. But what he was doing was making me even tougher. He knew I was a nice guy—I was peaceful, happy-go-lucky—and he was retooling me. I was becoming a different animal up here," he says, pointing to his head. "Those first three years in the NBA broke me down. He got me back to that animal status."

Equally important were his coaches, who not only gave him the space to develop his game but also encouraged him to be more aggressive. "Brendan Malone played me a lot. He let me play through my mistakes and deserves credit for that." He also watched his confidence flourish under John Shumate, an assistant coach for the Raptors between 1995 and 1998. "Some of the things he said to me I had never thought about. 'Damn, you're not just a shooter, you're a scorer too,'" Shumate told Murray. "'That's a rare bear,'" Murray laughs today. "That's another confidence thing that just sent me through the roof."

Suddenly, he was no longer just a bench guy, someone brought on to shoot a three here and there. Now he was a critical role player playing alongside *other* starters, including NBA vets like Willie Anderson and Alvin Robertson. "I knew about those guys. I had watched them for years, but now to get to be in practices and soak up the knowledge from them, it was huge." He even came to appreciate a newfound synergy with his former rival and the Raptors' rookie star. "I played against Damon Stoudamire when he was at Arizona. I was at UCLA. It was a bitter rivalry, boy. But when we teamed up together, that was a nice one-two punch. Damon was incredible."

That on-court energy filtered down from the top. Everywhere Murray looked in Toronto—from ownership to the end of the bench—he saw a group willing to go the extra mile to help the franchise succeed. It was clearly a team finding its feet, but it was finding its feet *together*. There was perhaps no better embodiment of that solidarity than the so-called Hood at the back of the team plane. "The 'Hood' was a bunch of guys that liked being around each other," Murray says with a laugh today. "Loud music playing, domino games, dice games, and card games at the back of the plane. We're all back there, vibing out, having a good time, enjoying each other's company. That's all that was. John Bitove Jr. was back there with us. And he's *the owner*. That's somebody who cares about the people on the team. That doesn't happen in the NBA. Owners are owners. Management, management. Not that year. Everybody genuinely cared about each other. Owners, general managers, coaches—everybody together. That doesn't happen in a regular organization."

That culture also cultivated a help-at-all-costs willingness. "Everybody was doing more than their job, even in the office, multitasking like crazy. That was the perfect crew." Doing more was essential. At the time, many argued that basketball could never succeed in

Canada. As Murray recalls, "When I first got there, hockey was all over the place. The Blue Jays had just won back-to-back World Series in 1992 and 1993. We were hardly even being talked about. We were fighting for visibility. We were fighting for eyes. We were fighting for an audience. We were fighting for fans."

The team took those challenges head-on, connecting with Canadians across the country. "We must have hit every city in Eastern Canada. Literally, from Nova Scotia to Barrie down to Niagara Falls. Whether it's preseason games, appearances, after practice, going with the Raptors' Dance Pak members and driving two hours somewhere for an autograph signing. We hit everything."

With increased playing time, Murray also understood that his role on the team was larger than the things he did on the court. "That first year we had to go above and beyond what we normally do to sell the game of basketball. It was a grind. People on the team had to be willing to go do more, but we had so much fun with each other. There was never a time that year where I felt like it was a job."

That grind also opened Murray's eyes. "I know what the stars do. I don't envy that. That's why they get paid the big bucks. They're in corporate meetings, they're helping put the team together, they're chairmen of charities, they're doing public service announcements, commercials, autographs—they're doing *everything* to sell the game and to help the organization flourish." As a shooter, he knew how to fill in gaps, even the promotional holes that opened up around the team's overtaxed star, Stoudamire. "I'd be in the middle of a nap. Sometimes Elaine Quan, a member of the community relations team, would be like, 'Dude, I need you.' I'm like, 'All right, where are we going? What are we doing? Let's do it.'"

By the end of the season, Murray unsurprisingly wanted to re-sign with the Raptors, the only team that had ever given him major minutes on court.

The only problem? Murray was so good that Toronto could no longer afford him.

Under both the Grizzlies' and the Raptors' expansion agreements, each team could only spend two-thirds of the league cap during its first few seasons. As a result, the Raptors could only offer Murray a 20 percent raise on his salary of $250,000—a stingy bump for an 82-game stalwart averaging more than 16 points per game and shooting 42 percent from behind the arc. Today, Murray is still steaming about the league's restrictions. "I fell under a *bullshit* rule. I got screwed out of the place I wanted to be, because I couldn't make more money. I already took a hit. I was making the minimum and being taxed like that up there. They couldn't even re-sign me to what I wanted or what I deserved. They needed to make a Tracy Murray exception!"

Toronto's hands were tied. "Isiah had a figure that he was able to go to." But it came with a catch. "You have to wait two years for it, pal," Thomas told Murray. He was torn. Toronto was the first team that had embraced him, giving him significant playing time and an important starting role. Plus, Murray felt like he was at home. "Toronto is unbelievable. It's multicultural. The restaurants are great. The people are fantastic. It was the cleanest city I'd ever been to. There was no violence. I was in heaven up there. They embraced me, so I loved them."

That internal struggle got a lot harder when the Washington Bullets, renamed the Wizards the following season, swooped in with a juicier offer: a seven-year deal worth $17 million. Once again, it was Thomas looking out for his guy, even if it hurt his team. "During negotiations, I was always talking to Isiah and I said, 'Washington came with that figure.'" Thomas understood, encouraging his mentee to accept the plum deal: "Man, go take care of your family."

In the span of one season, Murray had made the leap from peripheral bench guy to in-demand starter. But it was hard to celebrate his success. "I was in tears when I left Toronto. It was the most bittersweet—with an emphasis on *bitter*—deal, which I had to take. I didn't want to leave the only organization and city that embraced me like that."

His love of the Raptors also showed over the years in the box score. "If you treated me shitty, then oh yeah, you're on my hit list. I'm circling you on the schedule. So Portland always got it; Houston always got it. But I didn't have any animosity towards Toronto."

In Washington, Murray was also never as happy as he had been with the Raptors. After four years in DC, he was traded to the Denver Nuggets just before the start of the 2000–2001 season. Just a few months later he was moved again—and, in a stroke of luck, returned to his adopted home. In January 2001, Murray was sent back to Toronto.

He suddenly became the rarest of the rare in an organization that had only existed for a few years: a two-time Raptor. Between those stops, he could see how the team had changed. The organization had perhaps lost the us-against-the-world grind that had made it special. But it was also taking important steps toward becoming not just a legitimate NBA team but a model franchise. "Toronto was so groundbreaking. They were the first ones to provide pregame meals, during and after shootaround, to have a massage therapist, and to give access to the practice facility—anytime I wanted—to shoot and work out in the weight room. That's one thing I've always respected about the organization. They always did stuff slightly different from everybody else. It was awesome."

From the outside, all those changes weren't so easy to see at first. But publicly, the Raptors had entered a wholly new epoch. "It was the Vince Carter era. Now you had a superstar. We had come a long way. It was awesome to see Vince night in, night out."

Like the organization, though, Murray had also changed. He was now an older player, with a raft of injuries behind him, from a torn ligament in his shooting wrist to lingering hip problems, including bone chips and spurs. An aging vet, he simply had to slow down. "I didn't come back the way I was before. I had to shorten up my routine because, as you get older, you need your legs. You can't go out there and do an hour of shooting. I couldn't do the same routine and still go out there and give you the same results during the game because my legs weren't the same."

Sadly, his second stint in Raptors purple lasted only a year. In the summer of 2002, Murray was shipped to the Los Angeles Lakers. It hit him hard again. "I didn't want to leave, even the second time around. I wanted to finish my career there." Still, he embraced the new challenge. "I was going home, back to LA, back to the Lakers. I thought it was going to be a good move. But it was downhill from there." When that big seven-year contract finally expired at the end of the 2003 season, he signed as a free agent with the Trail Blazers. His second time back in Portland was short-lived, however, and the team waived him later that fall, putting an end to his NBA playing days.

Today Murray is back in LA, calling Bruins games as an analyst with the UCLA Sports Network. He was even inducted into the UCLA Athletic Hall of Fame as a member of the 2021 class. Three decades later, he still looks back fondly on those hardscrabble days of the Raptors' first season. "We had a bunch of guys on the team that nobody wanted. We were all guys at the end of the bench. We were all guys in search of a second chance—with the exception of Damon and Jimmy King," the Raptors' second-round pick. "We all needed a shot somewhere to establish ourselves." The Raptors gave them, and him, that shot.

2

Jimmy King (1995–1996)

It was the summer of 1993, in Ann Arbor, Michigan, and Jimmy King couldn't believe what he was hearing. "An NBA team in Canada? In Toronto? No way." And yet it was coming straight from the horse's mouth: Isiah Thomas, former Pistons Bad Boy, an NBA champion, one of the greatest point guards of all time, and a future Hall of Famer.

Even still, the words didn't make sense to King. By then he was going into his junior year at the University of Michigan as a member of the "Fab Five" alongside Chris Webber, Jalen Rose, Juwan Howard, and Ray Jackson. Together they had revolutionized college basketball both on and off the court, becoming the first team of freshmen to start in an NCAA championship game in 1992 and one of the greatest D1 recruiting classes ever.

Yet here was Thomas telling King about some hypothetical Canadian NBA team. "I was in Ann Arbor and Isiah was there in business attire," the former Wolverine told us. "We just started rapping. He said, 'I'm going to be vice president of basketball operations for an NBA team in Toronto.'" It was all a bit hard to swallow—especially Thomas's unexpected promise to King, who was still years away from the pros. "If you are still on the board," the future Raptors exec told the college player, "I'm going to draft you."

Rumors about Toronto getting a professional team had circulated since the late 1980s, with the NBA even confirming a planned expansion north in 1992. But the official announcement wouldn't come until November 1993. "At the time, I was like, 'Toronto?'" King recalls, shaking his head. "I hadn't heard anything about a new team yet. So in my head, I was like, *Yeah, whatever. That's not going to happen.*"

Still, it was hard not to contemplate what he was hearing from Thomas, somebody who had served as a mentor to him ever since King had first arrived in Ann Arbor as a wide-eyed teenager out of Plano, Texas. During the summers in Michigan, Pistons players would gather at St. Cecilia's Gym in Detroit for open runs. It was a basketball rite of passage. "St. Cecilia is like the Mecca of basketball for Detroit," King explains. "Any hooper that comes through there—out-of-town hoopers, hoopers that are native to the Detroit area, even the pros—has to grace the courts of St. Cecilia. It's like Rucker Park in New York."

It was no different for King and his Michigan costars, including Howard, from Chicago, and Webber and Rose, two Detroit natives. Before they were the Fab Five, even before they were Michigan freshmen, the future Wolverine sensations could be found at St. Cecilia's Gym alongside various Pistons, including Thomas, Joe Dumars, Mark Aguirre, Bill Laimbeer, Dennis Rodman, John Salley, Vinnie Johnson, and James Edwards. "In the late summer, prior to our freshman year, before we actually even got on campus, we never had official practice," King says. "We were just having open runs at St. Cecilia."

Going head-to-head with one of the most feared teams in the NBA was both thrilling and eye-opening. "It was the *whole* squad," King recalls. "Playing against Isiah and Joe, arguably one of the best guard duos in the league, one of the best defenders and rebounders in the league in Rodman, one of the most underrated big men in the league in Bill Laimbeer, and great role players like Vinnie Johnson, the

Microwave. Those guys were monsters. It was a dream come true. You don't really process it, though: 'You're here with the Bad Boys.' You're just playing basketball with perennial NBA All-Stars and you're grateful for the opportunity to learn from them in real time."

Those runs would also reveal the jump that the Fab Five would need to make, not only from high school to college hoops, but eventually from the NCAA to the pros. "We would have games where we'd go back and forth. Then it would be game point and they would kick it to another gear—a pro gear that we had no clue about," King says, thinking back to those daunting battles. "Those were the moments that we were like, 'Oh my God. There's a whole different gear we have to rise to if we want to be recognized as great basketball players or a great team.' We cut our teeth early and appreciated it."

Over the years, those summer runs would continue in both Detroit and Ann Arbor against the Pistons. Along the way, King grew closer with the team and especially Thomas, who proved a willing mentor to the budding stars. "I developed a relationship with Isiah and the rest of the Bad Boy squad. They really helped us set the path to what we wanted to be as the Fab Five. Battling against the Bad Boys on the court gave us great confidence. And then learning from them off the court—the little intricacies of the business of basketball—those things were invaluable."

Thomas in particular was always willing to coach young guys up. "Those are the things that Isiah is known for," King said. "He takes mentoring seriously. He loves it. He's always been that way. He was that way when he was still a player. He was showing guys proper techniques and things that can help them in their careers."

Along the way, King and Thomas remained in contact as the younger player's career at Michigan flourished. Webber left Ann Arbor for the NBA in 1993, followed by Rose and Howard the next year. By the time King was a senior, during the 1994–95 NCAA season, he was leading the team alongside Ray Jackson while averaging

14.7 points, 5 rebounds, and nearly 3 assists per contest. Like Webber, Rose, and Howard before him, King had his sights firmly set on the NBA.

Now it was the night of the 1995 NBA Draft—and it was happening for the first time ever outside of the US, in Toronto's SkyDome, to mark the inception of the league's newest franchises: the Raptors and the Vancouver Grizzlies. King was uncertain where he would land. "There were a couple of teams that I was talking to during that time," he told us. "The San Antonio Spurs, the Phoenix Suns, the Chicago Bulls, and a few other teams sprinkled in there." King didn't expect to go in the first round—some draft experts had even left him off their draft projections altogether—so the four-year college player sat tight, watching the picks tick by, one after another, all the way into the second round.

Then the Raptors were on the board with the 35th pick. Thomas, by then executive vice president for the team, kept his promise to King from so many years earlier. "When the spot came up with Toronto, Isiah drafted me." The fans in attendance roared their approval. "That was the greatest moment of my life," King said.

Shockingly, King had forgotten his old mentor's promise—all that pie-in-the-sky nonsense about an NBA team in Toronto, Thomas running it, and King's guaranteed selection. "I completely forgot about it. I remembered it when I actually took my first official visit to Toronto after being drafted. We were in the office walking around, meeting all the employees, and Isiah reminded me of the moment he put the bug in my ear. He was like, 'I told you I was going to draft you if you were on the board.' And he did."

King was finally in the NBA. But as a second-round selection, he knew he was facing an uphill battle to earn a spot on the roster. "As second-rounders, we didn't have guaranteed contracts. You got to make the team." Being drafted late also had knock-on effects.

He was the second-ever Raptors pick, but he was also, therefore, playing behind the team's first-round pick, Damon Stoudamire. "I had to fight for minutes. Damon set a rookie record of playing forty-one minutes a game, which is crazy. I worked my tail off in practice, at any position that I might fit in, to get those six or seven minutes on court. When I walked into practice, that was my game time. I made sure: I'm going to show you I deserve to be on the court. Ask Damon today: Who was one of thc hardest players he ever played against? It was me."

Throughout his year in Toronto, King's relationship with his coach, Brendan Malone, remained positive and productive. He also proved a formative mentor during King's—and what turned out to be the coach's—lone season with the Raptors. "I was a rookie, trying to find my place. He always had a great way of making you feel comfortable. The relationships I had with Brendan and the rest of the coaching staff, including assistant coaches John Shumate and Darrell Walker, those guys helped me learn the pro game. The experience was great."

Being a second-round pick presented one set of challenges. But transitioning to the NBA as a former member of the Fab Five was something else. "We all had different battles to fight," King recalls. "Chris was traded immediately after winning Rookie of the Year. Juwan had a hundred-million-dollar contract but became a journeyman. Jalen was drafted as a lottery pick by the Denver Nuggets, but he hardly played his rookie year, and then they traded him to Indiana."

Like his fellow Wolverines, King had been freighted with the impossible weight of his own celebrity. He was, and would always be, part of the Fab Five, something for which he would be both celebrated and seemingly punished. He was not Webber, not Rose, not Howard, the logic went, but one of the other two: a mere supporting player on college basketball's most electric squad. Jackson, in fact, went undrafted and spent several years in the Continental Basketball Association (CBA) while shuttling between the pros in France, Argentina, and Venezuela.

"Being a part of the Fab Five was detrimental to my career, and it was harder for Ray and me," King explained. "We were toiling and flipping and floundering, trying to scrape to get on a team. We were looked upon as being subordinates at Michigan and I was looked upon as a supporting player. That's something that I had to fight. Every time I went to a camp, they were always surprised at all the other things that I could do, because of the sacrifices I had made at Michigan."

Though the NCAA spotlight had given the players fame, the media attention soon soured, with the team being punished for the very qualities that had made them so attractive both on and off the court. One would have thought that the Wolverines' starting lineup, dressed in baggy shorts, black socks, and black sneakers, were the Five Horsemen of the NCAA Apocalypse. "The ones who were put off thought that we were cocky or brash," King recalls. "But the truth is that we were confident. We weren't kids who were disrespecting the game. We respected the game. We put the hours in. We didn't cut corners. We didn't cheat the game. We didn't do anything detrimental on the court. We didn't get into fights. We didn't spit on people. We didn't step on people. We didn't kick people. We didn't trip people. We played the game. We just didn't give a damn. We were different. And for all of that stuff, we were vilified."

In retrospect, it is hard not to read the reception the team often got as coded racism—at least from some—with all the fumbling, ambiguous talk about "respecting the game" being little more than a weak front for skeptics who were threatened by the idea that five unapologetic Black freshmen were becoming the face of collegiate athletics. Even worse, in light of the US Supreme Court's 2021 decision in *NCAA v. Alston*, which confirmed that the NCAA's restrictions on compensation violated antitrust law, paving the way for name, image, and likeness (NIL) deals that are everywhere in college sports now, it's hard to argue that the Fab Five's advocacy on behalf of their own future financial security was anything more than a prescient understanding of the NCAA's systemic injustices. While still at Michigan, all five players understood that they were being used by the university, the NCAA, and the corporations that had benefited from their electrifying play and on-court panache. "They would come in and bring us huge duffel bags of gear that they couldn't sell," King recalls. "We would sift through that gear and, anything we liked, that's what they ended up selling. We didn't get a dime for that. That's why we wore shirts without names or monikers or trademarks. That was our way to protest what was going on."

The sartorial protests rubbed onlookers the wrong way. So, too, did their calls for fair compensation. "It was a weird time. We started speaking out about what is now NIL. We knew the odds of all five of us making it were slim. It was just a safety net. And honestly, that's just good business. We were no dummies; we could see what was going on around us—the exchanges, the money, the benefits—and we were not getting anything."

The five players understood the NCAA's rules, but nonetheless hoped to secure some financial security for the decades that would succeed their collegiate and pro careers, if they were lucky enough to make the NBA. "We wanted to have a meeting with Nike. We went to Steve Fisher, our coach, and asked him. We cooked up the grand idea of coming up with a stipend, in case none of us or some of us didn't make the NBA. That's when we started getting pushback and started getting vilified. It took a month or so just to get the meeting."

According to King, when the Wolverines finally sat down with Nike execs, the conversation went nowhere, with the team's sponsors using the NCAA's antitrust provisions to shield them from compensating college basketball's most valuable assets. Those gestures of resistance and the Fab Five's outspokenness hurt the players' careers, even after four of them had broken into the NBA. "Even when I got into the league, players called me at times, respectfully and disrespectfully, 'Fab Five.' There was a lot of jealousy and a lot of hate."

Life as part of the Fab Five was not all bad, of course, and the glaring spotlight had even set King up for his NBA future. "The transition wasn't difficult for me. I was prepared, being at the University of Michigan with all of the media attention. I already had the experience of four years of that at the highest level in college as media darlings and media villains. When I got to the NBA, it was second nature." More importantly, he was in the NBA. "I was still living the dream. I was still on the team. I was still playing. I was still learning the professional game and I had great mentors—Alvin Robertson, John Salley, Darrell Walker—and just great teammates like Tracy Murray, Acie Earl, Willie Anderson, and Oliver Miller."

During his lone season as a Raptor, King was willing to do anything for floor minutes. He recalls one opportunity, late in the season, when the Raptors, down to eight active players, faced the Knicks at Madison Square Garden. There was only one catch for the 6'5", 210-pound shooting guard. "We had some injuries, so I was in as our forward—against Anthony Mason. I gotta lock up with a 6'8", 250-pound guy on the other end?" Despite going head-to-head with Mason, the 1995 Sixth Man of the Year and a versatile bruiser, King played well, scoring 9 points and dishing out 8 assists to go along with 2 rebounds and a steal. It even included a personal highlight. "I got a tip dunk on Pat Ewing—on Big Pat!—and the ref called it goaltending," King recalls, savoring the highlight and yet still burning from the bad whistle. "It was *clearly* not goaltending."

The performance in the Garden encouraged the rookie after a long season of scattered minutes. "I thought, *If I can finish like this, even at power forward, then I can do this.* It wasn't like I was getting the opportunity and failing. I just didn't get enough opportunity." Despite the limited floor time, King's numbers today bear out his intuition. His per-36-minute projections fill the stat sheet: 11.6 points, 4.3 rebounds, and 3.6 assists—all starting-caliber averages in an age before sports analytics had taken over.

During the offseason, Thomas traded King to Dallas for Popeye

Jones, but the second-round pick never faulted his old mentor for the deal. "I didn't take it personally. Isiah came to me at the end of the year. He traded me to get what he felt he needed for rebounding, and he also felt like he sent me a place where I could go to play."

Despite Thomas's hopes, King was waived by the Mavs. The following season, he signed a ten-day contract with the Denver Nuggets but spent the remainder of his career bouncing around the CBA, D-League, American Basketball Association, and World Basketball Association, while playing on teams in Venezuela and Poland. Along the way, King kept his NBA dream alive, often showing up to—and showing out at—various team tryouts. "I went to so many camps—the Lakers, Indiana . . ." he recalls, trailing off. "It's a big-boy league," he says with a shrug. "Ain't no crying in basketball."

What-if moments define many pro careers, but King's is filled with tantalizing hypotheticals. What if Malone had played King more rather than riding Stoudamire so hard that rookie season? What if Dallas had found in him a reliable second-unit guy? What if King was never a member of the Fab Five—and was never loaded down with the notoriety and expectations that came with being part of the most exciting lineup in college hoops? What if the Fab Five were not a phenomenon of the 1990s but of the 2010s? "It was before the embrace of the culture of hip-hop," King told us. "Corporations, advertising, marketing—that's something that they wanted to stay away from. They were more buttoned-up." Run the simulation again and again, and perhaps you get a different career for King, one defined by a first-round draft pick, more money, a guaranteed roster spot, and a chance to compete on the merits of his play rather than under the weight of his college legacy.

Those are hypotheticals, though, that King doesn't think about today. He also doesn't second-guess his time in Toronto. "I've been to a lot of places—New York, LA, Miami, Chicago—and I tell people this to this day: Toronto is one of the top five cities in the world. Easily. You got a great atmosphere, great restaurants, great entertainment. It's a different type of feel, an international feel, and I appreciated that. And particularly the people, they made me feel like home. I remember doing a lot of community appearances all over the city and being interwoven into the fabric of Toronto, learning the culture and learning how things jive there. It was a great experience and it's a special place."

3

John Thomas (1998–2000)

Basketball had always offered John Thomas a way to forge connections, whether it was with his teammates or with his family—and above all, with his own father, Morris Thomas Jr.

Born in Cape Coral, Florida, two-month-old John decamped in 1975 with his mother, Patricia Sever, and his brother to Finland, where his father was playing professional basketball. Two years later, they were on the move again, this time to Turkey for another pro hoop gig. This one stuck and the family stayed put for six years.

When Thomas was eight years old, his father retired from the pros and his family relocated back to the US, settling in Minneapolis. But life out of the spotlight, and especially off the court, was tough for his dad. Eventually Thomas's parents split and Morris returned to Florida, where he struggled with homelessness for a period. His parents' relationship and his father's post-pro challenges also hit Thomas hard. "You look at your parents as superheroes," he told us. "But as a kid, you don't understand the complexities of an adult relationship. My parents tried to reconcile, but it just didn't work."

Despite the distance, it was clear to Thomas that his father wanted to be in his life. By the time Thomas was in junior high, Morris was back on his feet, and basketball became a way for the two to maintain their relationship, something that came as a surprise to Thomas. As a kid, the sport had simply been a bit of fun. It was only at the age of fifteen that he fully committed to hoops, though it was not for a pure love of the game. "I wanted to maintain a connection with my father, that ability to make him proud in his absence."

With his large frame and natural athletic grace, Thomas proved a master of the paint. Both were the unspoken gifts his father had given him, gifts that Thomas had nurtured as a way to maintain Morris's legacy. At Roosevelt High School in Minneapolis, Thomas became a basketball star. It was during this period, in the early 1990s, that Morris returned to Minneapolis and the two began actively repairing their fractured relationship. Thomas decided he would never let it lapse again. "That's the reason I chose the University of Minnesota," he explains today. "I just wanted to stay connected to my father." With his dad in the stands, Thomas became a star for the Golden Gophers. His four-year college career even included a Final Four appearance in the 1997 NCAA tournament.

During those formative years, forging connections and maintaining relationships through the sport set him on a path: a hunt for mentorship. "Coaches became father figures for me." At the same time, Thomas came to understand his strengths as a player. "Basketball had a way of testing me with discipline, hard work, and sacrifice. I kept my nose clean and I just did a lot of stuff that other people didn't. I surrounded myself with eagles and not crows. If they're soaring that high," he asked himself, then "what are the habits, the traits, and the characteristics that they have that I might want to take on?"

The same spirit of emulation continued throughout his pro career. Thomas came increasingly to think of himself as a supporting player, someone who could chip in where he was needed, making the whole of the team greater than its individual parts. "There's something about having to be able to use your gifts in a way that helps to complement the collective through perseverance, dedication, and self-sacrifice. It's the ability to belong to something that's bigger than yourself, the opportunity to compete against the best players in the world, and the chance to establish meaningful, long-standing relationships."

Even today, the retired big man misses most this social element of the game, what Thomas calls "the camaraderie in the competition." As he said, "That's just part of who I am. I care about people. I look back, and think: *Did I really love the game?* I liked it a lot and loved it at times, but what I really loved about it was how it got me closer to people."

Selected 25th overall in the first round of the 1997 draft by the Knicks, Thomas's jump to the NBA was no easy feat. Luckily, he found new mentors in New York. "Classic true bigs," as he puts it, a who's who of the key's greatest players. "Patrick Ewing, who basically put his arm around me and said, 'You're going to be my rookie.' Charles Oakley, who ended up becoming my teammate again in Toronto, but a guy who had an impeccable work ethic and was just a beast. Buck Williams, the tenured OG who was a consummate professional." Those greats could be intimidating at first glance, especially for a young player hunting for minutes and a contract, but again and again, they proved themselves to be bighearted big men. "The moment I showed up for my physical in New York, wide-eyed and wet behind the ears, I saw Larry Johnson. He shouted in the loudest voice possible, 'Big fella!'"

Today he's grateful for their mentorship, both on and off the court. "I was soaking up all the knowledge from the vets." But the leap to the pros was a challenge for a player who had a history of staying put. "The truth was, I only knew one program from college. It looked like a perfect fit in New York, because it was a front-court-bruiser type of team."

Brendan Malone, the former Raptors head coach and by then an assistant with the Knicks, early on misunderstood the quiet rookie. "He at first thought I was this prima donna because he was thinking that younger guys were *all* prima donnas. I said, 'Give me a chance. I want to work.'" And that's exactly what happened. "We worked out all throughout the summer and I became one of his favorites."

Just over a week before the start of the 1997–98 regular season, the Knicks were in Boston for a final preseason game. Thomas was in his hotel room when he got a knock on the door from his head coach, Jeff Van Gundy. "He came to my room and asked, 'John, do you have a minute to talk?' I said, 'Yeah,' and he said, 'Do you mind turning the TV off?' Then I knew it was serious." Van Gundy broke the news. "John, I'm here to let you know you've been traded to the Boston Celtics." The deal stunned Thomas. "I called my agent and I was crying. It was a shock to my system." Even worse, the rookie didn't know what to do next. "You're clueless. There's no blueprint. There's no manual. Getting traded is not easy. You got seventy-two hours to take your stuff and go. And all the relationships you built, they're gone."

One day a Knick, the next day a Celtic—who's playing *against* the Knicks. The phantasmagoric swap left him disoriented. "I was on the Celtics bench watching the guys that I just went through training camp with. I was in a fog. I was like, 'This is insane.'" He even passed his old teammates in the tunnel to the court. "I was trying to keep myself from crying."

The changes kept coming. Where Van Gundy's smash-mouth Knicks offered a perfect fit for a grinder like Thomas, Rick Pitino's Celtics system was like speaking a foreign language. "I didn't really fit in Pitino's halfcourt-pressing system." It didn't match his style. It didn't even match his body. "According to Pitino, I needed to slim down. I wanted to hit you. I wanted to establish position more so than I wanted to run and trap and press." It was another lesson for the rookie, about fitting in and adjusting to a new system. "Pitino ran it like a training camp. It was two-and-a-half-hour practices. You were going to train. You were going on the treadmill *before* practice. You were going on the treadmill *after* practice." For all the conflict Thomas felt, he still saw it as a "healthy tension" between him and his new coach. "I couldn't figure out the relationship that I could establish with Pitino. And then, ironically, I started to adjust. My confidence went up."

Just a few months later, though, he was on the move again. A day before the 1998 trade deadline, Thomas was shipped to Toronto with Chauncey Billups, Dee Brown, and Roy Rogers for Popeye Jones, Žan Tabak, and the Raptors' newly acquired guard, Kenny Anderson, who had refused to report to Toronto after being traded from Portland. When Thomas finally landed in the Great White North, he encountered an organization nothing like the hallowed institutions he had witnessed in New York and Boston. "You get to a team that is a young team that's trying to figure it out. It was chaos. The last part of that season in 1998, the team was in shambles. It was a bunch of guys that probably at that time didn't want to be there."

For all the heartache of that first rookie year in the NBA—as a player constantly on the move and then as part of a Raptors team stuck in the basement of the league—Thomas caught a glimmer of hope. It started, again, with a mentor: the team's head coach, Butch Carter. "He had a vision for what he wanted. Butch did a good job of rallying everybody in the offseason and making sure that everyone was consistent with what they were trying to accomplish. It just seemed we had to position the team the right way in order to see his vision come to fruition."

Unfortunately for all of Carter's grand plans, the NBA was in a lockout by the start of the 1998–99 season. With no games to play, Thomas returned to Minnesota and the hard work that had sustained his career so far. "I did everything from tough workouts to playing a lot and playing against really good players like Kevin Garnett. We set up these runs and then guys would fly in to play." Staying ready also paid off. "Once the season started, I think it was my most consistent and probably my best year in the league, because I was confident in myself."

Thomas's teammates also made Toronto feel like home and, in the process, made the Raptors feel like a family. Through that closeness, he was encouraged to compete for minutes. "It's not personal. It's my job to kick your ass and your job is to kick my ass. And guess what: Some days you're going to do it and some days I'm going to do it. *And* I'm gonna tell you about it. And you're going to be so competitive that the next day you're gonna try to reverse the tide. That's what that competition does."

Toronto, too, helped make the adjustment to his new life and team easier. "My experience in Toronto was fantastic. When I first came to Toronto, I was like, 'It's a clean New York!'" As always, though, it was about people for Thomas—not just those he played and worked with, but the fans of the teams and the residents of the city itself. "You've got a multitude of people from various cultures that are there. All these different types of cuisines. It's metropolitan. We all genuinely appreciated what it meant to be in that city. The fan base is super passionate and knowledgeable about the game and they're invested. They show up in droves. I don't recall seeing empty stands in Toronto ever since the ACC opened."

During his time with the team, he even earned a nickname: Big Kitchen. It all started innocently enough. "There was a little kitchenette in the back of the locker room at the ACC that was close to the video coordinators' station. That little kitchenette was the place that I would go if I needed a quick bite. One day, I'm making peanut butter and jelly sandwiches, and Danny Aning, the video coordinator, was like, 'Why are you always in the kitchen? Damn, Kitch, every time! You're Big Kitchen!'"

At first, the nickname was just an in-joke among staff and players. Then a window opened up, thrusting Thomas into the limelight, when the team's center, Kevin Willis, went down with a shoulder injury in March 1999. By that point Thomas had been with the team just over a year, coming off the bench and doing a bit of everything: dropping a few buckets, gobbling up rebounds, grabbing steals, and guarding the paint. Suddenly the bench stalwart was a starter. "I started playing well and got confidence because there were consistent minutes. We went on a winning streak. I remember a newspaper headline one time said, 'Everything but the Kitchen Sink.'" By late

March, Willis was back in the lineup and Thomas was back to his lunch-pail role coming off the bench, but the name stuck, and to this day Thomas is still known as Big Kitchen in Toronto.

Things were also coming together on the court for the Raptors. The team finished the shortened 1998–99 lockout season 23-27, the franchise's best record yet. Finally there was something to build on, especially through the team's two young stars, Vince Carter and Tracy McGrady. During the 1999–2000 season, Toronto went 45-37—the team's first winning record—though they fell in the first round of the playoffs to the Knicks.

Despite the early playoff exit, Thomas, by then a third-year player on an expiring contract, was looking to secure his future with the team and in the NBA. From his point of view, the Raptors should have ponied up. The year prior the team had given Michael Stewart, his fellow big, a whopping six-year, $24 million deal. "In my head," Thomas recalls, "because the amount of time that I had played was comparable to what he had, I became incensed over the fact that my agent couldn't get that same deal. I didn't feel like the team valued me." Those hurt feelings are understandable, but Thomas realizes he was too green at that time. "I did not have enough patience to understand what free agency even meant. There's a pecking order. You fill your gaps with the biggest pieces first. They're not going to say, 'You know what, John, I'm going to sign you right away.' No, they've got to figure out those other pieces first."

As he admits today, Thomas just couldn't see the bigger picture. "I chose to go down a path of negativity and worry about other people's money instead of worrying about me and taking a moment to pause and reflect and think about how great of an opportunity it was to be in Toronto. This noise starts to creep into your head that they're trying to hold you down." Eventually, that noise became so loud that Thomas did the unthinkable, leaving the NBA altogether. "I let the noise, whether it was outside or it was self-created, get to me and I chose to walk away from the game. I walked away from Toronto."

Even more shockingly, it was a choice. "From what I understood, Glen Grunwald was willing to re-sign me, but I had already made up my mind, and by the time he was ready to re-sign, I had just given up. I became disenchanted with the business of sports without understanding that it is the business of sports."

And just like that, Thomas was out of the league. During that first season away from the NBA, teams still came knocking, including the Lakers, who would go on to win the NBA championship in 2000. "They wanted to sign me. My excuse was I didn't want to play in the triangle." Today he knows it was nothing more than sour grapes on his end. "The truth was I was missing the game. I was always watching it."

By the time he was ready to play again, the NBA had turned its back on the young big, still only in his mid-twenties. Desperate for another run, Thomas went to China. "That was a terrible experience, but one that I needed." Then he was back in the US, playing in the Continental Basketball Association under future NBA coach Dave Joerger, before decamping to Spain the following season. At the end of the 2003–04 season, Thomas was back in Minneapolis. "I came home and I watched the Timberwolves in the Western Conference Finals. With the electricity in that building, I was like, *I'm getting back in the league*. As soon as their season was over, I went to their assistant coach and asked, 'When are you guys in the gym again?'" Thomas put his nose to the grindstone and even managed to snag a roster position. All did not go to plan, however, as the aging big man was repeatedly signed and waived over the next two seasons, first by the Timberwolves and then by the newly relocated Memphis Grizzlies, before stints with the Atlanta Hawks and the New Jersey Nets.

Today Thomas is philosophical about his story and willing to recognize what he failed to see as a young man. "Leaving the NBA is a big regret that I have. I was just ill-informed and didn't understand the bigger picture of what it could have meant in terms of an opportunity for me to continue my career in Toronto." Thomas recalls the team's critical transition in 1998, one that set the groundwork for the Raptors' later success. "All those little things around the team, the culture and the environment, speak to why they were able to capture a championship in 2019." Thomas points in particular to Masai Ujiri, former president of the Raptors, and Teresa Resch, who had been named vice president of basketball operations for the Raptors in 2013, but who left the franchise in 2024 to work for Kilmer Sports Ventures, the Larry Tanenbaum–led group that brought the Toronto Tempo to the WNBA. Resch also worked closely with Thomas once he transitioned to the corporate side of the NBA. "I think the world of her. They're just quality people who are smart and who make decisions that are sound."

Over the years, he was able to witness that leadership from afar. "The last time I went back to Toronto was in 2016 for the All-Star Game. It was freezing, but it didn't matter. Because you think about the show that happens inside of the ACC, and then you compare it to the twenty-nine other teams across the league. It's a vibrant place to play. There's energy." For Thomas, despite its bitter ending, his Raptors experience remains a high point in his career. "I've only got positive things to say about Toronto. It was my favorite experience hands-down in the league. I miss it a lot."

Today it's Thomas's own journey, one defined time and again by the connection and mentorship he sought and received, whether from his father, his coaches, or even front-office staff like Resch, that has got him to where he is now. Thomas spent more than half a decade as vice president of community impact with the Minnesota Timberwolves and served as vice president of basketball development for the Timberwolves and Lynx, managing the organization's Basketball Academy, before transitioning to director of sports marketing at Beautylish in 2024. In turn, mentorship has come naturally to Thomas. Once a young man searching for a role model, he is now mentoring his own son and looking to his father's example from so many decades ago. "He provided me with guidance and advice, and in many cases, it helped me to understand the game a little bit better. I've been able to pass that along to my son."

But even mentorship comes with its own lessons. "What I'm finding is that, when the student is ready, the teacher will appear. You have all the resources as a former NBA and overseas player. I've been in a ton of leagues across the globe as a journeyman, but I've also been an NBA and WNBA executive, so I understand the business. There are all these nuances that I have that I've got stored in me that, honestly, I'm dying to share with my son, but it's got to be when he's ready, and he may never be ready. And the truth is, it's okay, because it's not my life. It's his. I just try to be patient. Maybe at some point he will be ready, but it's his journey. It's his life. As it was mine."

4

Doug Christie (1996–2000)

After being acquired by the Raptors just before the 1996 trade deadline, Doug Christie was finally meeting his new boss. He also just happened to be one of his heroes, Isiah Thomas. "I have an affinity for Isiah maybe more than the average person," Christie told us. "I liked the way he played. And the Bad Boys, him and Joe Dumars, were two of my favorites." The fifth-year wing was also impressed by how quickly his new boss, who had retired just two years earlier, had risen in the front-office ranks to become executive vice president of the Raptors. "He was still relatively young. Watching him transform from a player to the management side was definitely very interesting. Looking at Isiah, an African American in that position, we didn't see a lot of that."

Now Christie was about to play a game of one-on-one with the former Bad Boy at Toronto's Glendon College, which served as the team's makeshift practice facility. Thomas, who was only thirty-four years old, wanted to test the mettle of his newest acquisition. What better way than firsthand? Christie, too, was ready to compete. "My approach to the game was a little bit nasty," he admits with a laugh. "We ended up playing one-on-one. My wife came to the gym. I knocked Isiah down, and later we get in the car. She was like, 'Isn't that your general manager? What the hell are you thinking?'"

Christie was less worried, recalling Thomas's hard-nosed Pistons teams. "I think Isiah knew that he got the right guy, because I was gonna mix it up."

He was right. Thomas was impressed with his new wing right away and offered Christie a chance to grow with the Raptors. "Isiah told me, 'I've been following you. I want you here, I want you to play, and I want you to mess up. Some nights you're going to play forty-eight minutes. Most nights you're going to play thirty-five to forty minutes. Don't worry about mistakes—just try not to make two mistakes in a row. Find yourself and find your game because I know that you belong in this league. I understand the ups and downs of what you've been through.'"

Thomas's directness struck Christie right away. "His honesty, for me, I had never experienced anything like that before." Thomas's acknowledgment that Christie had had ups and downs also helped. "That type of conversation and confidence was all I needed to hear. I always tell him to this day: It was the wind beneath my wings that I needed as a professional."

With the fits-and-starts beginning to his career, Christie needed the boost. Coming out of a three-year stint at Pepperdine University, the Seattle-raised kid had been selected by his hometown team 17th overall in the 1992 draft. He and the SuperSonics had failed to reach a deal, however. With contract talks at an impasse, Christie decided to play in Italy.

Later in the NBA season, the SuperSonics traded Benoit Benjamin along with Christie's rights for Sam Perkins to the Lakers, who signed Christie to a multiyear deal. It was a dream come true, if deferred, for the untested rookie, who would get to play alongside a twenty-four-year-old Vlade Divac and a raft of vets, including Byron Scott, James Worthy, and A.C. Green. After leaving his Italian squad, Christie joined the Lakers in March, playing 23 contests off the bench. He also earned a few scattered minutes during the first round of the playoffs. The Lakers ultimately lost that series in five games to the Phoenix Suns, who were led by Charles Barkley and Kevin Johnson.

Christie was finally in the NBA, finally earning the money he believed he deserved as a first-round pick, and finally playing. But his court time fluctuated throughout the season and playoffs, and he was largely an afterthought on a Los Angeles team on the verge of a rebuild after 17 straight playoff appearances that included multiple trips to the Finals and five championships. The next season was, by Lakers standards, a disaster. The team went 33-49 and missed the playoffs. It went a little better for Christie, who played in 65 games and even started 34 of them, but struggled throughout the season with a sprained ankle. As he admits today, he wasn't prepared to make the most of his Lakers experience. "I wasn't ready for Los Angeles as a young kid, and it was a perfect opportunity. Jerry West was spectacular . . . I got injured and I just couldn't find my way. I wasn't a pro's pro yet."

Before the start of the 1994–95 season, the Lakers decided to trade the third-year player to the New York Knicks. Once again, Christie found a supportive developmental environment under another great. And this time around, he made the most of it.

"I went to New York and got slapped with the highest level of ultimate professionalism with Pat Riley." The Knicks threw Christie into a relentless regimen. "I would get in there at 8 a.m., run two miles, lift weights, and go work out on the court. Then we would practice, and practices were out of control—like next-level intensity. Then afterwards, I would shoot. I did that every day because Pat told me, 'You need to find your way.' I figured my thing was: If I worked harder than everybody, because I knew I had talent, it would figure itself out. I went from not being ready to the polar opposite: being *forced* to work my butt off."

The Knicks, and especially Riley, were good for Christie. But real opportunities were still scarce on a team that had just gone to the 1994 NBA Finals. Riley, for one, was clear. "When I first got there,

Pat told me, 'You're not going to play. I got my guys. But work hard and find your way in this league.'" Riley was good to his word. Christie played in a mere 12 games that season as the Knicks went 55-27 before losing in the Eastern Conference Semifinals to the Indiana Pacers. Riley abruptly decamped to become lead executive for the Miami Heat and the Knicks brought in Don Nelson to coach. The changes didn't bode well for the 1995–96 season.

"Right away, I could see I wasn't going to play. I called my agent and said, 'I want to get out of here.'" In the meantime, Christie held tight, playing in 23 games under Nelson, but averaging less than 10 minutes per contest off the bench.

Finally, the 1996 trade deadline rolled around. As Christie recalls, "There was a knock on my door, and it was a longtime trainer for the Knicks. I answered, and he told me, 'You just got traded.'" *Finally,* Christie thought. *A fresh chance to play.* There was only one question. "I was like, 'Okay, do you know where?' And he goes, 'Toronto.'"

Christie was ready for the new challenge, perhaps more than the average NBA player in 1996. In the first place, unlike many of his now fellow Raptors, he had actually spent some time in Canada. "I'm from Seattle, so Vancouver is a place you might travel up to from time to time. Before I started playing organized basketball, I played soccer. We had traveled there for a home-and-home. So I had a little bit of an understanding of Canada." Still, being traded in February had its downsides. "I'm from Seattle so I know a little bit about cold, but Toronto is the Great White North—it is totally different—and it was cold as hell when I got there."

Christie was also ready in a more important way—he was prepared, finally, to put to use everything he had learned in Los Angeles and New York under Thomas. "By the time I got to Toronto, I had a higher level of understanding and professionalism mixed with the confidence that Isiah gave me. In many ways, it was a perfect storm."

Thomas hadn't lied about playing time. During his four and a half seasons as a Raptor, Christie became an iron-man starter. He played in 32 games in his first half season with the Raptors, starting 17 of them, and logged increasingly heavy minutes throughout the remainder of the season. It was a far cry from his role with the Lakers and Knicks. The following year, he was installed in the starting lineup, where he played 81 games, averaging almost 39 minutes per contest. From then on, it was more of the same. Christie started 78 games during the 1997–98 season, all 50 games in the shortened lockout season, and 73 games in his final season in Toronto.

Throughout his time as a Raptor, Christie remained in awe of Thomas. Playing for the face of the original Bad Boy Pistons was one thing. But Thomas was also innovative and forward-thinking, offering a glimpse of the NBA future. "Isiah was so far ahead of the curve," Christie argues. "A lot of the things that I see in basketball today, Isiah was trying to do with us back then. And he was right. It's here today, except he was freaking thirty years ahead. People were looking at us like: 'The hell are you doing?' But I saw it, and I was like, 'I'm in, bro.'"

One of those shifts is today a staple of the NBA. "He was thinking positionless basketball. We could all switch. We were pressing. He was already telling us, 'Forget about point guard, shooting guard, small forward, power forward. I want the best players on the floor.'" Christie, an athletic and defensive-minded 6'6" wing, fit perfectly into the system Thomas was building. "He thought that I was one of the best players for it, and I bought into what Isiah was doing. I could totally see it. From the way that we played to the type of players he was bringing in to how he was breaking down the game, my man was doing genius-level stuff."

Thomas was never afraid to do things unconventionally, even leaning on his players when making executive-level decisions. During his second season with the Raptors, Christie recalls Thomas asking for his feedback on a potential draft pick. "Isiah and I lived in the same building. He called me up to his condo, so I come up and he's sitting on the back of the couch, just chilling, and I'm thinking, *Man, this is* Isiah Thomas. *This is totally cool.* We're sitting there and he goes, 'I want you to watch this. Tell me what you think.' He pops in a videotape in the VCR—I'm dating us—pushes play, and doesn't say anything. We're sitting there and all of a sudden, a highlight tape comes on. We watched for a few minutes and you can see immediately. I was looking at it going, 'Damn, whoever that is, get him. I want that dude. No doubt.' The highlight tape stops, and I look at him and ask, 'You got a chance to draft that dude?' Isiah was like, 'I'm thinking about it.' I was like, 'That's a no-brainer, bro. You got to draft that guy.' It was Tracy McGrady."

Thomas proved an essential guide during Christie's first couple of years in Toronto. But his vets also helped. "You need talent, obviously," Christie explains, "but you also need mentorship. Isiah understood the mix. Young players need veterans, guys that they're going to respect and look up to." It was something Christie saw time and again over his years in a Raptors uniform. It was especially clear after the newly drafted Vince Carter arrived, via trade with the Golden State Warriors, and when the Raptors, after only five seasons in the NBA, made the playoffs for the first time. "That jump with Vince didn't happen until the veterans had come in and begun to stabilize the team."

At the same time, Christie himself was not only a starter, but also the most veteran player on a young team that was looking for leadership. "Part of what Isiah taught me was how to pay it forward. From Derek Harper to James Worthy to Kevin Willis and some of the guys that helped me—it is so valuable. Then I could pay that forward to your Vinces and your Tracys. I didn't look at myself as a veteran; I looked at myself as a vessel that had knowledge and it was my responsibility to tell him how to get over the screen, how to play a certain guy, all of those things. That's what a veteran does."

In Toronto, Christie had a chance to redefine himself, garnering in the process a new reputation in the league as a lockdown defender. He had a chance to put those skills on display during a game from the team's inaugural season that Raptors fans would also cherish: beating the 72-10 Chicago Bulls at SkyDome in front of 31,131 screaming fans.

It was a special moment for Christie. He had been with the team for fewer than 20 games and was still coming off the bench. But his 26-minute performance in the win confirmed everything that Thomas had told the young wing. His stat line was one thing—13 points on 4-of-6 shooting, and 3-of-3 from beyond the arc, alongside 3 rebounds, 2 assists, 2 blocks, and a steal—but it was on the defensive end where he made his mark and where he had the toughest assignment in the league: guarding Michael Jordan.

Thomas had believed in Christie, encouraging him along the way that season, but it was locking horns with the best of the best that gave him the in-game boost of confidence he desperately needed after so many years of hunting for his place in the league. "I was guarding Mike. I'm battling him and hitting him and he's hitting me back. I gained so much respect for him, because he never cried to the ref." It was that back-and-forth that led to an iconic image Christie still cherishes today. "I still have the photo: I stole the ball from Mike and I went down and dunked it. He's trailing and looking up at me. You can see Phil Jackson in the background. That was supercool, because for me as a player, it was probably the moment that let me know that I really belonged in the league."

It was also clear that Christie's teammates had come to believe in him during the course of the game. "It came down to the last possession. I had been guarding Mike for the whole game." During the huddle, assistant coach Darrell Walker told Alvin Robertson, their veteran shooting guard by then in his final season in the league, "On this last play, you got Mike." The team paused. As Christie remembers it, "The huddle goes quiet—we were pretty close-knit—and

Alvin says, 'Coach, I'm going to be honest with you. The young fella has really guarded him good. Let him work.' Right then it was like, *Wow, you're legit anointed.* That was when I knew my teammates believed in me."

It was hard to believe—a brand-new franchise taking out Jordan's Bulls, who were on their way to their second set of three straight NBA championships. It was almost as unbelievable as what Christie's three-year-old asked him, in the moments following the pinnacle of his still-young career. "Afterwards, my daughter, Chantel, asked me to go get Mike's autograph. I'm looking at her—you do anything for your kids—but I don't really do that. I learned from Pat Riley: It's us versus them. I'm not trying to be friends and it's Michael freaking Jordan. I was like, 'Man, we just beat the hell out of each other. I don't know if he wants to see me right now.'" Still, the pleas of his daughter were impossible to ignore. "I go in the locker room and Mike has the scrum around him. They're in there, smoking cigars, and he sees me and he was like, 'You guys, watch out,' and he moved all the reporters and had a moment with me. He gave me some advice and signed an autograph for my daughter. He was so gracious. I was blown away."

When he was finally traded to the Sacramento Kings during the 2000 offseason, after four and half seasons with the Raptors, Christie was ready to go. It was no longer the same organization, and Thomas's decision to leave the team in late 1997 hit Christie particularly hard. "He was part of the reason that I started finding my way and now I didn't have that backing—I didn't have that person in my corner."

Christie could at least look forward to the prospect of playing for the Kings. "By the time I got to Sacramento, I was ready for the moment and I was excited for my career, but as a person, and being in the community and dealing with the people, I was sad, because I really enjoyed my time in Toronto." Still, the trade offered a great opportunity, including a chance to win at the highest level. The team went 55-27 during Christie's first season before losing in the Western Conference Semifinals to the Kobe-Shaq Lakers, who would claim the 2001 championship title. Moreover, in Sacramento he also finally earned league-wide recognition for his defense, including four straight nominations to first and second All-Defensive Teams and even votes for Defensive Player of the Year in 2001 and 2003.

After four and a half seasons in Northern California, Christie was traded to Orlando, where he finished out the 2004–05 season but played little thanks to bone spurs. He stayed on for two more years in the NBA, first with the Mavericks and then with the Clippers, but a nagging ankle injury, even after surgery, limited his availability, and Christie decided to retire in 2007.

At heart, Christie remained a Raptor and appreciated how the organization regrouped under Larry Tanenbaum, team owner and chairman of the newly formed Maple Leaf Sports & Entertainment (MLSE), which purchased the Raptors in 1998, after he had left the team. "The level of everything totally changed. His vision was incredible." He was also able to look on with pride as the team took care of that "unfinished business" almost twenty years later, in 2019. "Watching them win the championship, I was so freaking excited for them." It was the culmination of many years of work and part of a legacy Christie still sees today. "Watching them win the championship was probably the first time that it really hit me. When you look at the Canadian national team now, there's a lot of NBA players on it at a seriously high level. I think a lot of it started with that era, as basketball began to put down roots in Toronto."

Looking back, Christie is still grateful for everything the Raptors gave him—an opportunity to start and play significant minutes, an opportunity to become one of the best backcourt defenders in the league, and above all an opportunity to make mistakes—and flourish. "I credit my career to Isiah. Isiah was the catapulting piece." As head coach for the Sacramento Kings, he is still paying it forward, sharing the lessons Thomas had taught him decades earlier. "I didn't come in as a superstar; I've walked the path that these guys have walked. Even now, as a coach, I think that's one of my biggest gifts. I understood how to work, and outwork people, and find my niche. Those are valuable lessons, because mostly that's what the league is made up of. You can lose confidence in yourself and lose confidence in your game. In those moments when you might question yourself, or respond in a negative way, you need somebody to have your back."

Raptors Moment

February 21, 1999: The Raptors' First Game at Air Canada Centre

It was a makeshift start for one of the NBA's two newest teams. Yes, Toronto finally had its own NBA franchise to go along with its other professional teams: the Maple Leafs, the Blue Jays, and the Argonauts of the Canadian Football League. But the Raptors still lacked a permanent home—they were renters, forced to practice in college facilities across town and to play at SkyDome, a massive baseball and football stadium with a retractable roof.

First opened in 1989, SkyDome was a state-of-the-art facility, but a less-than-ideal place to play a basketball game. For John Thomas, a Raptor between 1998 and 2000, the vast stadium required an adjustment. "Playing in domes is really hard," he explained. "You don't have a solid background, so when you shoot the ball, your depth perception is off." It was bad enough for shooters. But the breadth of the interior in certain sections hardly helped fans far above the court, some of whom had to rent binoculars to follow the action. The Raptors played three seasons in SkyDome, alongside assorted games at Maple Leaf Gardens in Toronto and Copps Coliseum in Hamilton, an hour drive from downtown.

Still, hooping in SkyDome, renamed Rogers Centre in 2005, wasn't all bad. Some players even liked playing in the megastadium. Jimmy King, who played one year with Toronto during the team's inaugural season, was all smiles when discussing the Raptors' first home. "I thought playing in the 'Dome was live—I loved it—because we had a large crowd," he explained. "We had close to thirty-five or forty thousand people in the arena and they were always loud and rocking. I thought it was sweet."

For players like Alvin Williams, a Raptor between 1998 and 2006, the fuss around the team's temporary home was just one more pseudo-complaint about playing in Canada. "There was just so much hoopla over BS. People will always have excuses for not wanting to go to Toronto. They practice at a local college, or the taxes, or the weather, or the metric system, or the language. None of it impacted basketball. When I got to Toronto, I was there to play basketball. And fortunately enough, that's what I got an opportunity to do. I would have never left Toronto because we played at SkyDome."

Then, after three years as houseguests, the Raptors finally had their own home, one they would share with the Maple Leafs, when Air Canada Centre opened in early 1999. It was a massive change. "When they opened the ACC, you could start to see the vision of what was happening with Toronto basketball," Thomas told us. Antonio Davis, a Raptor between 1999 and 2003 and again in 2006, agrees. "To get the arena," he told us, "to be a part of the magic of that history, makes me feel good."

Following a lockout that delayed the 1998–99 NBA season, the Raptors finally played their first game at the ACC on February 21, 1999, against the Vancouver Grizzlies. In front of 19,800 fans, the hometown team won, 102–87, soundly beating their fellow expansion franchise. The game also inaugurated a new era in Raptors basketball, one that had begun just a season earlier, when the Golden State Warriors drafted a three-year player out of the University of North Carolina fifth overall, before sending him immediately to Toronto: Vince Carter. He showed out at the arena's opening, playing nearly 42 minutes, scoring 27 points on 11-of-16 shooting, while going 3-of-4 beyond the arc, alongside 6 rebounds, 5 assists, 4 steals, and 2 blocks. It was the beginning of Vinsanity. Air Canada Centre was finally in flight.

For the players, too, the new arena offered a true home court in Toronto, a place they could come and go as they wished. "The ACC was the shiny penny at the time," John Thomas explained. "It had a lot of cool features. One of the things I really loved is we got access to the gym whenever we wanted it. You got a nice little music system in there, so you can put your music on and go and shoot. I remember Chris Bosh used to fire up Dru Hill back in the day. That was a lot of fun and a part that I appreciated: the convenience, the ability to be in your element. I think that's the most important thing when it comes to facilities; it is less about how it looks and more about the convenience and the ability to feel like it's home."

PART II

VINSANITY, 1998–2004

In 2024, Vince Carter was inducted into the Basketball Hall of Fame. A month later, his number 15 was retired, first by the Raptors and then, in early 2025, by the Brooklyn Nets. Despite these accolades, it's easy to forget, all these years later, the effect that Carter had on basketball in Canada.

Vinsanity meant more than just the physics-defying athleticism that was crystallized for all the world to see during his performance at the 2000 Slam Dunk Contest. Carter, in fact, drove winning itself, with the Raptors making three straight playoffs appearances between 2000 and 2002—no small shakes for a team that had existed for a mere five seasons before going on that run.

He also changed how seemingly everyone viewed the city of Toronto and basketball in Canada more generally, from players across the league to the broadcasters who were just as giddy as the fans about his hardwood highlights. With Carter on the team, Toronto too started to think about the Raptors in new ways. "Before Vince, we would go places and no one knew who we were," Alvin Williams recalls, shaking his head. "But with Vince coming to town, you started to feel things picking up."

Behind Carter, the team at first flew high before struggling for consistency, as three winning seasons gave way to three losing ones. For years, Carter had battled injuries that had hampered his athleticism and limited his court time and scoring. The fans, in turn, who had grown accustomed to an endless reel of highlights and dunks couldn't understand his inconsistent play during the first months of the 2004–05 season.

By late 2004, the mood in Toronto had shifted. When rumors emerged that he allegedly wanted out, the city that had once embraced Carter as a minor god turned on their hero. The rumors were just that—rumors—and years later, in 2024, Coach Sam Mitchell confirmed that Carter had actually wanted to stay, but said that GM Rob Babcock wouldn't back out of the deal he had already brokered. Whatever the case, the seemingly inevitable eventually happened, even if it still caught everyone off guard: Vince was traded to the New Jersey Nets in December 2004.

Carter's exit left a bitter taste in the mouths of some fans. "I think the moment it really sunk in for me was the first game when he came back with the Nets," Matt Bonner recalled. "When Vince walked out for two lines of layups, I just remember thinking, *Holy mackerel.* I have never seen anyone get booed so loudly and so harshly in my entire life as a basketball player."

The reconciliation between city and player would only come years later, in 2014, when the Raptors finally honored the man who had put basketball on the map in Canada. By then Carter was a reliable vet off the bench for the Memphis Grizzlies, better known for his locker room leadership than his breathtaking athleticism. The Raptors' commemorative highlight package was a time capsule, taking the fans back to those same impossible dunks that had once wowed the entire league. It was those same fans who now applauded the player that they had once booed so relentlessly every time he touched the ball. On court that night at the ACC, with tears streaming down his face and his hand over his heart, Carter raised his fist in the air to the crowd, a gesture of mutual recognition, grateful to be taken back into the fold after so many years in exile.

5

Alvin Williams (1998–2006)

It's February 12, 1998, and another tough night for the 11-37 Toronto Raptors. They're at home in SkyDome, hosting the Cavaliers. The Raptors drop the matchup 103–94, good for their 38th loss in fewer than 50 games.

That same night in mid-February, something special is happening in the Sonoran Desert, a little less than 2,200 miles away. The Trail Blazers' rookie guard, Alvin Williams, is going off against a stacked 32-15 Suns team in a 115–110 Portland win. "I had my career high, nineteen points," he recalled to us. "They had Jason Kidd, Steve Nash, and Kevin Johnson, and I'm playing against all three of those guys in one game."

The very next day, Williams found his reverie broken. "I got a call from my agent, saying, 'You got traded, though it's not certain yet.'" Alongside Kenny Anderson and Gary Trent, Williams had supposedly been sent to Toronto. He was hardly surprised, knowing how the rumor mill worked. "I told my agent, 'All right, whatever. I've heard all this before.'"

Having brushed it off, Williams went about his day. "I went to get a new pager. I remember the woman working at the store was like, 'You're Alvin Williams?'" Yeah, he answered, perhaps basking just a bit more in the afterglow of his Phoenix performance. "You just got traded," she continued. "She ended up really solidifying it," Williams said, recalling his surprise. "This is somebody *outside* of the circle telling me that I was traded. I thought I would be in Portland my whole career."

First shock, then confusion. At that point, Williams was still new to NBA protocols. "I was so green, I ended up going to the game, acting like I could get one more run before I left. I didn't know that I was supposed to move. I didn't know *how* to move." Toronto, moreover, was a culture shock. "I was so young that I had no expectations coming to Toronto. That was my first time there. I remember checking into my hotel after a game. I was watching curling on TV. 'What the hell is this?'"

The shock waves of the trade continued to reverberate—and not just for Williams. Toronto's new general manager, Glen Grunwald, had taken a massive gamble in the deal in shipping off not only Carlos Rogers and Walt Williams but also, most shocking of all, Damon Stoudamire—a former Rookie of the Year, still only in his third season, and the team's best player. Fans were crushed, and the Raptors' coach, Darrell Walker, even quit in protest.

Back in Portland, more surprises were to come. Along with Williams, the Trail Blazers' starting point guard, Kenny Anderson, had been dealt to the Raptors. There was only one problem. "I'm not going there," Anderson told Williams. He was good on his word—which led to the next shock. "Gary Trent and I were getting off the plane in Toronto and Glen was waiting. He saw me and Gary, but he was looking over our shoulders, like, 'Where's the third guy?' And we looked at each other and said, 'Kenny didn't come, man.'"

Anderson, it seems, had never planned to show, even though he was the prime mover in orchestrating his exit from Portland. "Kenny wasn't happy in Portland and he had a lot more power than I had," Williams explains. "He was an established player and he was playing at a very high level. He had a very powerful agent in David Falk. I think they were controlling the destination where Kenny wanted to go." Canada, in 1998, was not it. "Remember," Williams says with a laugh, "at that time, *nobody* wanted to go to Toronto."

After landing in Canada, Trent and Williams headed straight to SkyDome. "I'm getting off the plane, ready to hoop. Next thing I know, everyone's looking at my knees. I didn't pass my physical." Those supposed knee problems were news to Williams. He had never had a complaint and was coming off a near flawless 40-minute performance in Phoenix the night before. Ultimately, Williams needed minor arthroscopic surgery.

At the time, he couldn't help but suspect Falk and Anderson had a hand in directing attention to his knees, in the hopes that the deal would be rescinded altogether. "I would say that it was an attempt to block the trade until a destination for Kenny opened up that he would be happy with."

Despite Williams's knee problems, the trade went through. And with Anderson a no-show, Grunwald had to scramble to move the recalcitrant guard only a few days before the 1998 trade deadline. Luckily, he found a willing partner in the Celtics in a multiplayer deal that netted the Raptors Dee Brown, Roy Rogers, John Thomas, and Chauncey Billups, the third-overall pick in the 1997 draft and future Finals MVP for the 2004 champion Pistons.

Nonetheless, Williams's knees—and the rumors about them—continued to plague him throughout his career. Years later, in January 2000, the Raptors attempted to trade the guard to the Celtics, but the deal was ultimately rescinded when he failed his medical.

Grunwald called Williams. "I got good news and bad news. What do you want first?"

"I want the bad news," Williams responded.

"You failed your physical in Boston."

"Damn. So what's the good news?"

"You're coming back to Toronto."

Early on, Williams struggled to find his role on the team. He finished the 1998 season coming mostly off the bench while battling for minutes at guard alongside Doug Christie and Dee Brown. It was easy to keep pushing forward with support from his fellow Raptors. "I was fortunate. My teammates always encouraged me, especially the older guys like Muggsy Bogues, Dee Brown, Dell Curry, and Doug Christie, like 'Keep your head up, young fella. Keep playing. Keep going to work.' The biggest vote of confidence comes from your peers."

Even still, watching his new team lose that season was not easy for Williams. Following Anderson's trade to Boston, the Raptors went 5-28, finishing 16-66, good for the franchise's worst record in team history.

Luckily, the team's losing ways had their perks. The first and most enviable: high draft picks—and two faces that would forever redefine Raptors basketball. The season prior, in the 1997 draft, the Raptors had scooped up Tracy McGrady straight out of high school. Williams immediately saw his potential and marveled at T-Mac's growth. "He was like a Swiss Army knife. He could guard multiple positions. He could play multiple positions offensively. You could start him. He could come off the bench."

The Big Bang, though, happened in the 1998 offseason. This time around it was a sparkling first-round pick, taken fifth overall, by the name of Vince Carter. The real shock for Williams was watching Vince, a player he had battled years earlier in the NCAA, grow into the face of the team. "I played against him twice when he was a freshman at the University of North Carolina and I was a junior at Villanova. In college, all I saw was an athletic guy. It wasn't until I started seeing him day after day that I saw how good his ballhandling was and how good of a shooter he was. He showed all those guard skills and he had a high IQ—he understood the game."

The next season began with the 1998 lockout, during which Williams returned to his hometown of Philadelphia. There he played pickup with various 76ers, including Allen Iverson. As an unrestricted free agent, Williams didn't know where he would end up. "To be honest, I didn't even think we were going to have a season."

By the belated opening of the 1998–99 season, though, Williams had re-signed with Toronto and was in the Raptors' starting lineup. Things went better that shortened season, with the team improving to 23-27, and yet Williams struggled as a starter. "I was playing like shit," he bluntly admits. "My confidence was rattled. I was out there playing so as *not* to make mistakes. I had to figure that out. I had to find myself. I had to get my confidence back."

There was also a bigger problem. "I was still hesitant about Coach Butch Carter. We just didn't connect, and I wasn't one hundred percent sure of our dynamic. I was starting, but I wasn't playing starter *minutes*; I wasn't playing that starter *role*. I'm not blaming Butch at all. Butch was a great coach. But I had to prove to the coach I was the starter."

Those tensions with Carter nonetheless crept into the following season. Williams started a little more than half the games, but saw his minutes diminish. Even worse, he was getting DNPs—dozens of them—for the first time since his first months in the league.

Part of the problem, as Williams now admits, was his own approach, pointing to a selfishness that defined him early in his career. Finding a role actually meant playing within a team concept. It was also hard to complain when the concept was working. First, the Raptors were finally winning—and winning heals all wounds—finishing the 1999–2000 season 45-37. More importantly, the team was heading to the playoffs for the first time in franchise history.

That first run didn't go to plan, with the Raptors losing in three straight games to the Knicks. The series nonetheless marked a critical turning point in Williams's career. Later that summer, the Raptors fired Carter and hired Lenny Wilkens, a former point guard and multi-time All-Star who had already spent two and a half decades coaching in the NBA.

It was under Wilkens that Williams finally figured out who he was and who he could be for the Raptors. "Lenny was the key," he explained. "I had to earn his respect, but he gave me the basketball, gave me confidence, and let me play through my mistakes." Williams was no longer playing scared; instead he was taking the kinds of risks that were central to the point guard's duties. "Lenny had confidence in me. I've always had coaches who yelled and were high-strung, ever since little bitty-bop basketball and all the way up to the pros. But Lenny, he was one of those mild-mannered guys and he had a calmness about him. When I looked over to the sideline, after I made a mistake, he looked back like, 'Don't worry about it. Keep going.'"

Following their first-round loss to the Knicks, the Raptors signed Mark Jackson as a free agent. Other young guards might have sweated what that meant for their minutes. But going into the 2000–2001 season, Williams was growing, as a player and as a person, and recognized what the veteran brought to both him and the team. He was now effectively doing an internship under one of the best point guards in the league. Plus, how the team handled the transaction spoke to the club's growth and professionalization. "When they signed Mark Jackson, Glen Grunwald called me and told me. 'We have you in our plans, but this is the direction we're going in.' It was a level of communication that I'd never had before. That's when I started realizing Toronto was starting to get it—starting to get how to communicate with their players—because that's how you get the most out of them."

Playing behind Jackson, and under Wilkens's tutelage, Williams began shoring up his skills. But he also needed to show his coach that he deserved an enhanced role. That was another lesson he learned: the importance of making sacrifices. Summer League had typically been reserved for rookies and first-year players eager to prove their worth. At first Williams resisted attending, but he soon realized how those sacrifices to dignity might pay off. "I just wanted an opportunity to play. I was probably the longest-tenured Summer League player—I played about four years of Summer League."

In turn, Coach Wilkens recognized his young guard's growth. Through the first two-thirds of the 2000–2001 season, Williams still came mostly off the bench, logging steady minutes. But Wilkens was there the whole time, coaching up Williams. "I have a picture with me and Lenny looking eye to eye and he signed it, 'It's a pleasure coaching you.' It's of me, asking, 'All right, tell me something, Coach.' And he's just calmly talking to me. It's one of those face-to-face pictures that speaks a thousand words about the dynamic between a coach and player and what Lenny gave me. It's a dope picture."

Then, following a close 113–111 loss to the Nets, Wilkens told one of his assistants that Williams was ready for more responsibility. Everything changed the next day, on February 22, 2001, while Jackson and Williams were driving together. Shockingly, Jackson had been traded, and they both found out while listening to the radio.

The veteran point guard had been shipped to the Knicks along with Bogues. Williams was losing two mentors, but he was also gaining a vote of confidence from Raptors brass and a new mentor in Chris Childs. Suddenly Williams was the Raptors' starting point guard, a position he would assume only a day after the trade deadline at home against the Kings. He rose to the challenge in the triple-overtime loss, 119–118, playing almost 58 minutes with 18 points, 13 assists, and 4 steals. It was a great stat line, but a tough ending, one that rubbed Williams the wrong way.

Wilkens's faith once again helped to calm his guard. It also recalled a piece of advice Williams had received years earlier from Portland's head coach, Mike Dunleavy Sr. "I had a conversation with

Coach Dunleavy when I was a rookie. He told me two things: 'You always want to be involved with an organization where the coach trusts you and where the owner will take care of you.'" In Toronto he had finally found that support. From Wilkens, his coach. From Larry Tanenbaum, team owner and Maple Leaf Sports & Entertainment chairman. And from Grunwald, the Raptors' GM. Williams had finally found his role. Now he only needed to vindicate their faith.

Williams started the remaining 27 games of the season, averaging 12 points and 8 assists. The team finished 47-35, its best record yet, and headed to the playoffs for a second consecutive year. There Williams got a chance to prove Wilkens, Tanenbaum, and Grunwald right.

The Raptors got a rematch with the Knicks. It was also a chance for Williams to scratch an itch that had nagged at him the entire season. "That first year, I didn't play. I was sitting on the bench and looking around MSG, at all the stars and feeling the energy. I'm like, 'Before I die, I have to play in a playoff game here.'" The very next year, that fantasy came true. "It's something you couldn't even script," Williams recalled, still in wonder. "And I was starting and playing against the person they had traded, Mark Jackson."

The series proved a hard-fought Ping-Pong match. In a close first game in New York, the Raptors lost 92–85, with Williams bagging 19 points and 8 assists in 41 minutes. The Knicks outplayed them, Williams recalls, and the Raptors' ever-tenacious Charles Oakley called out the coaches and players: "We weren't prepared enough." Thanks to Oak, the team regrouped. "The practice after game one was so intense," Williams said. "If Charles Oakley wasn't on that team, then we would've got swept."

The next game, Williams played nearly 44 minutes at MSG, fulfilling his dream and scoring 23 points on deadly shooting. It was a decisive victory, 94–74, and the Raptors' first-ever playoff win. Back in Toronto, the team dropped the third game to the Knicks, only to beat them in the fourth.

Everything came down to a decisive game five back at MSG. With a minute left, Toronto was up 87–83. The Raptors' Antonio Davis pulled down a rebound off a missed Latrell Sprewell jumper, outletting it to Williams, who brought it up the court. Just outside the three-point line, Williams slipped. Vince Carter recovered the ball and hit a suddenly open Williams, who drained a deep two, putting the Raptors up 89–83. For Raptors fans, it was probably the most iconic shot in team history, until Kawhi Leonard's corner three against the 76ers in the 2019 Eastern Conference Semifinals. The next play, off a lazy pass by Charlie Ward, Williams stole the ball at halfcourt. He was immediately fouled, with 32 seconds left, pushing the Raptors into the bonus. Williams walked to the line and calmly hit both free throws, putting the score at 91–83, sealing the win and capping off his 9-point fourth.

If his performance in the clinching game against the Knicks didn't secure his place in Raptors lore, then the following series, against Allen Iverson's 76ers, did. The Raptors ultimately fell to the 76ers in a heartbreaking 88–87 game-seven loss. Despite the pressure and spotlight, Williams played well throughout the series. He averaged over 11 points per game on efficient shooting with handfuls of assists and steals throughout. For Williams it was also a homecoming of sorts, for the kid born and raised in Philly—a chance to show everyone back home just how far he had come.

Williams's time with the Raptors lasted longer than others, but the team never again showed the same promise. The next season, the team was plagued by injuries. By mid-March, with the Raptors at 30-38, limping toward the season's end, Wilkens decided to shut down the ailing Carter and Williams, who was nursing an ankle injury. "I asked the coach, 'Are we mathematically eliminated?' He said not yet, but we had to win twelve out of fourteen." "Until we are eliminated," Williams told Wilkens, "I'm going to keep playing."

He was good to his word. "We always had grit and that ability to believe that we were going to win in any situation. I remember guys like Tracy Murray, Morris Peterson, Chris Childs, and Dell Curry really stepping up. We just started rattling off wins and ended up crawling into the playoffs." Unfortunately, by the start of the post-season the Raptors were out of juice. Carter was still hurt, and the Raptors fell in five games.

The team wouldn't make the playoffs again until 2007, but by then Williams's days as a Raptor were done. After suffering through recurring knee injuries, he was waived by the team on July 26, 2006. He eventually signed a ten-day contract with the Clippers, but his knee injuries continued to plague him, and he ultimately chose to retire.

It was a sad finish for Williams in Raptors purple, but his time with the team was hardly over. In 2009, Jay Triano hired him as an assistant coach and in 2010 he became Toronto's director of player development. That return offered a chance at reconciliation with the team. "There was a big-time disconnect between me and the Raptors because of the way I left as a player. The Raptors were going in a different direction and I just wasn't in the plans. I give a lot of credit to Jay Triano. He offered me an opportunity to come back and it reminded me of how great the city was. It reminded me of Glen Grunwald, letting me know that I really do want you here. It reminded me of Mr. Tanenbaum, and how he and his family always supported me. I think back to when my dad was sick, and after a game Mr. Tanenbaum said, 'Go see your dad,' and he provided me with transportation to go fly and see my dad and come back. As an owner, as a friend, as a person, that really means something to me."

Eventually Williams migrated to the media side. In 2015 he was hired as an analyst with Rogers Sportsnet, and since the 2021–22 season he has done color commentary on Rogers Sportsnet broadcasts of Raptors games. “I have no regrets,” Williams says, looking back at his time as a player, coach, and member of staff for the Raptors. “Toronto was one of the biggest rewards for playing in the NBA. I’ve been fortunate in always getting these opportunities to be a part of Toronto and the Canadian community.”

6

Antonio Davis (1999–2003, 2006)

Antonio Davis was in his second year as a Toronto Raptor during the 2000–2001 NBA season. To put it mildly, he was hoopin'. Davis had even been named a starter in his first and only All-Star Game, alongside his teammate Vince Carter. His nomination was also a coup for a frontcourt player known more for his defense and rebounding than gaudy scoring.

His stats, moreover, testified to just how well he had rounded out his game during his first two years in Toronto. Davis started 77 games at center during his second season, averaging 35 minutes per contest, almost 14 points and 2 blocks, and more than 10 rebounds. He was playing well, the team was winning, and, for the first time in his NBA career, he was starting. That, too, was a major change.

After a four-year stint playing for the University of Texas at El Paso Miners alongside Tim Hardaway, Davis had been drafted 45th overall by the Pacers in 1990 but spent the first three years of his professional career in Greece and Italy. After signing with Indiana in 1993, Davis played for the Pacers for six straight seasons as a backup power forward.

Life in the warm embrace of the bench wasn't all bad, of course.

There was less spotlight, less scrutiny, and simply less pressure to perform at the sweatiest moments. "When I was in Indiana, praise God for Reggie Miller," Davis recalled thinking, having witnessed the demands of leading a team in the playoffs. "I didn't want that ball with four seconds left. I accepted that that was who I was, and I supported Reggie to lead us in any way that I could."

Even still, by the end of his sixth season with the Pacers, Davis was looking for a change, including more playing time and, above all, greater responsibility. He knew that his growth wasn't going to happen in Indiana.

"I had already talked to my agent, Bill Duffy, that summer," Davis recalled of the 1999 offseason. "I told him I just wanted an opportunity to be the best that I could be. I'm not coming off the bench *and* being an All-Star; it was just never going to happen. I still had some apprehension about leaving a situation where I knew we had worked our tails off to have an opportunity to win, and I felt like I was leaving my brothers and in some ways being selfish, but all of my Indiana teammates understood. So I said to the Pacers GM, Donnie Walsh, 'Am I going to be playing behind Dale Davis, Rik Smits, and Derrick McKey for the rest of my contract?' Donnie wanted me there because he knew I was a part of that team and a great supporting cast. But he also understood what I was saying. It was such a blessing to have a GM who understood both sides."

His conversations with Duffy and Walsh set the trade machine immediately in motion. "Next thing I know," Davis said, "I get a call from Bill: 'There's an opportunity in Toronto for you to possibly start.'" It was great news, no doubt, but it also caught him off guard. "My first reaction was 'Toronto? Hold on. Wait a minute.'" It was hard to blame him. The Raptors had finished the lockout-shortened 1998–99 season 23-27. Admittedly, that record was the team's best finish yet, but it was still a young franchise in the process of building. Did Davis, going into his seventh NBA season and turning thirty-one, really want to be one of those foundational blocks?

"I was still trying to make a decision," Davis remembers. "The next person I talked to was Butch Carter," the coach of the Raptors. "He called me out of the blue. I told him that I was going back and forth with this whole thing." But before Davis could even wrap his head around the situation, he had been traded. "Next thing I know, Bill called me and was like, 'It's done.'"

Ready or not, Davis was a Toronto Raptor. He immediately embraced the change and challenge. "I was extremely excited about all the opportunities in Toronto. I wanted to establish myself as someone who could lead a team and be a big part of winning. Plus, the guys, man, the *guys* that were there: Vince, the superstar, and Tracy McGrady, who was going to be a superstar. It was crazy. I was so excited that my wife, kids, and I immediately packed our stuff up and flew to Toronto and bought a house."

It was a massive step up for Davis, and a real opportunity to contribute, start, and lead a team, but it was also a step into the unknown. Could Toronto develop into a competitive organization? In the summer of 1999, neither Davis nor his new teammates could know. Only time would tell, but Davis had his sights set firmly on the future. "Man, I *never* looked back."

Davis immediately excelled under the increased workload and the pressure of his new role as a vet and a team leader. He started 78 of his 79 games that first season at center, averaging 30-plus minutes and filling the stat sheet with 11.5 points, nearly 9 rebounds, and 1.3 blocks and assists. More importantly, the team was playing well, going a promising 17-12 by New Year. He could hardly believe his good fortune. "I can remember so many days coming in, sitting in my chair in the locker room, looking around and thinking, *Wow, I'm here.*"

His on-court success was also a pleasant surprise, at least to Davis. He of course wanted the challenge. But he didn't know if he had what it took to be not only a starter but a team leader. "I'll put it on record," he told us candidly. "There were times that I struggled with self-confidence. I didn't have that inner confidence to feel like I could do it."

If the first season boosted his confidence, then the second proved to him what everyone else in the league had already come to know: Davis was not only a starter but a top-tier frontcourt player who had rightfully earned a spot in the All-Star Game.

That second year was also a chance for the team to take care of unfinished business. The previous season had closed with a bitter pill. After going 45-37, the Raptors fell to the Knicks in the team's first-ever playoff appearance. The loss stung, but the team regrouped for the coming season. "I didn't feel bad about getting swept," Davis told us. "I had my moments where I was *pissed*, but it forced me to go into the summer and put in some work. *That's* what I was excited about." He was hardly alone. "The next year, guys got to training camp earlier," he recalled. "You're like, 'Okay, *now* y'all get it.' We were all more committed."

Through the leadership of the team's new head coach, Lenny Wilkens, and thanks to the roster building of Glen Grunwald, the 2000–2001 Raptors were also a better-rounded squad, with a healthy mix of young guys, like Carter, Alvin Williams, Morris Peterson, and Jerome Williams, and seasoned vets, including Charles Oakley, Kevin Willis, Dell Curry, Tracy Murray, and, eventually, Chris Childs. "The pieces that they had at the time made me feel like I could go to Toronto, fit in, do my part, and create an identity for myself in this league. Plus, Charles Oakley and Kevin Willis were icons to me and I learned so much from them every single day in Toronto. The first day I got there, Oak was like, 'We got work to do, but it's going to be good work.' He gave me so much confidence. I would never say this to anybody back then, but I was scared to death, bro. It was a huge adjustment, mentally, to be ready, and Oak was there, in my ear and with his no-fear attitude."

For Davis, it all boded well for the season—and the playoffs. "In bringing in those veteran guys, who had playoff experience, we always knew that if everything goes the way it's supposed to go, then we're going to be back in the playoffs. But our goal wasn't just to get out of this first round. During the year, we started talking about some of the other teams and how playing them meant a little bit more. It wasn't just another game; now, when you play, it's a chance to lock in, because we knew we might see those guys again in the playoffs. We were still wild, we still had a lot of fun, and we were still crazy. But our mindset and the way we went about our day was different."

The 2001 playoffs started with unfinished business: a first-round battle with the Knicks. Both Davis and his teammates welcomed the rematch. "It was on and poppin'," he says with a laugh today. Davis was also ready, teeming with a newfound confidence after his two years as a starter. "I wouldn't turn down any shots. I'm not making an extra pass. If I wasn't going to do it, it wasn't going to get done. That was my mentality. I think it was the first time I ever felt that. In Indiana, it was always 'Reggie's going to knock down a big shot. Just set a screen, roll to the basket, and be ready to rebound.'"

The Raptors–Knicks rematch came down to a decisive game-five battle in front of a hostile New York crowd at Madison Square Garden. Channeling Miller, Davis and the Raptors dispatched the Knicks, closing out the series on an iconic twenty-foot jumper by Alvin Williams that extended the team's lead and iced the game. Like his teammates, Davis too had risen to the challenge during the series, coming third to only Carter and Williams in points and minutes played, while leading the team in rebounds (60) and blocks (10).

Perhaps even more unbelievably, the Raptors were headed to the Eastern Conference Semifinals to face the Philadelphia 76ers in the franchise's sixth season. As Davis told us, "Getting to the playoffs was always our thing—get there and give ourselves a chance—and then we beat the Knicks and took the Sixers to game seven. It's crazy, right?" Davis and the team were confident going into the Philadelphia series, but the team's big man remembers the almost uncontrollable enthusiasm he felt. "It wasn't like any other playoff game I had been in. I was so hyped about that series. I walked into a lot of my playoff games with Indiana with this sense of calm. But I found myself against the 76ers having to take a deep breath, like 'Calm down, bro.'"

The Raptors ultimately fell to Philadelphia in seven games. It was a tough break in an otherwise miraculous season. But Davis's performance in the series only provided further proof that he could help lead a competitive team. Despite the nerves, he was second behind only Carter in both minutes played and points scored. He also led the team in rebounds (73) and dished out 16 assists, grabbed 7 steals, and blocked 12 shots. The critical game seven was, moreover, a true showcase. In Davis's 41 minutes on the floor, he led the team in scoring with 23 points, going 11 of 15 from the field, with 9 rebounds and 2 blocks.

If there were any lingering doubts that Davis was a top-tier starting center in the league, his performance across the playoffs had decidedly quashed them. "I didn't shit my pants," Davis says today. "I knew what I was going to have to do in those series. My mentality was different, and each and every game it progressed. I stepped up to the moment and did everything I could to help the team win. I was very proud of myself. It was the best span of basketball that I ever played."

Win or lose, Davis was loving his time in Toronto. "Being there really was this huge peak in my career," he said. "I was embracing being a part of the team and I felt more of a part of it—building that culture and being in the city. People always ask, 'What were your best years?' Indiana was great, but I felt like I was just part of a supporting cast. I got to Toronto and I was forced to take on a bigger role, which also forced me to grow."

Life in Toronto proved a welcome surprise to both Davis and his wife, Kendra. "In Indiana, we had settled in and had so many friends. We got married there and we were a short drive from my wife's hometown. There were so many things that were great about Indiana from that perspective. But now I'm uprooting all of that and going to Toronto and the unknown. That was tough. I had to go to Kendra and literally be like, 'I don't know what this is going to be, but what I do know is it's an opportunity for us to change our lives and our kids' lives.'"

Almost immediately, things started to come together for the Davis clan in Canada. "That first season, halfway through, I looked around and thought, *We're having a pretty decent year and we're winning some games. Things are going good.* Our house felt like home. My wife was getting adapted. My kids went not just to a good school, but a great school; we lived in not just a good neighborhood, but a great neighborhood. That's really all you want: to have all those things come together and to have so many good things happening."

Then, while renegotiating his contract in 2001, a gross misunderstanding emerged about Davis's attitude toward the metric system, of all things. Really.

In an interview with Jim Rome, Davis expressed his concerns over how his twins, Antonio Jr. and Kaela, might eventually re-adapt to life in the US after so many years in Toronto. "It's just that Canada teaches a lot of different things," Davis told Rome. "You know, the metric system, when they go to school every day and they're singing the national anthem. As they grow older, there are some different things they need to learn. I'm a little worried about it now because they're really starting real school—first and second and third grades—and I think those grades are very important in their learning process."

In Toronto, and Canada, this led to a small but largely overblown furor. In truth, no one inside the organization actually cared. Glen Grunwald, the Raptors GM who was in the process of re-signing Davis, shrugged it off with a joke: "Tell Antonio that I will volunteer to tutor his kids in pounds and ounces and gallons and pints (if he re-signs)."

Davis could hardly believe the blowback. "I got ridiculed for saying that," he recalled, wincing at the memory. "Anybody who questioned me just really did not understand. I went there, I bought a house, and I bought in; I didn't half step in and half step out. Kendra and I had several talks about it, and there was such an upside to the conversation; it was never anything negative. Just to get that kind of backlash was a little unsettling, but understandable to a degree. I didn't trip out."

Plus, the hullabaloo hardly affected Davis's—or the Raptors'—decision-making. He re-signed with Toronto, inking an extension worth $60 million over five years. It was the most lucrative deal of his career and more than doubled his annual salary. It also meant at least a few more years with the metric system. Unsurprisingly, Davis didn't seem to mind.

Davis played well throughout his third season with the Raptors, but the team finished only 42-40. Carter missed the final 14 games of the season and the playoffs with an injured knee, which required surgery, and an overmatched Raptors team predictably fell to the Pistons in the first round of the playoffs. After that, the Raptors never regained their winning form. En route to a 24-58 season during Davis's fourth with the team, in 2003–04, the team traded him, Chris Jefferies, and Jerome Williams to the Chicago Bulls in exchange for Lonny Baxter, Donyell Marshall, and Jalen Rose.

Life with the Bulls was going well, but then rumors of another trade emerged and Davis was sent to the Knicks. He had been in New York only five months when he was traded again. Back to the Raptors. It was another blindsiding trade, and Davis was feeling burnt-out between stresses at home and the upheaval of being unexpectedly dealt again and again.

By the time he rejoined the Raptors, the thirteen-season vet was thirty-seven years old, and his second stint with the team proved an impossible homecoming. "When I got shipped back to Toronto, I was just done mentally at that point. It wasn't fair to Toronto; it wasn't fair to me; it wasn't fair to anybody." After just eight games with the team, Davis couldn't continue on. He went to the Raptors' GM, Bryan Colangelo, and told it to him straight. "I said, 'Bryan, I'm beat up mentally and physically. My body's not recovering. I'm not playing, bro. You and my agent can figure it out.'"

Just a month and a half after returning to Toronto, Davis decided to hang up his sneakers, on March 23, 2006. It was a hard way to end an otherwise remarkable playing career. He had even served as vice president and then president, between 2005 and 2006, of the National Basketball Players Association and had played a crucial role in explaining the collective bargaining agreement to his peers and more junior colleagues, while sitting on negotiating teams for the NBA's Competition Committee and even speaking in front of the US Congress.

Today, Davis is reflective about his time in Toronto. "I hope Toronto got as much as I was given. I hope they know that. So many great things happened there: being an All-Star and being a part of a team that went to the playoffs three years in a row. All of that on a personal note meant a lot more to me than anything I had ever done in my career. I was happy to be able to celebrate that with the fans. They embraced me and they came along for the ride. I always love to come back no matter what the occasion is."

His pride in the team and his own accomplishments as a Raptor were only solidified during Toronto's run to the Finals in 2019. "To be a part of the magic of that history makes me feel good. You're the only team in the country. I watched a lot of those 2019 Finals games, and I was just so excited. I was literally rooting for the Raptors, and everybody thought I was crazy, because you *never* saw me rooting for anybody, but I was rooting for them and I was very excited when they won. I feel an attachment to that team in a way, but more than that, to the city and the country and to Larry Tanenbaum, who I have so much respect for. Those were the kinds of things that crossed my mind when the Raptors won the championship. To see the fans go crazy, I was like, 'I can only imagine what it's like up there right now—how great of a feeling.'"

Raptors Moment

May 20, 2001: Game Seven of the Eastern Conference Semifinals

Going into the 2000–2001 season, hopes were high. Vince Carter had become the face of the Raptors as one of the most electric players in the league. The season prior he had been named to the All-Star Team, been voted Third-Team All-NBA, and even garnered votes for Most Valuable Player. Not bad for a second-year player, to put it mildly.

Now, it was only the Raptors' second time in the playoffs. The season prior, Toronto had lost in the opening round in three straight games to the Knicks. One year later, Carter and the team mowed down New York in a first-round rematch, a series sealed by Alvin Williams's iconic, game-clinching shot. With the win, the Raptors had gotten over a major hump, earning their first playoff series victory in franchise history. But on the other side of that hill were the 56-26 Philadelphia 76ers, led by Allen Iverson, by then a fifth-year player and that season's MVP. After splitting the first six games, the Eastern Conference Semifinals came down to a decisive game seven in Philadelphia. The Raptors struggled early on, ending the first quarter down 10 points, 31–21, but held the hometown team to a meager 19 points in each of the next three quarters. Ultimately, their stifling defense wasn't enough. The Raptors fell to the 76ers in the final moments of the 88–87 loss, when Carter's deep two clanged off the rim as the buzzer sounded.

The loss in Philadelphia was a tough end to the season and, for some onlookers, a premature exit from the playoffs. But it was also testament to just how far the Raptors had come in only six seasons. That, unfortunately, is not often how the series is remembered, especially game seven, when Carter decided to fly to his college graduation the morning of the game.

Eric still remembers the chatter at the time. Toronto, Canadian, and even US sports media were in a tizzy, second-guessing Carter's decision. Even today, Eric still hears from the naysayers. It's easy for some to claim, in hindsight, that Carter made the wrong choice. But it's worth remembering that the team's star had hardly gone rogue. Carter actually took the short flight to North Carolina on MLSE Chairman Larry Tanenbaum's private plane, left the two-hour graduation ceremony after only twenty minutes, and arrived in Philadelphia by noon, five hours before tip.

It's also worth recalling that there's another story to tell about that series. There's Carter's 35 points in the opener, good for a win against a hostile Philadelphia crowd. There's his 50-piece and a win in game three. There's his 39-point performance back in Philadelphia, down 3–2 in an elimination game, for another win. And there's the reality of game seven: Carter flirted with a triple-double—going 20-7-9 with 3 steals and 2 blocks and playing *all 48 minutes*—and was just a few inches too long on a deep two that would have won the entire series at the buzzer.

And inside of those inches, there are plenty of other possibilities to consider.

Imagine Vince makes that shot in Philadelphia. He's a twenty-four-year-old All-Star, Second-Team All-NBA prodigy, who has led a veteran squad to the Eastern Conference Finals in his third season, on the morning of his college graduation. That alternative history would have changed everything: The Raptors become a Conference Finals team, facing the Bucks, after less than a decade in the league, with a chance to go to the Finals for a showdown with Kobe Bryant's Lakers.

It's a tantalizing hypothetical. All of a sudden, perhaps, the talk would not have been about Carter and his graduation but about the team itself, defined by a core of talented players around a budding superstar and a new face of the league, a player who had earned his bachelor's degree the morning before hitting a game-winning, buzzer-beating, series-clinching shot. It's easy to imagine the Just-Do-It poster today: "Vince Carter: Do *all* of it." That, though, was a story never written.

Game seven against the Sixers simply raises a lot of what-ifs. For Antonio Davis: "It was an opportunity that we let slip away. We had a chance to win, definitely." Alvin Williams agrees—"I felt really confident that we could have beat the Bucks as well," he told us—but was less certain that he would have been able to chase down the competition's offensive spark plugs the entire postseason. "That Philly series was a dogfight. I've never been so exhausted after a game, physically or psychologically. I probably slept for two days. If Vince made that shot, I was thinking, personally, *Did I have enough juice?* I was dead tired. First round, Allan Houston. Second round, Allen Iverson. Third round, Ray Allen. All these goddamn Allens," he laughs. "They would have been torturing me, man." Chris Childs doesn't know how that postseason would have progressed. "If we would have got to the Eastern Conference Finals, and got through and played the Lakers, it would have been a struggle, but man, all you gotta do is get there."

Today it's easy to ask questions about game seven. What's not up for debate among his former teammates, however, is Carter's decision to attend his graduation. Childs, for instance, tells it straight. "The graduation didn't affect *nothing* that happened on the court. What the media wrote and quoted players saying—that's bullshit. We all talked to Vince. Vince came to each person individually, and we said, 'Brother, go ahead. We got your back.'"

Antonio Davis recalled a similar interaction alongside Charles Oakley. "I remember it like it was yesterday. Me and Oak were in the bathroom. Vince came in after game six and said what he was going to do. All we could do is give him our blessing. I would never say I was mad about any of that." So little did Carter's decision to attend his graduation matter to his teammates that Alvin Williams didn't even realize that Carter had gone to his graduation until later that day.

In any case, the series wasn't won or lost on a single shot. "We had opportunities throughout the game to go up," Childs argues. "We had two turnovers in the fourth quarter. *We* lost the game." In addition, Davis added, Carter was the team's leader who had shown up in clutch moments again and again. "At the end of the day," he rightly observes, "we don't get to game seven without Vince. He gave us a shot."

7

Chris Childs (2001–2002)

Chris Childs had finally hit rock bottom. It was 1993, and the twenty-five-year-old point guard had spent the night out gambling and drinking, trying to string out the three hundred dollars he netted each week playing for the Quad City Thunder of the Continental Basketball Association (CBA).

"I fell asleep in my son's bed. I woke up and his feet were in my face," he told us. "My son had this look in his eyes—the most embarrassed or surprised look. It might've been nine or ten o'clock, and I was usually up at six, making the family breakfast and then going to practice. At that moment, I looked at my son and I made a promise that he would never have that look on his face again."

Childs knew he needed help. His first call was to Dan Panaggio, his coach, and then to Anne DeLong, the owner of the Quad City Thunder, who flew her troubled point guard on her private jet to Houston and enrolled Childs in John Lucas's Wellness and Aftercare Program, a substance-abuse recovery program for athletes.

As a former NBA journeyman and coach, Lucas had seen it all since founding the program in 1986. Today, Childs doesn't split hairs about his experiences there. "That program is to save your life, and a lot of people didn't make it. When you're coming into the league at eighteen, nineteen, or twenty years of age, you know you can play, but can you manage the twenty out of twenty-four hours when you're not playing, practicing, or getting treatment?"

At the time, despite knowing he needed help, Childs hadn't yet come to terms with his struggles. "It was the hardest thing I've ever done. I thought, *I don't have these problems. I don't sit out on the corner with a can, getting drunk or falling over.* But through Lucas's program, I saw it was a psychological issue. You have things that you don't know how to live with. When something gets hard, you try to find satisfaction in material things when your family and God are the only things that can satisfy you."

Childs also realized he was failing not only himself but his family. "My dad had always told me and my siblings, 'When you walk out the door of our home, you're always auditioning for somebody, so be the best version of yourself.' I always carried that with me. John was the same way. He used to make us look in the mirror every day and would ask us, 'Do you like what you see?'"

The lessons he was learning were about himself. But through that mentorship, he was also seeing how the person he was off court shaped who he could be on court. "John Lucas told me, 'You're going to have so many different people on your team with different personalities. Can you handle those personalities?' He was always giving us these recipes, and it was up to you to cook the meal. John told me, and Magic Johnson told me the same thing: 'You can play the game, but can you lead men? Can you get other men to follow you? Stop trying to be everybody's favorite. They don't have to like you, but they damn well better respect you.' Hearing that from two point guards who've played at the highest level changed the trajectory of my career."

It took time, though, for those lessons to sink in. "During my first stint, in Houston, I was there for thirty days in the rehab facility. Then I went to a place in Miami because me and another player were still drinking and disrespecting the program. John made me go to Miami, which was court-ordered. You're either going to this program or you're going to prison. I stayed in that program and it made me the basketball player that I became. Once I got out, John picked me up. I said, 'Take me to the gym; just drop me off. I will make my way home.' I locked myself in the gym for three months back home in California to get my body in the best shape."

It was a turning point for Childs. After returning to the team, the Quad City Thunder went 34-22 in the 1993–94 season, and Childs was named CBA MVP. Under his leadership, the Thunder also went on a decisive playoff run, dusting the Omaha Racers 4–1 in the Finals and claiming the CBA championship. Childs stood out in the playoffs, averaging 17.9 points and 7.6 assists, and was even named Finals MVP.

For his outstanding play, the undrafted four-year player out of Boise State, who had already spent half a decade in the CBA, caught his first glimpse of the NBA. After the Quad City Thunder won the championship, Willis Reed, the general manager and vice president of basketball operations for the New Jersey Nets, contacted Childs and gave him the chance he desperately longed for: a chance to fight for a roster spot in the NBA.

Coming out of Foothill High School in Bakersfield, California, Childs already knew what it meant to face the consequences of his own choices. He was a highly touted prospect, and top D1 programs across the US had taken notice. "During my junior year, I had approximately thirty to forty scholarship offers. During the summer prior to my senior year, I protested the SAT because I thought it was biased towards minorities. The questions on those tests are not conducive to the environment that I grew up in or anybody of color. I said, 'I'm not taking this test.'" His father, James Henry Childs, backed his decision. "My dad at the time was a city councilman. He said, 'If this is what you strongly believe in, then I'm going to support you.'"

His stance courted immediate blowback. "They started writing in the papers, 'He's militant, he's a troublemaker, blah, blah, blah.' A lot of the colleges took their offers off the table." Just like that, Childs watched his ticket to a free college education and a gateway to the NBA vanish. It was his father who again stepped in to counsel his young son. "Maybe ten days before the signing period, my dad said, 'Listen, you got to get a scholarship. You made a stance, you stood by it, now go ahead and take the test.' So I took the test and blew it out of the water."

Before long, those retracted recruitment offers started to rematerialize. "All those schools tried to come back. I wrote each and every one of them: 'I appreciate you having more interest in me now, but at this time, I don't think I'm a good fit for your program. I'm just going in a different direction.'"

There were also new offers, and Childs weighed his decision carefully. "Bobby Dye, who was the coach at Boise State, said to me one thing that stood out. 'I'm not going to promise you a position, but I promise you that I'm going to allow you to fight for a starting position. If you outplay this person, you'll start.' So I went to Boise, because Coach Dye gave me a fair shake. I ended up beating the senior out for his position and starting all four years and was all first-conference and all-conference every year. *Sports Illustrated* named me one of the best guards coming out of the West." Childs's careful decision-making had paid off. So too had Coach Dye's gamble. Childs led the team to three of the Broncos' best seasons in school history.

But it was déjà vu all over again when making the leap to the NBA. "Where I made the mistake was when I was going to pre-draft camps. When you go to a smaller school, you do not have the leeway of somebody going to a North Carolina or a UCLA. They want you to humble yourself and to know that at any given moment everything can be taken away." Childs failed to kiss the ring, and it showed on draft night. "I went from being a mid-first-round pick to a late-first-round pick to not getting picked at all. Being ranked one of the best guards coming out the West to not get drafted. It wasn't my play. It was all these rumors that guys were spreading because they didn't like me coming from a small school and getting notoriety."

On draft night, the ugly truth finally settled in. "We had a draft party at my house in Boise—mom and dad, brothers and sisters. They called everybody's name in the draft, but they didn't call mine. I left the room, crying, and people wanted to see me. My father said, 'No, just leave him alone. He'll be out in thirty minutes. I know my son.' I'm in there, pity pie, just feeling sorry for myself, and then thought, *Everybody who got drafted before me, I'm gonna make them pay*. I took a T-shirt, cut off the sleeves, and wrote on the T-shirt everybody's name that got drafted. I wore that shirt every day for the five years that I played in the CBA. I made all-league teams, got all these different accolades, but I never got called up."

Four years in college. Five years in the CBA, with four different teams. Personal trials and struggles. A recovery. And finally: a shot in the NBA with the Nets and another battle for a roster spot.

Scraping and grinding, Childs had finally found his way to the NBA at the age of twenty-seven. He spent two seasons at the Meadowlands, where he established himself as a reliable contributor and a steady floor general. During his first season, he served as a backup guard but gradually earned more playing time thanks to his tenacious defense and canny playmaking. The next season, Childs played in 78 games, eventually starting and averaging 12.8 points, 7.0 assists, 3.1 rebounds, and 1.4 steals—all career bests.

Following his breakout 1995–96 season, Childs was a free agent and signed a massive six-year, $24 million deal with the Knicks. The money was one thing, but even better was the spotlight in the Big Apple. "There's not a lot of people in this world who get to hear the announcer say your name starting for the New York Knicks." As a playmaking point guard, it was also a rare opportunity to feed some of the game's all-time greats. "I got Patrick Ewing, Allan Houston, and Larry Johnson. They need the ball."

His distributor role also played into his vision of himself on the court. "I was all about the best for the team. 'How can we be better?'" During his time in New York, his commitment to the team showed, including his willingness to come off the bench. Childs played more than 50 playoff games with the Knicks, as both a starter and a backup, including two runs to the Conference Semifinals, one Conference Finals, and one Finals appearance against Tim Duncan's Spurs.

During his fifth season with the team, the Knicks were looking to retool—and the clock was ticking on the 2001 trade deadline. "I'm in Hackensack, New Jersey, at a barbershop," Childs recalls. "The trade deadline was at midnight. It's a blizzard outside and it's 11:52 p.m. 11:55. 11:58. 11:59 and thirty seconds, and my phone rings. My buddy answers the phone. He said, 'Man, you've been traded to Toronto.' I'm like, 'What? Toronto?' I was all in my head. I didn't talk to anybody. I was in shock."

Childs gathered himself, though, and prepared for the next challenge. It also didn't hurt that the Raptors had slowly become one of the most talented—and exciting—teams in the NBA, with one of the best fan bases and, above all, an emerging star in Vince Carter. "To experience the love that the fans of Toronto and the city of Toronto gave to the players—once the players saw that excitement and when Tracy McGrady and Vince Carter came, that's when that team took off. That team just happened to mesh with great management and ownership."

He also saw that team leadership firsthand. "I sat down to have a conversation with Glen Grunwald. This guy, he didn't come off like he knew more than you. He was like, 'I'm new at this. You're going to be new at this. Let's help each other.' That had never happened to me before." The team Childs joined in late February 2001, on closer inspection, was stacked. A starting lineup of Carter, Alvin Williams,

Charles Oakley, Antonio Davis, and Morris Peterson, supported by a Swiss Army knife of role players: Tracy Murray, Keon Clark, Dell Curry, Jerome Williams, and Eric Montross. As a seasoned big man and former Knicks bruiser, it was Oakley who set the terms for the team, consulting with Childs, who was by then a thirty-three-year-old vet himself. "Oak said to me, 'I take care of the big guys. You take care of the guards. Just know that we're going to have to put in extra work in the weight room to get these guys to buy into what we did in New York.'"

Pushing that buy-in also meant mentoring the Raptors' young starting point guard, Williams, whom the vets knew as Boogie. "The first person that I went to was him. I told him, 'This is your show. I'm here to lend my expertise and my experience. I'm going to be your brother—no matter what time of the night, the day, whatever.' I wanted to help Boogie to be a better player and bring some stability and leadership." There was work to be done not only in the gym. "In practice they didn't watch a lot of film when I got there. I made sure we had VHSs and DVDs on the road. We watched film together; we broke down defenses. That was a big component of giving yourself the best opportunity to go out there and succeed."

Childs's view of Williams wasn't merely some smoke to hype up the young guard. "He's one of the five most underrated point guards that I've played with or against," Childs argues today. "Alvin was very important to the Raptors, in the same realm as Vince, T-Mac, Kawhi, Damon Stoudamire, Siakam—all these guys. I have the utmost respect for Boogie."

The team was bursting with potential, but Childs could see that he and Oakley needed to push the squad to get better. "I'm like, 'Dang, these guys are very athletic, but have they ever been hit midair?' We get to practice and I say, 'Lenny, let me guard Vince. Let me see what he's made of.' Vince went to the basket and I followed him. I wasn't going to hit him, but I went to nudge him and he flinched. He still made a double-clutch shot, but he flinched."

Childs needed to get to the bottom of it with the team's young star. "We lived right across from each other in condos off Lake Shore Boulevard, so afterward I knocked on his door and said, 'Man, you got a minute?' He said, 'Yeah, come on in.' I said, 'Why did you flinch?' Vince said, 'I didn't flinch.' I said, 'Vince, why did you flinch and why do you shoot threes when you start the game?' He said, 'I gotta see it go in so I can be comfortable.' And I said, 'Do you want to be the best player in the NBA?' He said, 'Yeah, I do.' I said, 'Then that can't happen. You're too great. You're too great to be lax.' I saw the light turn on in his head and every damn practice after that I guarded him unless I was on the first-team offense. I've never seen a person do the things that he was capable of doing. I knew he would make us become something else and that's when I fell in love with the team."

During Childs's first season with the Raptors, the point guard didn't have much time to acclimate. Toronto finished 47-35 and, within just a few months, they were in the playoffs, facing off, for the second time in as many years, against the Knicks.

Childs was suddenly on the other side of the ball, with an opportunity for a showdown with his old team. His hasty midnight trade to Toronto still stung. "It's like, *How dare you trade me from the Knicks when I gave up my starting position for the betterment of the team? This is how I'm rewarded?* That was my mindset. Once it sunk in that I was a Raptor, there was no way we were losing to the Knicks in the playoffs. I saw the makeup of that team with Vince; we were deep. I looked at the Knicks. Yes, they have Latrell Sprewell and Allan Houston, but I've guarded those guys, so I already knew that me and Alvin would control Spree and Allan."

Childs was good to his word. The year before, an unseasoned Toronto team had dropped three straight to the Knicks in a best-of-five series. This time around, the Raptors rose to the challenge. "We beat them and it was so gratifying," Childs recalls. "I talked a lot of trash in the Garden to the fans, and they were giving it to me as well, but I was ready to battle and do whatever I needed to help my team."

Toronto's luck would famously run out in the 2001 Eastern Conference Finals against Allen Iverson and the 76ers. To Childs's surprise, the Raptors were unable to build on their momentum going into the 2001–02 campaign. "The team just didn't go as far as they could coming off the Philly series and going into the next season," he recalls. The Raptors struggled with injuries, including to Carter, who was in his fourth season. A nagging left-knee injury (which ultimately led to arthroscopic surgery) saw Carter miss the All-Star Game, stretches of the regular season, and all of the playoffs. "If we had Vince, with the makeup of our team, we'd have won," Childs argues today. Being bounced in the first round stung. "It was embarrassing."

At the end of the season, Childs was also once again a free agent. The thirty-five-year-old guard signed with his old team, the Nets, but it would be his last year in the league, when New Jersey waived him the following spring.

Today, despite the heartbreak of those two playoff appearances, Childs looks back at his time in Raptors purple fondly. "In a perfect world, I would have stayed another two years in Toronto. I wanted to make sure that my time in Toronto was special—that I didn't take the city for granted. It was an incredible city then; it's an incredible city now; and it's going to be an incredible city down the line, because of the influx of people from all over the world. Canadians are so humble and so gracious to others that aren't from there; they make us feel welcome. I was there for only two years and some change, but I know the impact that city had for me."

8

Jerome Williams (2001–2003)

In late February 2001, the 35-17 Sacramento Kings were in town, led by two skilled Euros, Peja Stojaković and Vlade Divac, a showy mixtape guard by the name of Jason Williams, and their superstar forward, Chris Webber (who, luckily enough for the Raptors, was out with an injury).

In comparison with the Kings, the Raptors were less sure-footed, playing .500 basketball and on the hunt for consistency. It was also a new-look squad. Toronto general manager Glen Grunwald had already sent Tracy McGrady to Orlando during the summer in a sign-and-trade and shipped Muggsy Bogues and Mark Jackson to the Knicks at the deadline in exchange for Chris Childs.

On the floor for the Raptors was nonetheless a formidable starting five: Vince Carter, Alvin Williams, Charles Oakley, Antonio Davis, and Morris Peterson. A versatile lineup of scoring and defense and a mix of developing players and established vets, supplemented by a raft of quality bench guys, including Dell Curry, Tracy Murray, and Keon Clark.

That night, just a day after the 2001 trade deadline, Raptors faithful also got to catch a glimpse of another newbie. With two minutes left in the second quarter, Jerome Williams, the Junkyard Dog, stepped on the court for the first time as a Toronto Raptor.

The crowd rose to its feet, giving the gritty forward a standing ovation. Not bad for a player who had spent his first four seasons in Detroit coming off the bench, averaging just 7 points per game. By the time he stepped on the court, though, less than twenty-four hours after being traded to Toronto, Williams was already a fixture in team lore, all thanks to a long drive through the night.

By the time the trade went through, it was already late at night on February 22. Williams had been exchanged with his fellow Piston Eric Montross for Tyrone Corbin, Kornél Dávid, and Corliss Williamson.

The Raptors had practice scheduled for 10 a.m. the next day. It was too late to get a flight, but Williams was raring to go—ready to start his new run as a Raptor. "I'm packing as we speak," he told Doug Smith of the *Toronto Star*, who caught Williams late that evening. "The planes don't fly but I can put gas in my truck."

So in the late hours of the night, Williams hopped in his Chevy Blazer and began the wintry six-hour haul from Detroit to Toronto. He pulled into town at 4:30 a.m. and was on court for shootaround the next morning. The legend of the Junkyard Dog grew. The reporters and fans ate it up, this instant dedication to his new team, this hurried desire to be in Toronto.

But that journey was not all smooth sailing. "I'm driving on the 401 and the snow's coming down pretty thick," he recalls. He's in his 4x4 SUV, but the truck, all low-profile rims and tires, is better built for drag-race fashion than wintry function. Still, Williams is pumped, his gut a swirl of "mixed emotions" and "butterflies," as he recalled to us, at the thought of being traded for the first time. He pushed on, speeding through the snowy night.

Eventually, those tires failed him, and the Blazer nearly skidded off the highway. It was a wake-up call. Williams pumped the brakes and refocused, recalling the patience that served him throughout his young basketball career. "I need to just make sure I'm going extremely slow," he told himself, pulling in behind a tractor trailer.

Today that moment is a part of the legend that he keeps to himself. "I was thinking, 'That's not a good story: Driving off the road, in a snowstorm, trying to get to practice.' I never told anyone that."

Back on the 401, the thought of playing for the Raptors calmed him. In December 1994, while he was a junior at Georgetown University playing alongside Allen Iverson, Williams and the Hoyas had matched up against the Memphis Tigers in a game at Maple Leaf Gardens in Toronto.

It was the first time Georgetown had ever held a regular-season game outside of the US, and the players had no idea what to expect. "On our schedule, it just said 'Memphis,'" Williams recalls. "We didn't even know we were going to Canada until we got on the plane." All they knew was that they needed their passports as they boarded their flight in Washington, DC. "When they told us we were going to Canada, everybody kind of sat back in their seats like, 'Oh, this is going to be a long flight.'"

Another supposedly endless journey to the forbidding north.

At least that's what it looked like to Williams, who thought back to the maps of North America he had seen as a kid. "That's eight to nine hours to get to," he recalls thinking. "I didn't grow up watching hockey. Back then, we didn't know a Toronto from a Calgary or a Vancouver or a Montreal." In 1994, the whole country was a big unknown. "We would just say, 'It's Canada.'"

So it came as a welcome surprise when the flight attendants announced that the plane would be touching down fifty minutes later. "I was like, 'Wow, that's pretty close!'" On the ground, too, Toronto turned out to be more familiar than expected. "It was a city! So our perceptions changed. I remember we wanted to get out on Yonge Street and just walk. Me, Allen, everybody." The shocks kept coming, the biggest surprise being just how familiar Toronto felt. "I remember going to Popeye's Chicken and thinking, *They have a Popeye's Chicken. In Canada!*" Today, that first visit holds a special place in Williams's heart. "I still have a Canadian two-dollar bill we had all signed."

That maiden trip to Canada immediately came to mind, back in the wee hours of February 23, 2001, while driving along the icy 401. "Toronto felt like an extension of home, because that was the only place we traveled outside of the country when I was in college." When he finally pulled up to practice, it was hard to tell him from the longtime vets. "I'm truly a Raptor," he told reporters that morning. "My heart and soul lies with the purple and red and white and the little dinosaur."

And that six-hour drive from Detroit to Toronto? That was nothing. As a college junior, remember, he thought it was an eight-hour *flight*.

Toronto ultimately dropped the game against Sacramento, Williams's first as a Raptor. It was another loss, but a good one, with Toronto offering a glimpse of the tenacity that would buoy them through the rest of the season and carry them to the Eastern Conference Semifinals.

Williams only played three minutes, but he, too, liked what he saw and already knew the role he could play. In Detroit, where he was drafted late in the first round in 1996, he developed a reputation for his work ethic and motor. It was also there that he earned his nickname, the Junkyard Dog, given to him by his teammates Grant Long and one of the original Bad Boy Pistons, Rick Mahorn, who was also known for his punishing play. To Williams, being called a "dog" never felt so much like a compliment.

The fans in Detroit also lauded Williams's unerring energy. He even had his own fan section, the Dog Pound, which followed him to Toronto. As Williams told us, Raptors fans "brought in posters—'Junkyard Dog, we love you!'—and all these creative things. I used to look at the fans from the court and say, 'Man, you're wearing *my* jersey.'" That love for the gritty bench guy made sense, a bit of reciprocity between a second-string player and a place with its own second-city mentality. "The fans in Toronto are very appreciative of the underdog. I think they're even more underdogs in Canada because of the lack of respect Canadians get in the US. That is one of the main driving forces for them to appreciate the underdog even more, because they know that's a mirror image of themselves. They had to get there by grinding. That really propels the fans to identify with a person who's trying to do everything they can to help the team win, more so than the guy who's just out there getting up shots."

Williams knew what it was like to live on hustle and heart rather than a deadeye shot. Growing up in Germantown, Maryland, just outside of DC, he was an accomplished high school player but undersized, standing at just 6'2". Looking for a chance to keep playing, Williams attended Montgomery College, a nearby junior program, where he paid his own tuition. There, both he and his game grew. Over his two seasons as a Montgomery College Raptor (the other *avian* type), Williams averaged 26 points and 17 rebounds per game. He also shot up to 6'9".

Nearby Georgetown noticed, offering him a full athletic scholarship. With it, though, came a new role on the team, one that downplayed his offense. Over his two years at Georgetown, in fact, Williams averaged only 10.5 points per game. But he wasn't there to score. That's something the team could leave to its star, Iverson. Williams's job was to defend and to gobble up rebounds. He welcomed his supporting role, just as he later embraced his job in Detroit and Toronto. As the longtime Hoyas coach John Thompson remarked at the time, admiring Williams's quiet alacrity for the dirty work, he was "Dennis Rodman without the attitude."

Being part of the Georgetown system also had its perks, including summer runs in DC with college alumni turned NBA pros—guys like Patrick Ewing, Alonzo Mourning, Mike Sweetney, Othella Harrington, Dikembe Mutombo, and AI. "We talked so much trash during those pickup games," he recalls with a laugh. "We didn't call fouls at Georgetown, so I'd get fouled half the time. Dikembe's there, blocking everybody's shot, waving his finger, 'Jerome, you will *never* dunk on Mount Mutombo.' He used to love that. I was like, 'Dikembe, you are never going to say that to me again.'"

His time at Georgetown and then in Detroit helped him to hone his skill set as a guy willing to come off the bench to energize the team—and the fans—through a combination of tenacious defense and grab-everything rebounding. Toronto simply offered the perfect landing spot. "Teams need players like me. I did have skill, I could dribble, I could dunk, I could shoot a little bit. I wasn't just a screener and a rebounder. They call guys like me a 'ball shifter.' I felt like that was my role and what I needed to do. And that's what I was there to do."

Toronto also offered Williams the chance to play with Vince Carter. His own excitement came out of watching the hallowed 2000 Slam Dunk Contest, when Carter showed the whole world his bag of high-flying tricks. "When I first got traded, I was like, 'I'm getting ready to play alongside one of the greatest dunkers of all time, arguably the best in-game dunker.' That was the most exciting part of the game for me. You have to put Vince up there with the Shawn Kemps and Michael Jordans and Dominique Wilkinses. The degree of difficulty for a lot of his in-game dunks was insane."

In Carter, Williams also saw a true star. "I played alongside AI in college, then my rookie year I played alongside Grant Hill in Detroit. These were the faces of the NBA. Then to see a young Vince. You know that you're getting ready to play alongside another player that's comparable to MJ." The Jordan heresy is hard to resist, even today, and everywhere Williams looked he saw the inklings of a potential superstar. "That was some exciting basketball to watch. Vince had one of the quickest first steps. He didn't kill you with crossovers or dribbling moves. When he gathered himself, you were in trouble too. You literally could be on a poster. He had so much ball control and could palm the ball like MJ and Dr. J. He could manipulate and move it whenever he felt like it. How are you going to defend that?" For Williams, playing a supporting role to Vince was the best way to maximize both of their skill sets. "The excitement was just being able to really help build something alongside a player like Vince."

Vince was one thing. But the squad was also good. "Our team was the first-ever Raptors team in history to get out of the first round. People need to understand that Vince, Antonio Davis, Alvin Williams, Jerome Williams, Charles Oakley, Morris Peterson, Keon Clark, Chris Childs—we were those *goons*. That was the start of some good basketball in Canada, where people were respecting us as soon as we came across the border, like, 'Oh, this is trouble coming to town. This is not the Raptors teams of old. These guys are fully loaded.'"

The team could also feel that newfound awe and respect on the road. "Traveling, we were a rock band. And, as far as all of Canada being behind us, that was one hundred percent true. The fans, the kids, and the support when we left Canada was at an all-time high. I remember going to every stadium in the US and having Canadian fans there. Repping jerseys, *my* jersey, Vince's jersey. We were two of the top-selling jerseys of that era of Raptors basketball."

That excitement started to build even before the games. "We had electricity as soon as we came in the gym. As soon as we came in the stadium, people were like, 'We're going to see something. Don't leave your seat.'" The team fed on that enthusiasm, and the crowd fed on the players' energy in return. The Raptors even had a special pregame routine: a layup line dunk contest. "Vince and I were obviously the two best dunkers. I could have the crowd going on two or three dunks. I'd be doing 360s, windmills, stuff like that. But that's about as far as I could go. Vince would take it easy the first couple dunks. He would always wait till his last dunk, which would be between the legs." The fans loved it, but so did the team. Williams recalls the oohs and the aahs. "Everybody's, 'Man, did you see that? Did you *see* it?' And I got to see that every night. We would all be just so hyped when he would do it."

Plus, when Vince was dialed in, you knew he had his legs. "If he did that dunk in the layup line, it was like, everybody's in trouble tonight." During a game, after one such dunk contest, Williams remembers, "Alvin threw Vince a lob and it was totally out of the lane. You didn't even see the basket. The ball was just floating out there. And you're like, 'There's no way Vince is catching that. That's *dangerous*.' And he caught it and did a windmill. I'm sitting there, thinking, *This is insane*. Vince would always make stuff look so effortless. We could just throw balls anywhere and he would go up there and figure it out."

As the 2000–2001 season wore on, the new-look Raptors found stability—and, most importantly, started winning, going 19-8 to close the season. After plowing through the Knicks in the first round, the Raptors ran into the 76ers and Williams's old college teammate, AI, the 2001 MVP, only to lose the series in the final moments of game seven.

Those memories ended up being bittersweet. A great series for the best Raptors team ever to that point, but still the lingering feeling of unfulfilled potential. During the Vince era, the team never made it again to the Eastern Conference Semifinals. And before long, Vince was gone, shipped off to the Nets.

Soon Williams was gone too. After three and a half seasons with the Raptors, the Junkyard Dog was traded to the Chicago Bulls in December 2003. Then he was on the move again, this time traded to the Knicks, who waived him at the end of the 2005 season. That proved a hasty close to his career. "Two years after leaving the

Raptors, I was gone from the game." Still, looking back, Williams has only fond memories of Toronto. "I was only there for a little under three years, but those three years I gave it my all. I gave it everything I had and the fans appreciated it. When people think of my legacy, they look at Toronto."

PART III

THE BOSH ERA, 2003–2010

Eras never start and end cleanly, and by the time Chris Bosh joined the Raptors, Toronto was witnessing the collapse of its first-ever superstar empire under Vince Carter. When the lanky southpaw was selected fourth overall in the 2003 draft, Carter was still the face of the team. Eventually the Raptors pivoted, in late 2004, unceremoniously trading Carter and rebuilding around Bosh, who was by then in his second season.

It was during this period that the Raptors fan base was solidified. It wasn't the thrill of the new anymore or even the gravitational pull of Vinsanity. It was about identifying with a team, one that had been interwoven into the very fabric of the city, becoming a touchstone for a generation of young Raptors fans who had suddenly grown up.

Any casual fan could also look around Air Canada Centre and find ample sartorial commitment in the stands: waves of purple jerseys with the names and numbers of so many of the guys featured in this book. Stoudamire, Carter, and Bosh jerseys were there, of course, but so too were less-heralded players: Matt Bonner, José Calderón, Mike James, Charlie Villanueva, T. J. Ford, Anthony Parker, Jason Kapono, and Jorge Garbajosa.

All those names also speak to something that marks out the Raptors fan base. It was these secondary players—the part-time and regular starters, the role fillers, the glue guys, the bench units—that the fans glommed onto, whether they spent six months in a Toronto jersey or seven years. Win or lose, Raptors nation found its feet under Bosh.

This is all the more remarkable because being a fan during Bosh's seven-year run as a Raptor was no easy feat. It was a period marked by a few highs and plenty of lows, including roster churn, changes in the coaching and executive ranks, and a struggle for stability and success.

Amid all that was Bosh, a leader on the court and in the locker room, respected by teammates and beloved by fans. He was the portrait of consistency, starting throughout the era, playing through injuries, and holding down almost nightly double-doubles. That elite steadiness did not go unnoticed. He went to the All-Star Game five straight times between 2006 and 2010 and even garnered MVP votes in 2007 and 2010. Bosh was a rock.

In 2010, after another losing season in Toronto, he decided to take his talents to South Beach, joining Dwyane Wade and LeBron James as part of the much-reviled "Heatles." In Miami, Bosh played an important but slightly diminished role, one that would help the Heat to two championships and would lead to a career-defining highlight. With only eight seconds left in a must-win game six of the 2013 Finals against the Spurs, and with the Heat down three, Bosh somehow corralled an arcing rebound off a missed James three, finding Ray Allen in the corner, who hit the game-tying shot. The play was classic Bosh: a hustle play leading to an assist that helped seal the game and series, but something easy to overlook within the chaotic celebration of Allen's clutch three. That was the kind of quiet leadership that also defined the Bosh Era in Toronto.

Bosh's time in the NBA would sadly come to a premature end in 2017, when blood-clotting issues would put a stop to his playing days. In 2021, Bosh was elected to the Naismith Memorial Basketball Hall of Fame. By then Raptors fans were chanting "We the

North" game in, game out, during seemingly annual playoff runs. Many of those fans were the same ones who cut their teeth on the Bosh Era, when they came to love a team better known for its odds-and-ends roster construction than its playoff prowess, a squad so visibly held together by the gangly power forward who quietly did a little bit of everything on the court.

9

Matt Bonner (2004–2006)

In the summer of 2003, all eyes were on the most stacked NBA draft class in years, if not decades. LeBron James, Dwyane Wade, Carmelo Anthony, Chris Bosh, and, most infamously, Darko Miličić, the Serbian big man chosen second overall. The Raptors sat in the fourth slot that year thanks to an injury-riddled 2002–03 season and selected Bosh, a southpaw big man tasked with the seemingly impossible: turning around the struggling squad and replacing Vince Carter when he was traded to the New Jersey Nets a year later.

Watching the draft that night from his hometown of Concord, New Hampshire, was another future Raptor, though not a name at the top of any team's big board: Matt Bonner, a four-year college player out of the University of Florida. "I hoped to make it to the NBA," he told us, "but I didn't know if I would." At best, he thought, he might get scooped in the second round, a low-risk pick, seasoned through four years of NCAA play and ready to spread the floor from the four, something largely unknown in 2003. After a few exhausting weeks of team workouts all over the US and Canada, he had reason to hope. "It's a grind: six days a week for three weeks, doing a workout for a different team every day in a different city."

After a week of flights and grueling sessions, though, his performance in Toronto was less than stellar. "The Raptors were on a

Friday. By then, you're not getting the same scores you did on Monday when you were rested. The workout went okay, but it wasn't anything special." Luckily, he was more optimistic about another workout. "The team that I thought was going to draft me was the New York Knicks. I worked out for them twice. I was unconscious. I literally didn't miss a shot and annihilated everyone I was up against, including a projected lottery pick. I beat him so bad in the one-on-one drills that he quit the workout."

Those performances came as a huge relief to Bonner, so the evening of the draft he planned to head to a local sports bar in Concord. "I called a few of my friends like, 'Let's go watch the draft at the Capitol Grille.'" His dad, Dave Bonner, overheard and wanted to join. He also had a request: "You mind if I invite some people?" Matt agreed, thinking little of it. "I show up at the Capitol Grille and it is packed. Like hundreds of people—and Concord's not that big. Because he was a mailman there for thirty-five years, he knows the entire city. And my dad told *everybody*. There were no decorations or signs, but it was just a frack-ton of people there. I'm like, 'Oh, great. Here we go. It's a full-blown draft party now.'"

By the start of the second round, Bonner was sweaty with anticipation. "I was still thinking the Knicks were going to draft me. But with the Knicks' second pick, they didn't take me." At 30th, New York tagged Maciej Lampe, a Polish big man. "Their thirty-ninth pick, I'm like, 'This is it.' And they don't take me." Instead, it was Slavko Vraneš, a 7'6" Montenegrin giant.

As the draft ground on, Bonner started to panic. "Now they were going to forty, and I was like, 'Aw, crap. This could be embarrassing. Half my hometown's here to watch me get drafted, and I might not.' Forty-one, not me. Forty-two, not me. Forty-three, not me. Forty-four, not me." As the numbers ticked higher, the mood at the bar shifted from an excited buzz to subdued murmurs, before the draft coverage mercifully went to commercial.

After the break, with the 47th pick, the Jazz selected Mo

Williams. And Bonner sank even further. Then, a draft-day miracle. "In the background of the broadcast, you could hear someone say my name." Sure enough, the commentators backtracked, clarifying that, during the commercial break, the Chicago Bulls had selected Bonner with the 45th pick. "I got drafted *during the commercial.* The whole bar went nuts."

Thirty seconds later, Bonner got a call from his agent, Arn Tellem. "You're not on the Bulls," he explained. "You're on the Raptors. They traded the pick." Bonner was just as surprised as anyone, recalling his crummy workout weeks earlier. It turned out that the Raptors' GM, Glen Grunwald, who was friendly with the Knicks' front office, was also at the New York workouts. "Apparently Glen watched me annihilate the lottery pick. Based on that workout, they decided to select me."

Bonner was over the moon. Celebrating in a hometown bar, with his friends, his father, and seemingly his dad's entire mail route. It didn't matter where; Bonner was bound for the NBA. "Let's do it!" Bonner yelled to the bar. "Let's go to the Toronto Raptors!"

Long Beach, California. The Fourth of July, 2003. The Raptors were hosting a minicamp before Summer League began. Finally, NBA basketball under the big lights. "It was at the Pyramid in the LBC," Bonner recalled, a naive rookie still wet behind the ears. "It was Long Beach, the home of Snoop Dogg! I was starting to feel like, 'Holy crap, maybe I'm good enough to play in the NBA.'"

That sun-soaked California outlook changed quickly, however. "I didn't understand at the time that, as a second-round pick, you're not guaranteed to be in the league, especially as a forty-fifth pick. You're not guaranteed a contract. There were no two-way contracts. They couldn't even put you on the G League team, because there was no G League back then. They owned my rights, I was on the team, but I didn't have a contract or anything."

The competition, moreover, was daunting, with few opportunities early on to show off what he had to offer. "We started Summer League with *twenty-three people* on the roster, and every play was run for Chris Bosh." Even still, Bonner pulled down near double-doubles in his first couple games. Not everything went to plan, though, in the team's third contest. With only thirty seconds left against Dallas, Bonner coughed up a game-tying turnover to Josh Howard, the Mavs' first-round draft pick, ACC Player of the Year at Wake Forest, and ACC All-Defensive Team small forward.

The Raptors' new coach, Kevin O'Neill, immediately called a timeout. "Coach O'Neill took me on the sideline and just ripped me a new one for the turnover," Bonner recalled. The rookie then walked back toward the court only to get another earful from O'Neill. "He put me on the bench and didn't play me the next two games."

Bonner's late-game benching also led to a bit of soul-searching. "I was always a hard worker: 'Yes, Coach, what are my marching orders?' I was rarely reflecting on big-picture stuff. That third game was one of the rare times I did actually think, *What am I doing here? What is going to happen? Why is this not working out for me?* I had a moment of clarity that recentered me mentally."

The war of attrition that is Summer League ground on, with Coach O'Neill's bench continually dwindling. "By the last game of Summer League, we had seven guys on our roster because everybody had quit, left, or gone back to Europe. So now Coach *had* to play me and I had my best game. I had twenty-five points and redeemed myself."

Despite leaving Summer League on a high note, Bonner heard nothing from the team for the rest of the summer. Finally, toward the end of August, he got a phone call from his agent, who explained: "They have seventeen guaranteed contracts on the roster and there are only fifteen roster spots. Plus, they're over the cap. They don't have room for you on the roster. They want you to go play in Europe for a year, and then when you come back, they'll put you on the team because a bunch of the contracts will expire."

Bonner took it as a gentleman's agreement. "Cool," he thought. "I guess I'm going to Europe." Before long he was on a flight to Palermo to play in the top tier of the Italian league. There he worked on his game, plotting his return to the NBA. A good year overseas, a chance to play professionally, and a chance to get paid. Then *boom*, he thought: *I'm back in the NBA*.

Some of that turned out to be true. Some.

Back in Toronto, though, things were not going well. The Raptors finished the 2003–04 season 33-49. Then Grunwald, the GM who drafted Bonner, and Coach O'Neill were both fired. Rob Babcock was appointed GM and brought on Sam Mitchell as the team's new coach. "I came back towards the end of May from Italy," Bonner recalled, "and the two guys who drafted me and told me I'd be on the team were no longer there. I had to start all over again." That meant Summer League, then training camp, then preseason. If all went well, he was looking at a roster spot and a contract. Again, a big if.

Luckily, he had Mitchell in his corner. A year earlier, before being drafted, Bonner had attended a pre-draft camp in Chicago—run by none other than his future coach. "He remembered me, and when I was struggling, he was great. He said, 'I know what you're capable of. Just play your game, Matt.' This really built me up, because I could be an overthinker on the court. I credit Coach Mitchell for getting me over the hump. He had my back, and he saw me busting my butt. I think he saw a little of himself in me as a hard-playing role player and gave me minutes and a chance in Summer League and in preseason."

Bonner once again made it through the meat grinder, from Summer League to training camp. Then, just a day before the season began, one of the staff told Bonner, "Rob wants to see you in his office." Bonner went upstairs, where Babcock was waiting with Coach Mitchell. Also waiting on the desk: an NBA contract. A one-year, nonguaranteed, rookie minimum. There was a catch, though, and Babcock told him straight. The Raptors only had two point guards, Rafer Alston and Milt Palacio, and if one went down, they would need to find someone on the open market. If that happened, then they'd also need Bonner's roster spot.

On top of that, Babcock explained, Bonner was not without options. "Top teams from Europe have been calling all week asking what we're going to do with you." The list was tantalizing: "Madrid, Barcelona, Rome—first-class cities in Europe where you can make way more money than this contract taxed at the Ontario tax rate. *And* they'll guarantee it. It'll be multiyear and you'll be the star of the team."

Babcock finally finished: "So what do you want to do?"

And Bonner paused.

Coach Mitchell saw his uncertainty and intervened. "Matt, when you were a kid, what was your dream: playing in Europe or playing in the NBA?" Bonner immediately responded: "Playing in the NBA." And so did Mitchell: "Then sign the damn contract."

It was all Bonner needed to hear. He immediately called his father, Dave, with the good news: "I made the team and the first game's tomorrow."

Dave, as Matt well knows, does nothing in half measures. "As soon as I get off work," his father told him, "I'm driving straight there." Good to his word, Dave jumped in his car and drove through the night to Toronto. Crossing the border, he went out of cell phone coverage, and Bonner had no idea where his father was. "I didn't see him because it was game day. I had done my walk-through, taken my pregame nap, and didn't see him the whole day. My dad is very social and makes friends with everyone. Somehow, he talked his way down to courtside. I kid you not, we did 'hard work on three,' ran out for two lines of layups, and he was right there on the court in the tunnel while I ran on the court for my first NBA game. He gave me a high five with tears streaming down his face."

To most NBA fans, Bonner is known as the Red Mamba, a nickname gifted to him by none other than the Black Mamba himself, Kobe Bryant, for his shock of red hair. In 2013, Bryant was rewatching his famous 81-point performance against Toronto from January 2006. During the matchup, Bonner hit a three. Bryant couldn't resist, tweeting out Bonner's new name. "I was as shocked as anyone," Bonner recalled. "I had a million people texting me. It went like wildfire on social media and just stuck after that. It's definitely an honor."

In Toronto, though, he will always be known as the Red Rocket, a name given to him by the Raptors' play-by-play voice at the time, Chuck Swirsky, for riding the red and white Toronto subway to and from Raptors games (though if you ask Bonner, the name actually describes "the rocket athlete I am").

During his first season in Toronto, Bonner was just one more forward on the roster, playing behind Bosh, Carter, and Donyell Marshall. Then Marshall went down with a hamstring injury in November, offering Bonner two to three weeks to prove himself. And, once again, he did. The night that secured his place in team history occurred weeks later, on a cold December night in Toronto, against Kevin Garnett and the Timberwolves.

The Raptors were off to a rough start, going 8-16 to begin the 2004–05 season, already on a seven-game skid when the Wolves pulled into town, with Carter out with a strained Achilles. Even still, by the fourth quarter, the Raptors looked like they might be able to stave off their eighth straight loss. With only five and a half minutes left, and the Raptors up 86–79, the Wolves fed Garnett low in the post. He spun, dropping his defender, before coming face-to-face with Bonner.

That December KG–Bonner showdown wasn't even their first run-in. "I've had more important intersections with KG than any other player," Bonner says laughing. Before the season started, Minnesota had hosted a five-day Summer League with six teams, including the Raptors. "The first game we were playing was at the Target Center—twenty thousand seats—and there were three hundred people at the game. It was like a Tuesday at eleven a.m. in the middle of the summer, and this was before Summer League was even a thing, so there was *nobody* there."

Except one person in particular. "KG was sitting courtside on the baseline with his crew. It was so quiet and he just started heckling the crap out of me." At his peak, the seven-foot-tall, trash-talking KG was hard to miss. With only about three hundred people in the near-empty arena, a bellowing Garnett was also impossible to ignore. "Everyone could hear everything. He was talking all this crap, like four feet from me."

"Who's this bum?"

"Who's this redheaded bum?"

"Go at his ass! Go at him!"

"You can't guard *nobody*!"

"I remember I looked at him," Bonner recalls, "like what is going on? But KG was just locked in on me, talking all this smack. I thought, *God, is this how my NBA dream ends—getting heckled by Kevin Garnett?*"

Four months later, up in Toronto, late in the fourth and deep in the post, KG and Bonner met again. KG's baby hook clanged off the rim, back into his own hands. In the tangle for the rebound, Bonner suddenly found himself *behind* KG, who went up hard for the dunk. Bonner met KG at the apex of his outstretched arms, pulling down hard and sending KG to the floor.

The Toronto crowd erupted. For Bonner, he had no other choice. Protect the net. Protect the lead. If that took a little grit, so be it. And of course, Bonner had not forgotten the heckles. "I had some pent-up frustration with KG from Summer League and also that game," he admits. "My mentality was 'You're not getting the shot up.'"

Unsurprisingly, the Wolves' Latrell Sprewell came bounding in to protect the fallen big man. Then KG sprang up and started charging toward Bonner. He quickly assessed the situation. "I had this preconceived philosophy on fighting," Bonner explains. "I was not going to throw any punches because I couldn't afford to get fined. But if someone tried to punch me, I would just let them because my teeth were really crooked, and then I would get my teeth fixed for free."

Luckily for Matt and his dental insurer, but sadly for his smile, no punches were thrown. As the officials tried to work out what happened, the fans started chanting: "Bonner! Bonner! Bonner!" Finally, the decision came in. Bonner was hit with a flagrant two and ejected. As he trotted to the tunnel, the fans erupted again, and Bonner started handing out high fives, before pumping both his fists in the air, index fingers outstretched, basking like a top-rank wrestling heel in the cheers of the crowd.

Years later, Bonner and Garnett get along just fine. "I got to know KG pretty well during the 2011 lockout. I love KG. He's such a character. Pure entertainment. All heart and honesty. *And* he's hilarious. I played against him a million times. There's definitely mutual respect. He pokes and prods guys to see what they're made of, and if you stand up to it, then you got his respect. If you don't, he's just going to be relentless on you."

It was perhaps the greatest fight that never was in team history. And it secured Bonner's place in the fans' hearts, becoming a critical piece of Raptors lore: the image of the redheaded kid from New Hampshire, riling the crowd up, fingers in the air, as he walks to the tunnel to deafening cheers. "That morning, maybe five percent of the city of Toronto knew who I was," Bonner recollects. "After, like eighty percent of the city of Toronto knew who I was. It was on the front page of the paper and it was the number one highlight on all the shows. It was the turning point where the city made me their own. Everywhere I went it was: 'Red Rocket! Red Rocket! Red Rocket!'"

The next season, Bonner re-signed with the Raptors on a two-year deal. The contract meant something more to the hardscrabble player than just a suddenly swelling bank account. "It was a guaranteed deal and a home," Bonner said. "I thought I was going to be there my whole career."

Just a year later, though, his days in Toronto came to an untimely end, when the Raptors traded him in June 2006. "I was with a couple of my buddies golfing in Concord," Bonner recalls. "I had just hit like my fourteenth ball into the water." On the green, he got the call from his agent, who broke the news. "My initial reaction was like I just got shot. But then my agent's next sentence was 'You're going to the Spurs.' They had just won two of the previous four championships and were one of the best-run organizations in professional sports. So now I'm thinking: Tim Duncan, Tony Parker, Manu Ginóbili, Coach Pop. That's really exciting. *And* they wanted to trade for me."

Bonner flourished as a Spur, but the deal still stung. "I ended up rebuilding my life in San Antonio, staying there for ten years and winning two championships, so there's no regrets on that front. But that's the hard part about this business. You develop friendships and personal relationships with so many people, and then it's *poof*: 'I'll see you once a year when we come back to Toronto.'"

After his playing days finished, Bonner eventually moved back to Toronto. "I fell in love with the city and the people and that hasn't changed through the years. I loved living in Toronto—I love the vibe, the energy, the people—and the way the city embraced me, which is why I'm living here now."

His first trip back to Toronto as a player, though, happened sooner than expected. Just three games into the 2006–07 season, the Spurs traveled to the ACC. There Bonner was greeted like a returning hero. "That first game back in Toronto was awesome. Herbie Kuhn, the announcer, introduced me as the Red Rocket, and I got a standing ovation." The Spurs' shooting coach, Chip Engelland, couldn't believe the reception Raptors fans were giving a visiting role player, who had only played two seasons in Toronto, in a game featuring multiple future Hall of Famers. "Chip still busts my chops about that game. He said, 'This is insane. Who puts the opposing team's player on the ticket, introduces you with your nickname, and gives you a standing ovation on a road game?'" Toronto. That's who.

10

José Calderón (2005–2013)

By 2005, José Calderón was already a twenty-three-year-old star in La Liga ACB, the top professional basketball association in Spain. Then the Raptors came knocking.

From the outside, it was an obvious choice: money, fame, the NBA. Who could say no? "People thought joining the league was an easy decision," Calderón recalls today. But he had his reasons for staying put, including offers from teams in Spain and in Europe, and concerns about court time, let alone success. "I didn't know if I was going to fit in and I didn't know if I would play." The NBA simply represented the unknown.

Moreover, at the time, players, execs, and critics in and around the association knew that there were good basketball leagues and even some great players over in Europe, but many still doubted whether those same guys could cut it in the NBA. That was 2005.

For the Raptors, though, Europeans were a major resource when it was still tough sledding to convince American players to head north of the border. Calderón was just one more guy from an early generation of foreign-born and foreign-coached players who ended up in the league—and specifically with the Raptors—after successful careers overseas.

Calderón's own journey began in his hometown, Villanueva de la

Serena, in southwestern Spain. In a way, those early years prepared him for the momentous decision to decamp to Toronto. At the age of thirteen, he was invited to play in Vitoria, in Basque Country, for one of the minor league teams operated by the basketball club Saski Baskonia. From there he bounced across the entire breadth of Spain: from Vitoria to Alicante, and then from Fuenlabrada near Madrid back to Vitoria. He spent the next three seasons with Baskonia, winning the King's Cup (Copa del Rey) and playing in the Finals in both the La Liga ACB and the EuroLeague.

Staying in Spain offered a safe route for Calderón. In 2005, in fact, skepticism went both ways across the Atlantic. For foreign-born players, the NBA was a big question mark. Back in the 1990s and early aughts, even viewing games was difficult. "When you're a kid in Spain, the NBA is at two a.m. or three a.m.," Calderón recalled. "There was a section in the newspapers, here and there. The NBA is now everywhere. But when I was growing up, it wasn't my dream to go to the NBA."

The Spanish pros seemed like a more realistic dream. When looking for a model, it was players like his own father, a second-division pro in Spain, and national heroes like Juan Antonio Corbalán and Juan Antonio San Epifanio, who had won the silver medal in the 1984 Los Angeles Olympics, that sparked Calderón's imagination. "If you dream about something, it's something you can touch. So for me, the NBA was too far out. I wanted to play for my national team. Only in the last couple of years in Spain, when I was playing better and better, were people starting to ask, 'Hey, what about the NBA?' I'm like, '*Really?*'"

It was the people in his life who ultimately swayed Calderón, sending him from the sun-soaked shores of Spain to the Great White North. "It started with my wife, Ana Hurtado. We went away for a week on vacation." During the trip, Ana helped him work through the pros and cons of his potential life in the NBA. Canada was less certain. "We didn't know *nothing* about Toronto," he says today.

Thanks to those conversations, by the time he boarded his flight to Toronto Pearson International Airport, Calderón felt fairly confident. "When I arrived, I had already made the decision: It's going to be the NBA, unless something weird happens." His first visit to Toronto sealed it, showing him what the Raptors had to offer as both an organization and as a new family, one to supplement all those he was leaving back home. "I made the decision because of the trip. They picked me up in a limo at Pearson Airport. From there, it was just amazing how they took care of us. The best part was going to MLSE Chairman Larry Tanenbaum's summer house on a lake a couple of hours from Toronto. It was Tanenbaum's whole family: kids, grandkids, everyone, with me and my agent, who came from Spain with me, general manager Rob Babcock, and director of international player personnel Scott Howard. It was like, *These guys* really *want me*. I couldn't say no."

And just like that, José Calderón became a Toronto Raptor.

Right away, the leap proved tough. Despite being a seasoned vet from Spain, Calderón was just another new guy. When Toronto's coach, Sam Mitchell, first welcomed him to the team, he ran down Calderón's résumé, and even misnamed his old club, calling them "the Gato Team" ("Cat" Team) rather than Saski Baskonia, the FIBA European Cup and Spanish League champs. That first meeting set the tone. "Sam didn't know me at all. We joked about this a lot. Sam was like, 'This is a rookie from Europe. I'll play him a little bit here and there, but I don't know what he can do.'" Building trust took time. "We started to understand each other. He understood, too, that the players wanted to play with me, because I was able to pass the ball. He thought, *Okay, the kid's got something*."

Language also proved a problem. "That was the toughest part of my first year," Calderón said. "It was a headache, trying to understand what they were saying. I had to think in Spanish about what I wanted to say, then translate it in my head and try to say it in English. It was complicated."

True to form, the crafty point guard found ways to work around his linguistic deficits. Trick one: using what English he had. "I wasn't scared of speaking in English. I knew how to say *something,* and after I would add 'yesterday' or 'tomorrow' without knowing how to say future or past sentences. It was like: 'I like this. Yesterday,' or 'I like this. Today.'" Trick two: looking rather than speaking. At practice, he always waited to be the second or third in line for a drill, in order to see what the other guys were doing ahead of him.

Even still, Calderón longed to communicate better with Coach Mitchell. "Sam didn't let me practice when I made mistakes. We were watching video of one game. He got pissed because I made a mistake *in the video,*" he says laughing. Immediately, the veteran coach squared up to his veteran rookie: "You're not practicing." Calderón was shocked. "I was trying, like, 'Sam, it should be the other way around. If I make mistakes, I gotta practice *more,* not *less.*'" He got the same response each time: "Go to the bike!" "I'm laughing now," Calderón recalls all these years later, "because Sam was great and we have an amazing relationship. But the start of our relationship? Everybody practiced but me. It wasn't about me. He was trying to make a point, and I'm the rookie, so I'm not practicing."

Epic Tour de France sessions on the stationary bike and fast-paced practices in a foreign language were only two challenges. Another was communicating during games. "I was the point guard. I'm a guy who communicates a lot on the court. It was a tough few months until I started to feel a little bit more comfortable." Moreover, Calderón knew the most important language was nonverbal—the actions he took on and off the court. To get the respect of his teammates, he just needed to work hard and not complain. "The adjustment was tough. At the end of the day, it's a different culture, a different language, a new league, and a new job. Yes, it's basketball, and maybe between the lines I was feeling more comfortable because it was basketball, but it was difficult all around."

His earlier experiences in Spain had nonetheless prepared him for the change. "It helped me that I left my house when I was thirteen years old. It's almost like your kid years stop right away and you just got to become more of an adult. There is no other option." There was also the organization. "Ana and I were so lucky to have the kind of people that they were in Toronto when we arrived. That helped us too with that transition."

Nonetheless, during his first season, in 2005–06, Calderón struggled to find his feet in the NBA. Even understanding league business and protocols proved taxing. "Every day it was something. I remember the Jalen Rose trade to the Knicks. We were playing the Knicks that night. He did shootaround with us the same day. And that night, he's in the *other* locker room. I'm like, *He already knows what we're going to do! He's going to tell them what we're gonna do!* That was my thinking at that time as a kid coming from Spain, like, I've never seen this before."

On the court, too, he struggled. "It was weird in a lot of situations. I think it's just a perfect rookie season," Calderón laughs about it now. "I remember in my second game, I scored twenty points. The next day I go out and score zero or play only eleven minutes. And you're like, 'Okay, you cannot be this high, you cannot be this low. I gotta find a middle ground.'" Even the Raptors' challenges weighed on him. By mid-December, the team was 4-20. "I lost six games the whole season in Spain. I lost fifteen in my first month in Toronto."

Even worse: The three-point line felt as far away as Basque Country. After the season ended, Calderón checked his stats, shocked to discover he made only seven shots beyond the arc the *entire* season. It was a far cry from his NBA career three-point shooting percentage of 40.6 percent and his league-leading 46.1 percent in 2012–13. "I didn't expect to be that bad at shooting. I never was a great shooter in

Europe, but I wasn't a 16 percent shooter either. I struggled with that. I was able to get to the rim, but the shooting piece was important. It was something that was on my list: If I want to play here, I gotta make shots."

If shooting was one hurdle, then finding minutes was another, a challenge that Calderón faced throughout his seven-plus seasons in Toronto. The veteran-rookie was never guaranteed a starting job, let alone a place on the team. During that first season, he played in 64 games, starting 11 of them and averaging more than 20 minutes. Mostly he backed up Mike James, who logged heavy minutes all season. "Mike arrived and was playing really good basketball. He was scoring a lot, so I was the backup and we started sharing the court." Even still, Calderón could only see the silver lining. "I was lucky. Some of the guys who went from Europe to other teams, they never played. There was an opportunity to play in Toronto. You're going to be the backup point guard. You don't know how many minutes that will be—ten or fifteen per night?—but at least there are ten or fifteen per night."

In Calderón's second season, the primary facilitator role went to T. J. Ford, whom Toronto had acquired from Milwaukee in exchange for Charlie Villanueva. Everywhere you turned that season, you heard the same debate, among fans and in the media: The team has two point guards. Both could be starters. And then the inevitable questions: Is the team better with TJ as a starter? Or should José be out there? As Calderón recalls, "People were talking about it from the outside, even the media, creating a story about what's going on."

That was the story, but it was only half of it.

To this day, the two players still talk and, at the time, they worked together. Calderón was also straight with his supposed rival, telling him directly that his only goal was to improve and help the team. But getting better also meant making personal sacrifices, even after

Calderón had successfully filled in for Ford, who had suffered a brutal back injury that left him sidelined for a couple of months. "He was out for a long time. I started and we were playing really well. At some point, I actually told Sam, 'TJ's gotta go back to the starting position. It's better for everybody. He's more comfortable out there as a starter. My guys are on the bench, and I can play with them.' That was always my thing with the Raptors: 'I don't care. Whatever happens, I'm okay.'"

That was the underreported story Eric also saw playing out: Calderón approaching his position with grace and humility and with the team foremost in his mind. It was something Calderón also did time and again over the years, as team brass looked to strengthen the point-guard position. That's how he handled it when the team scooped up Mike James, before Ford. After Ford, it was Jarrett Jack, whom they signed to a four-year deal in the summer of 2009. Then it was Kyle Lowry, acquired by trade in the summer of 2012. In each instance, Calderón asked the same question. Not "How do I secure my role in the starting lineup?" but instead, "What role does this team need me to play and how can I help us win?"

"The team was first, and it wasn't about me playing more minutes or fewer minutes," Calderón told us, recalling his peace of mind. "I wanted to be a starter. Don't get me wrong. I was going to work as hard as I could to put the coach in the toughest decision possible. That's basketball. That's what *everybody* is trying to do. But that's a coach's problem. That doesn't mean I cannot be friends with my teammates. We're going to compete, but whoever plays, I want him to do well. If TJ was playing great, that's great for me. It's my team."

He saw the same attitude with his fellow Raptors. One such was Darrick Martin, a scrappy point guard who had gone undrafted in 1992 after a four-year stint at UCLA and who spent the last three seasons of his thirteen-year career in Toronto. As Calderón told us, "When D-Mart arrived, he was like, 'I'm here to help you. I'm not here to take any minutes.' I was lucky to have Darrick."

During his second season with the Raptors, Calderón appeared in 77 games, playing solid backup minutes behind Ford. He also assumed a new role. In his first season, he once again became a rookie; in his second season, he once again became a vet. "I knew a little bit more and was more comfortable with my language and on the court with my teammates. I could help people who were having the same struggles that I had seen the year before."

With one of those new teammates, it was more good news, at least personally, to start the 2006–07 season. During the summer, the Raptors signed another Spanish talent, Jorge Garbajosa, who joined the team after a celebrated dozen-year career in Spain and Italy. He was a rookie, "but like fifty years old," laughs Calderón. He had even played with Garbajosa in Spain years earlier. "We had been together so many summers with the national team. Bringing an old teammate to Toronto was great. Just having a friend there. That was amazing. For me, for my family, for everything."

For the team, things were also finally going to plan. Before long, whispers about a potential playoff appearance started to echo around Air Canada Centre.

No doubt the squad was riding high when they rolled into Boston in late March. They were a solid 38-31, coming off two decisive victories at home. Then disaster struck.

With about four and a half minutes left in the fourth against the Celtics, Garbajosa chased down a fast-breaking Al Jefferson. They got tangled in the air, and Garbajosa came down awkwardly, breaking his leg. Garbo's season was over.

The Raptors ended up dropping the game that night in Boston, but the team soon rallied, ripping off nine wins in the next ten contests, and eventually finishing the season 47-35, good for their first playoff berth since 2002, though the Raptors ultimately lost their opening series to the Nets.

That season's end is something Calderón still thinks about. "Maybe things would have been different with the Nets," he conjectures, pointing to the important role that Garbajosa could have played. "We were on the right path and we were playing really well. They had an amazing team: Jason Kidd and Richard Jefferson and Vince Carter. I think their experience is what beat us in that series. It was our first NBA playoffs for a lot of us. But with Garbo, I think it would have been even closer; maybe we would have won that one."

The following season, the Raptors again made the playoffs, only to be bounced in the first round by the Magic. Even still, it was another year of tremendous growth for Calderón, his third in the NBA, with rumblings of an All-Star Game appearance. More importantly, the deep-range woes of his rookie year were a thing of the past. Calderón even flirted with the pinnacle of efficient play, a so-called "50-40-90" season (for shooting percentages on field goals, three-pointers, and free throws) but was ultimately denied the honor on a minor technicality: he hit only 80 of the required 82 three-pointers. ("C'mon, I got it," Calderón smirks today, waving it away.)

After those two runs, though, the Raptors wouldn't sniff the playoffs again for six more seasons. The team never settled, however, and always looked to upgrade their talent on the floor. "We felt like we were going in the right direction," Calderón said. "It was like keep building, keep trying to get the right people."

Despite his early struggles and those untimely playoff exits, Calderón can only look back on his time with the Raptors with a smile. "I was so happy in Toronto," he says. "I could have stayed there forever, losing or winning." His career with the Raptors lasted seven and a half seasons—during which he even claimed the team record for assists—a remarkable run for a period with so many personnel changes on the team.

All good things come to an end, though. In January 2013, Calderón was traded to Detroit in a three-way deal with Memphis. Eric still remembers the emotions of that night. The team was in Atlanta. There was the usual media scrum, and the first few questions acknowledged that this was simply the business of the NBA. But then it turned emotional, not only for Calderón but also for the journalists and broadcasters who had covered him for so many years. "It was eight years of my life," Calderón recollects. "It's still the place where I lived the second most after my home in Spain. It wasn't about the business side of things; it was about how many friends I was leaving in Toronto."

The trade to Detroit also inaugurated Calderón's career as a reliable journeyman in the NBA, willing, as always, to play whatever role was needed. During the 2013 offseason, he signed with Dallas but was traded a season later to the Knicks. Two years later, Calderón was on the move again. First he was dealt to the Bulls in the summer of 2016, before being traded to the Lakers, who waived the point guard after the trade deadline in 2017. From there it was brief stops all over the NBA—with the Warriors, the Hawks, the Cavaliers, and again with the Pistons.

Today, after a fourteen-year NBA career, he's still a part of the league, serving as special advisor to the Cavaliers. Even still, his run in Canada will never be forgotten. "My relationship with Raptors fans is amazing. Every time I travel back to Toronto, it still feels like home, even now, and people always stop me in the street. The best reaction is from my kids. They're like, 'What's going on? Daddy, how good *were* you?' Now they're older. But in the beginning, they were like, 'We never saw you play at *that* level,'" he laughs. There's only one downside to his visits to Toronto as his playing years, and his time as a Raptor, inch further and further into the past. "Usually now the fans say, 'You were my *dad's* favorite player.' Other than that, I love it."

11

Mike James (2005–2006)

Mike James began his career as a standout but underrecruited high school player in Amityville, New York. There he was known as the Amityville Horror—at least until he got to Toronto, when he was rechristened the Amityville Scorer by then–Raptors' TV play-by-play voice Chuck Swirsky. James eventually ended up playing four years at Duquesne University in Pittsburgh, between 1994 and 1998. Despite a successful college career—his number 13 was even retired by Duquesne in 2017—James went undrafted.

A natural grinder, with a chip on his shoulder after having played at one of the less-storied NCAA D1 programs, James knew what it meant to be ignored by recruiters. He also knew that he had what was needed to make the NBA. He just needed a chance to show the league what he could offer.

Back home in New York, James played for the Long Island Surf of the United States Basketball League for one season. He then decamped to Europe, where he played in Austria and then France for three seasons, before returning to the US in 2001 as a member of the Rockford Lightning of the Continental Basketball Association.

James finally got his NBA break at the beginning of the 2001–02 season, when he landed with the Miami Heat. Just a couple of years later, though, he was on the move again in a pattern that defined his pro career. The end tally is a laundry list of pro teams: Miami, Boston, Detroit, Milwaukee, Houston, Toronto, Minnesota, New Orleans, Washington, Chicago, and Dallas, with stops in China, Turkey, and the G League along the way. Between 1998 and 2015, when he hung up his shoes, James played for twenty-one different squads in multiple leagues and countries.

Among those many stops, no stint stands out for James quite like that single year he spent with the Raptors, which proved a career-making season. Fans loved his brashness and spark-plug offense—and still remember him today—and the Raptors desperately needed a scorer during a difficult year of rebuilding. Stats aside, it was also a special experience for James. It was the first time a team fully recognized what he could do if only given the chance.

The idea of becoming a Toronto Raptor caught him off guard, though, at least at first. He had played well during the 2004–05 season for the Houston Rockets—his fifth NBA team in just four seasons—even blossoming under the bright lights. "I noticed something about my game in the playoffs," James told us. "Playing in that atmosphere did something to me, really. I was on something crazy that year."

He was there to stay—or so he thought. And not only that: He was already plotting his path to becoming one of the Rockets' greats, thinking about how he could contribute long-term to the team's success. "I used to walk through the tunnel in Houston going to practice every day. I always looked where all the players' jerseys were retired and thought, *My jersey is going to be retired right there.*"

He also had ambitious goals for the following season. "I was at Tracy McGrady's house and I said, 'Listen, I'm not trying to be Batman. I'm not trying to be Robin, but yo, every guard in the league is on assignment next year. Help me become an All-Star this year.'" The former Raptor, by then a repeat All-Star for the Rockets who routinely received votes for MVP between 2001 and 2008, couldn't believe James's bravado. "He looked at me and laughed."

When news of the trade to Toronto finally arrived, it blindsided James. "We had media day in Houston and I'm getting ready for practice the next day," James recalled. "I got the phone call from Rockets Head Coach Jeff Van Gundy. He says, 'Mike, you've been traded.'" James was shocked. "I said, 'Traded? Traded for who?'" Van Gundy gave him the news: Rafer Alston. James, never short on confidence, couldn't help but follow up. "I said, 'Then who *else*? It's impossible that you just gave me just straight up for him.'"

The emotions of the trade only hit later, a rare display from the usually stoic athlete. "This was the first time a trade really hurt me," James said. "I thought I had some roots and I was being cut off. I was taking my girls to school that morning and I started tearing up as I was driving. My wife was looking at me like I was crazy, because she had never seen me cry. My oldest daughter, she was five at the time, was shocked." Then, the worst of it, his two-year-old daughter, in schoolground singsong, taunting her father: "'Dad-dy's a cry-baby. Dad-dy's a cry-baby. Dad-dy's a cry-baby.'"

Amazingly, it was his daughter's innocent taunt that actually snapped him out of his doldrums. "At that moment, there was so much anger, rage," James admitted. But he knew there was only one way out: "Suck it up, go to Toronto, go do your thing, and stop worrying."

With that, James accepted his newest challenge. "There was still a rage that was going on inside me, but at the same time I embraced it." He was now a Raptor and determined to prove his worth.

James arrived in Toronto ready to show what he already knew: He was more than just a journeyman guard. He had always been known for his grit, a trait he cultivated during his first years in the league, and he knew that that was the best way to prove himself a legitimate NBA starter. "I always tell people, 'I was born in Miami and I was raised in Detroit,'" James recalled, pointing to his stint in South

Beach between 2001 and 2003 and his later championship with the Pistons in 2004. "I created a winning mindset in Detroit and my work ethic in Miami. I've always taken that with me wherever I went."

In Toronto, his work ethic would be put to the test. The Raptors were in the midst of a rebuild, still reeling from the departure of Vince Carter during the 2004–05 season. In his stead, the Raptors' third-year center, Chris Bosh, was having a breakout season, even earning his first All-Star nod, while averaging nearly 40 minutes a game on a packed stat line: 22.5 points, 9.2 rebounds, and 2.6 assists, with a steal and block per game thrown in.

Still, the young team was looking for leadership—and, above all, production. James was ready to step up, showcasing along the way his ability to score and distribute the ball effectively. "They let me off the leash that one time to go play with the other dogs," James says today, laughing as he warms to the metaphor. "They gave me the opportunity to roam the yard and they couldn't get me back on that leash. Every time they tried to run and go get me this way, I'm going that way. I said, 'I ain't going back on the leash and y'all can't make me.' I was the dog, brother."

It was all part of the squad's next-man-up culture, with every player pulling his weight when called upon. It was also something James and his teammates witnessed again and again, especially after Bosh sprained his left thumb in a late-March matchup against Milwaukee, which forced him to miss the last dozen games of the season. The core of the team was solid, with a few real prospects, but the truth was that they were still too green to fully compete. Bosh was only twenty-one. Charlie Villanueva was a rookie. Joey Graham, the Raptors' small forward, who had been picked 16th overall in the draft that year, was a raw talent fresh out of a four-year NCAA career at the University of Central Florida and then Oklahoma State University. There was optimism, of course, but it was a team still waiting to grow.

The season ended up being a career best for James. He averaged

20.3 points and 5.8 assists per game and even went on a scoring rampage in April that included four consecutive nights where he dropped 30 or more points. He could also see the writing on the wall. This was not a playoff-bound team, like the squads he had played on in Miami, Houston, and Detroit. They would try to win, of course, but even in a loss, why not at least entertain the fans? "I embraced the moment, every game. 'Get ya popcorn and ya soda. I'm about to really put on a show for y'all. Y'all gonna get ya money's worth!'"

In the end, it was a season marked by personal highs but team lows, with the Raptors finishing a disappointing 27-55 and unable to recover from their 6-22 start. Despite his best efforts to elevate his teammates, James often found himself battling the perception that he was a selfish player, more concerned with his stats than the Raptors' success. It's something that still rubs him wrong today. "It was always about winning. It was always about the team. It was never about individual goals. I really busted my tail."

On the court, James could be brash and fiery, all part of a persona he cultivated to overcome his natural introversion. "I started taking on a character," he explained. "When I played the game, I was entirely different from the person that I was off the court. On court I would just become angry. That's what that rage was—what made me such a good player."

However, his coping mechanism—this way of projecting something larger and more intimidating than his 6'2" frame—was also easy to misinterpret. "It was funny. So many times people used to see me out there talking to myself on the court and they would think I was talking trash. But I was talking to *myself*. The fight was never with no one else. It was always with me."

Those misunderstandings extended even to his closest circle. James remembers asking Jeff Van Gundy, while playing in Houston, what kind of player his coach thought he was. According to James, the reply was a surprise: "You're just an arrogant SOB. You think it's all about you."

Outsiders also missed how James used that persona to channel his anger and to play better. "One time I was playing pickup," James remembers. "A player was calling out all my plays. Then I scored and he said, 'Man, you ain't even like that. You ain't even *that* good.' I looked at him and said, 'You know what? You're right. I'm not that good. But I work so hard that I'm nicer than all of y'all.' I know if I'm putting in the work, my skill is going to be better than probably the majority."

That drive, that almost desperation to push himself and the team toward wins, also led to misunderstandings with the media. "Coming to Toronto, people probably looked at me like I was standoffish," James said. "Everybody thought I was some prick!" He knew the perception of him and understood how his on-court intensity, a residue of being traded from Houston, translated to the screen.

But those close to the team saw a different side of James. Eric was one of these people. This was a player who was professional, dedicated to his craft. He was the first one in the gym and the last one to leave, setting an example for the team's young guns—Bosh, Villanueva, and Graham. Sure, he could be prickly at times, but who wouldn't be, as the guy shouldering the load, doing all he could for a struggling squad, only to be labeled a ball hog? He might have had an edge at times, but that edge was the key to his on-court success.

Eric also saw James's professionalism and personability firsthand. As a broadcaster, Eric has always tried to maintain a professional divide between himself and the players. But one night in New York City, a day before the Raptors faced Jason Kidd and a stacked New Jersey Nets roster, Eric and his broadcast partner Paul Jones bumped into James and his Long Island buddies in the lobby of the team hotel and invited Eric and Jonesy out for dinner.

James and his friends were having no luck getting a cab out front of their fancy Manhattan digs—the Trump International Hotel & Tower, to be exact. Almost immediately, the point guard went into leadership mode, with his usual sense of flair, and hailed a *limousine.*

As the driver explained, he was on a tight schedule. James assured him he would be back there exactly on time. And James, good to his word, kept the crew on schedule. After dinner, Eric was halfway through his final drink of the night when James began ushering them back to the limousine. "I got Jason Kidd tomorrow," he explained. "It's time to go back to the hotel."

Moments like that paint a larger picture. Most people have never understood who Mike James is. Where coaches sometimes and the media often saw him as temperamental, James's teammates—and Eric and Jonesy—saw a guy with the self-confidence to lead a team in the midst of a massive transition. Simply put, it's not always going to be Kumbaya. But James got labeled a problem, that label stuck, and it was at most half the truth.

That night in New York was symptomatic of the person James was. "That was the way Mike treated people," Jonesy recalls. For Eric, it also spoke to James's willingness to prioritize winning and preparation above all. It was a sign of his openness—an openness not everyone saw from a distance. But that's who Mike James *really* is and was: a generous and thoughtful guy as well as a leader dedicated to performing his best. You could see that leadership, too, off the court. James was known for his dedication to his faith and his commitment to helping others through community events, using his platform to inspire and uplift those around him.

His lone year with the Raptors stands out as a defining moment in a long and eventful career. That season, he showcased his perseverance, his dedication, and his ability to seize an opportunity when it was presented to him. He always believed in himself and knew he was good enough to play in the NBA. He just needed a chance to show it—something he did that year in Toronto. His season with the Raptors also literally paid off. In the summer of 2006, James signed a four-year, $23.5 million contract with the Minnesota Timberwolves.

It was a financial windfall for a player who had long sought stability in the NBA, but James could only view it with mixed emotions, knowing that it spelled the end of his time in a Raptors uniform. "I wish it could have been in Toronto longer, but obviously things happen," he told us. "During the time that I was there, it was definitely home. I made sure that I treated the people like they were family." His combination of on-court performance and off-court leadership endeared James to the Raptors' fan base. "Toronto was a great year and a blessing," James says today. "I enjoyed my whole tenure there and the love that I get whenever I go back."

12

Charlie Villanueva (2005–2006)

Charlie Villanueva couldn't believe his luck. It was the summer of 2005, and he was on the cusp of being drafted. "Think about the numbers," he says today. "How many players are in the NBA that come from immigrant parents from the Dominican Republic? From New York City? And players who have alopecia? I think I was the only one at that time. The chances of me getting into the NBA, it's like zero to none. I wasn't even supposed to be there."

Yet there he was, not merely being drafted, but being drafted in the first round, thanks to his willingness to take his challenges in stride. "I always had the underdog mentality growing up and I always rooted for the underdogs. That's me all day." That tenacity served him well. While only a freshman at the University of Connecticut, he had won the 2004 NCAA national championship. The following season, Villanueva led the Huskies in scoring and was named team MVP, earning second-team All–Big East honors along the way.

For the Raptors, draft night in 2005 was just another extension of the major decisions the team was already facing. Toronto was coming off an underwhelming 2004–05 campaign, during which the team had dealt their first-ever—and perhaps greatest-ever—superstar,

Vince Carter. The squad was not without its bright lights, though, including Chris Bosh, by then entering his third season, who was improving every year. But to onlookers it was also clear: The team was at a crossroads. This was a rebuilding season, and canny picks mattered.

For his part, Villanueva was uncertain where he would land. "I really thought I was going to go to Charlotte, but then they went with Ray Felton. So once number seven hit, I knew Toronto was the spot, because I had a great workout in Toronto." Sure enough, Raptors general manager Rob Babcock made the call, selecting Villanueva seventh overall.

Unsurprisingly, he was both excited about his future and a bundle of nerves. "I was ecstatic. I knew a little bit about Toronto, but I had never spent time in the city." His excitement continued into the next day, as he boarded a plane to his new home. "I remember thinking on that flight, *Man, the hard work that I've put in, and where I came from to be in the NBA. This is crazy.* It was a dream of mine to be in the NBA and to actually accomplish that was nothing but amazing."

Then reality began to set in. "After you're done with all the festivities and celebrations, you sit down and really start thinking about what this looks like." Moreover, not everyone was thrilled with the pick. "I remember, the next day after the draft, I was on an Air Canada flight, sitting in first class, and they were handing out newspapers. And boom, right there: You see my picture in the newspaper. I was excited."

Then he actually read the article. "They were questioning the pick. They said that Chris Bosh and I play the same position. So it was like, 'Why draft another power forward?' It wasn't a good feeling." Raptors reporters weren't the only ones with their doubts. Bill Simmons, a columnist at ESPN and perhaps the most widely read sportswriter in America at the time, was even harsher in his so-called "NBA Draft Diary": "Charlie has a new claim to fame—he just became one of the top-five worst picks in the history of the NBA draft." It was Villanueva's first time under that kind of microscope. Even worse? "The guy sitting next to me was also reading the paper, and I'm like, *Oh my God*. I was trying to hide."

Still, Villanueva was ready to take on the haters—it was just one more hurdle that he would fight over. "My mindset going into Toronto was: I'm going to have this chip on my shoulder and I will show that I belong in this league and on this team."

Other surprises were more welcome, including his newfound life in Toronto. "I didn't even know where Toronto was on the map. Being raised in New York City, we don't leave the city. The border is right there, but Toronto just seemed far away." At first impression, the change didn't seem so radical. "There are a lot of similarities between NYC and Toronto: the traffic, the weather is terrible," he laughs. "But Toronto is a beautiful city." There was also a key difference. "No disrespect to my New Yorkers; I'm a New Yorker, too, by heart. But, to me, Toronto is similar to New York, but it's a lot safer and a lot cleaner, and it just seems like a lot of the people are friendlier in Toronto."

Those friendly faces, in fact, were key to his transition. "As soon as I stepped off that plane, even though the media might've had a different perspective on the pick, the fans embraced me. It was super welcoming. To this day, Toronto is still love, and I only played there for like six months. It felt a lot longer, to be honest. It felt like I played in Toronto for numerous years. The city was nothing but amazing. It embraced me with open arms."

The other thing that helped? As with so many players who arrived in the summer to Toronto, the answer is the same. "It was Caribana weekend," Villanueva laughs, referring to the massive festival, which showcases the music, dance, costumes, and culinary traditions of the Caribbean and includes a huge parade across the city to the sounds of calypso, soca, and reggae, attracting a million visitors to Toronto each year. "That did it for me. I was going into Toronto not knowing what the hell it is like. When I came back to look for a place, it was during Caribana." Even old Raptors helped him feel welcome. "Vince Carter had a club! I had a great time. I was like, *This is home*."

Life was shaping up for the against-all-odds rookie. "I had a nice penthouse," he recalls. "It was overlooking Rogers Centre—back then it was called SkyDome—so through my living room, when the dome was open, I could see the Blue Jays games. It was pretty cool. I was twenty years old. It's my first time in a different country, living with my older brother, Rob. Everything was just so new and fresh." The distance from New York and his family also worked for the young buck. "Everybody had to get passports! It was cool to have my family there, to come to a lot of games. It was an hour flight, so it was good that it was *close* enough but *far* enough, you know what I mean?" Toronto was also home to one of the most significant experiences of his life: the birth of his son, CJ, in 2008.

Part of the connection Villanueva made with his new Canadian fans came through his own work for people with alopecia. "It was my first time doing charitable work. I was very active in the community and I think a lot of people were able to relate to that, especially the kids that had alopecia." Villanueva also realized the reach he had as the lone player in the NBA with alopecia, playing in a city that had come to represent an entire country. "Vancouver wasn't around when I got there, so Toronto was the only team. There is a difference because, in Canada, it is a *whole* country. You got people coming from Vancouver, Montreal, coming from all these places, just to meet me. That hits different. Being active in the community won the city over. The love that I still get in Toronto is unbelievable. I'm never going to forget the people I impacted in the city."

After arriving in Canada, Villanueva immediately went to work preparing for the coming year. "I got there in August and I pretty much stayed there for the rest of the season. I was trying to get an early start." Eventually it hit him, if not right away: Villanueva was in the NBA. "It was the second game, against the New Jersey Nets," he says. "This was the New Jersey Nets when they were, like, the *New Jersey Nets*. Jason Kidd—I was almost starstruck with him. Vince Carter. Richard Jefferson. They were the real deal."

Villanueva was thrust back into his high school days, when he was just an NBA hopeful. In his mind's eye was the May 2002 cover of *Slam* magazine, featuring Kenyon Martin, Todd MacCulloch, Jason Kidd, Keith Van Horn, and Kerry Kittles. The title of the piece was pure bombast but represented the prevailing logic at the time: "New Jersey Nets: The Best Team in the World." The Nets had changed in the three years since, but Villanueva was still impressed. "I remember when we played them, it was like, 'Those Nets are on the court. This is crazy. I'm here.'"

The other wow moment came a couple of weeks later, when Toronto played Miami and Villanueva caught a glimpse of Alonzo Mourning. "He was at the end of his career, but he was one of my favorite players. I was a big Charlotte Hornets fan growing up. Him, Larry Johnson, Muggsy Bogues, Hersey Hawkins, Bobby Phelps. Seeing Alonzo Mourning was a surreal moment."

It was a tough season for the Raptors, but a formative one for Villanueva, and it was the fans, once again, who helped to buoy the team's spirits. "It was a rebuilding year. We were fully aware of it. The season started one-and-fifteen, but I remember the fans were still showing up. If it was me, I would have given up on this team. Like one in ten? But the fans were still there. It's like the more we lost, the more they were *rooting* for us!"

Those losses weighed heavily on the rookie. "I came from Connecticut, winning a championship, winning a Big East tournament, and then going to a team where I can't barely win one game." Still, he felt the team had potential. There was something, even, to build on. "We were definitely underdogs. Obviously, we didn't win many games, but could we beat the best on any given night? Absolutely, we could. We beat some good teams." Those teams included the 64-18 Pistons, the eventual league champions, the Miami Heat, and those hallowed New Jersey Nets, who finished 49-33.

On a personal level, things could not have gone better for the rookie. Villanueva played in 81 games, averaging 13 points and trailing only Bosh for rebounds. He even made the All-Rookie Team and finished second in Rookie of the Year voting behind his former McDonald's All-American teammate Chris Paul, who had been drafted by the New Orleans Hornets.

Among a season of highs and lows, one game still stands out in the minds of Raptors—and Bucks—fans from Villanueva's tenure. In late March 2006, Toronto rolled into Milwaukee to face another fellow rookie, the first-overall pick Andrew Bogut.

Villanueva rose to the challenge, even if early signs suggested a different outcome. "That night I didn't get no sleep. I was just tossing and turning. Then we go to shootaround and I still couldn't get to sleep. I was exhausted." Even worse for the Raptors: Bosh played only six minutes, before exiting with a sprained left thumb, an injury that would force him to miss the remainder of the season. "We ran a lot of things through Chris. Now it's like, 'Who's gonna score the basketball?' Me, I'm young, so I decided, 'I'm gonna step up.' It was just one of those days where the ball was going in, anything I threw up."

The performance was a stat-sheet-filling expo: 48 points on 20-of-32 shooting, including going 6-of-11 from three, with 9 rebounds, 3 assists, and a steal. The Raptors lost the contest, 125–116, but Villanueva set a franchise record for most points in a game for a rookie—a record that still stands today. Only one thing nags at him today about the game. "I ended up scoring forty-eight. My regret? I should have scored *fifty*. Fifty sounds better than forty-eight. 'I scored fifty in the league.' That sounds different."

Team brass also noticed Villanueva's contributions. By the time of his shooting expo in Milwaukee, the Raptors were already regrouping for the next season. In January the team had parted ways with their general manager, Rob Babcock, the executive who had pushed for Villanueva at the draft, and who passed away in 2019. "Rob Babcock was an amazing man. When some of the media experts were saying that I was the wrong pick, I remember him always speaking life into me."

Following Babcock's exit, the Raptors brought in Bryan Colangelo from the Phoenix Suns as their new general manager. He, too, liked what he saw in Villanueva. "I remember the next day after that forty-eight-point game, Colangelo and I had a great discussion and he was praising me for the hell of a game that I had." That conversation gave the rookie confidence that he might be part of the team's long-term plans. "So now I'm thinking, *I'm good here.*"

By the time the season ended, the 27-55 Raptors were back at the top of the draft board, with the first-overall pick. Unsurprisingly, Villanueva was eager to secure his future with Toronto. "I remember having a conversation with Sam Mitchell. He said to me, and I remember this word for word, 'If Michael Jordan comes out of retirement, it's the only way we'll trade you.'"

When the 2006 NBA Draft rolled around, Villanueva was in Toronto doing a promotional appearance with season ticket holders. "I'm at an event. They end up picking Andrea Bargnani first overall. I'm thinking, *He plays the same position as I do.* So now you got me, Bosh, and Bargnani. Jalen ended up getting traded to the Knicks midway through the year, and I was playing small forward. So now I'm envisioning: Maybe I can play small forward. Maybe they want to go big: Bargnani, Bosh, and me, at the three-four-five position."

During the appearance in Toronto, he ran into his GM. According to Villanueva, Colangelo explained the situation: "There are a lot of teams calling for you, but we're not going to trade you." Again, Villanueva liked the future he was imagining, even if he was being thrown into potential trade talks. "That's a good thing. That means you're doing something right. Another team wants you."

Then, the ugly truth. Just two days later, the Raptors traded Villanueva to the Bucks in exchange for T. J. Ford. "You're talking about hurt," Villanueva told us, almost twenty years later. "I'm going to keep it real. I was talking about *betrayal.* I shed some tears. Like when you get punched in the stomach and you're trying to catch your breath. No knock against Milwaukee, because I ended up loving Milwaukee. But when I first heard it was to Milwaukee, I wasn't excited right away. I was going from Toronto, a city that I love. I just planted roots there. I was just so committed to the city. It was just like, 'Man, you're taking candy from a kid!' That's why it hurt me so bad, because I was so into that city and so devoted to being there and helping this franchise win some games in any way I could."

That hurt wouldn't go away anytime soon. "I'm twenty-one years old. You have two grown men telling me one thing. And boom, not even forty-eight hours later, I was gone. It carried me all throughout my career," he admits now. "Every time I played against Toronto, I took it personally." His own sour grapes are just one measure of how deeply and truly he felt for Toronto, Canada, and the Raptors. For the sophomore player, it wasn't just NBA business as usual.

Over the next three seasons with the Bucks, Villanueva steadily improved, gaining more and more responsibility in a mix of starting and bench roles. Scoring, rebounding, shooting efficiency—all generally trended upward during his time in Milwaukee. Going into his final year with the Bucks, Villanueva showcased his ability to contribute significantly, averaging 16.2 points and 6.7 rebounds per game.

It came as no surprise, then, that plenty of NBA teams once again came knocking for his services as soon as he was available. Including Toronto. "When I became a free agent in 2009, once that clock hit midnight, the first team to call me was Toronto: 'We want you back.'" But Villanueva, even three years later, still carried that hurt. "I felt like I was cheated on. I took it extremely personally. So I was like, 'I can't go back.'" He even avoided talking to the Raptors. "I didn't even take the call. They ended up calling my brother Rob to try to get in touch with me, because I wasn't picking up." But his answer remained the same. "'Nope. Right away. I'm not going back. You had your chance.'"

All these years later, Villanueva has forgiven the team and even come to rethink the vendetta he carried with him on the court. "I was too young. I wasn't mature enough to really understand that business side of it. I was also in a different place in my career. I don't have any regrets, but if I was to redo something again, I would have actually taken the call from Toronto." Quite possibly, he might even have re-signed with his former team. "I already knew what they were offering. It was similar to the Pistons' offer," a five-year, $40 million deal. "Detroit was a little bit more, but I was okay with taking less because I loved Toronto so much. I have a son there. So it made sense to go back. If I was a little bit older, a little bit wiser, a little bit more mature, I would have taken that approach. That was my first Welcome-to-the-NBA-Business moment. Later in my career, I understood that the league is a business."

He has even come to realize that the trade to Milwaukee in 2006 wasn't about him, though he also admits his 48-point game had a role in the deal. "I don't think it's a coincidence that I got traded to Milwaukee and that's the team that I ended up lighting up." That trade to the Bucks, instead, was about the direction that Colangelo was trying to take the Raptors. "Being a GM is a tough job. That's a headache for sure. Colangelo was coming in and cleaning house. I never thought in a million years I'd get traded, because I had a pretty good year. But when a new guy comes in, he might want to do things differently. They were in need of a point guard. I know Mike James wasn't in the long-term plans for them, and they're not trading Bosh. My having a good year made me the next-biggest asset, and they needed a point guard. I get it now, but I didn't get it back then."

Those bitter feelings are all gone today, and his short time in Toronto has left a lasting impact on him as both a player and a person.

"Toronto is the beginning. It has my heart. I have a son that's Canadian that came out of me getting drafted to Canada. If I don't get drafted, I probably won't have a son, right? So that just means more. My connections will always be rooted in Toronto." The effect for Canada basketball might also be long lasting. His son, CJ, is an up-and-coming teenage Canadian prospect. "He's still playing. He hoopin'! He's got some work to do, but as long as he stays hungry . . ." Villanueva laughs, trailing off and thinking back to his own time in Toronto, on the court and off.

"I will always have ties in Canada."

13

T. J. Ford (2006–2008)

Ten games into the 2006–07 season, the Raptors were a humbling 2-8. This was not the plan. The team was coming off a rough 2005–06 campaign and was in the midst of a rebuild. In February 2006, the Raptors had hired Bryan Colangelo, a longtime exec for the Suns. In Toronto, he flipped player after player, reshaping the Raptors into a prototype of the future small-ball era.

Along the way, Colangelo made some tough choices, including the release of fan favorite Alvin Williams and dealing 2006 Rookie of the Year runner-up Charlie Villanueva to the Bucks for T. J. Ford, a fast and agile playmaker known for his ability to control the floor. Playing for Milwaukee, Ford had of course been in and out of Toronto, but his knowledge of the country and city was limited. He didn't know what to expect. As he told us, "Being over in the US, you don't really hear anything about Toronto. 'It is cold. It is Canada. You have to go to Customs.' That was the limited information that we had."

Luckily, being dealt in the offseason meant Ford had a chance to explore his new stomping ground. Later that summer, when he finally landed in Toronto with his brother, Tim, he immediately liked what he saw. "I fell in love with the city and with the vibe before I even played a game of basketball, before I even touched the basketball, and before I met any of my teammates. It was just about understanding the culture there."

Summer in Toronto also meant a huge surprise for Ford: Caribana, or the Toronto Caribbean Carnival, as it is officially known, a celebration of Caribbean culture. "When I arrived, I had never heard of Caribana. I didn't know anything about Toronto at that time. But I was like, 'Oh this is dope.' You got the costumes. You got the floats. I had never seen any of that stuff a day in my life." When he finally connected with another NBA player, it was his former teammate from Milwaukee, Jamaal Magloire, a Toronto-born hooper and future Raptor. "We were already close, and Jamaal took care of me and my brother that whole Caribana weekend. I was on his float," known as the Toronto Revellers, which still takes part in the festival parade to this day. "I was with him the whole time."

Riding high on the good vibes of Caribana, Ford was also optimistic about the Raptors' prospects for the 2006–07 season. Even the team's 2-8 start, at least for him, was no big deal. He knew how to face a challenge, having spent much of his career battling catastrophic back injuries, first in high school and then during his collegiate career with the Texas Longhorns. Disaster had even struck at the worst possible moment—right before the 2003 draft, when a bad fall left him with temporary paralysis. By then Ford was a major prospect—even, potentially, a top-five pick—but his injuries scared off teams at the top of the board, and the Bucks eventually selected him eighth overall.

During his rookie year, Ford suffered another potentially career-changing and even life-threatening injury. In February 2004, during a game against the Minnesota Timberwolves, he was fouled by Mark Madsen. The tumble to the court left Ford with a serious spinal cord contusion that led to temporary paralysis in his arms and legs. He eventually underwent spinal-fusion surgery, missing the remainder of his rookie year and his sophomore season. That he was able to play at all after the injury was a gift. As he told us, "All my spinal problems were a blessing in disguise. It made me appreciate the game more that I was still given a chance to play it at the highest level. That always made me want to give it everything I've got."

Coming to Toronto, Ford knew what it meant to face a challenge head-on. "Any player that gets traded, you got something to prove. It doesn't matter the team record. I think most of the situations that I was coming into, I wasn't going to a team that had any expectations that they were supposed to win. That was also me in college, going to a university like Texas that wasn't known as a basketball school. I was accustomed to building things and being a part of the foundation to get things on track." History, according to Ford, would repeat itself. "I did it in Milwaukee. I knew I could do it in Toronto too."

Shifting outside perspectives of the team also meant rewriting how the team viewed itself. Ford knew he had to lead by example. "My mentality went to another level; my work ethic and my workout regimen went to another level. I was focused and locked in, trying to prove people wrong about me while trying to be the best player that I could be. I think that's why we were able to revamp the culture pretty fast."

Ford saw a natural partner for rebooting the team's culture in Chris Bosh, the Raptors' fourth-year center and a fellow Texan. "Having Chris was the ultimate thing for me. We spent a lot of time together. When I came to Toronto while playing for Milwaukee, he would pick me up and we would go to dinner. When he came my way, we would do the same thing. It made things a lot easier, getting that phone call, saying, 'Now we got a chance to do some special things.' That made it very welcoming after I got over the emotions of somebody telling you they don't want you anymore."

On court, though, it was not as clear what type of team the Raptors would become, thanks to Colangelo's offseason reengineering. "You had a lot of guys coming from a lot of different backgrounds. A lot of guys were underdogs. A lot of guys were coming into the league from overseas. You had guys that had success in other places and this was them getting their shot. People didn't expect us to do things. We *all* had something to prove."

With such a diverse group of personalities, the organization worked hard to cultivate team unity. In part, that meant showcasing the team across Canada and even Europe, which included a training camp in Treviso, Italy, two preseason games in Rome, and a four-team tournament in Madrid, against the Memphis Grizzlies and two Spanish teams, Real Madrid and Estudiantes.

Such bonding measures also translated to the court. "Part of my game is understanding my teammates," Ford explains. "I spent a lot of time with guys off the court, even after practice, having conversations. Some of that is basketball-related; some of it is not. My success as a point guard is being able to just know a little bit more in depth about my teammates. That connection works for me *on* the court. If I don't really have that connection with you off the court, it becomes a disconnect on the court because we have to be on the same page. Getting guys to be able to trust that you will make them look good and be able to give them the ball and play the right way. It's the ultimate thing."

Ford also saw a leader in the Raptors' coach, Sam Mitchell, who had served as an assistant during Ford's rookie season. "I went under his wings my first year with the Milwaukee Bucks. We had a connection." Plus, it was hard not to be impressed with Sam Mitchell *the player.* An undrafted underdog, Mitchell had carved out a place for himself in the NBA after two years of playing in France in the late 1980s. The versatile forward was known for his work ethic, leadership, and toughness, all qualities he brought to bear at the tail end of his career in Minnesota, where he served as a mentor to Kevin Garnett, who had entered the league directly out of high school in 1995. For Ford, Mitchell embodied leadership. "Obviously I looked at him as a pro as a kid and knew the impact that he had with Kevin Garnett. Being able to play for him as a head coach—it was awesome."

Mitchell's demeanor also helped set the tone for the rebuilt squad. "The way Sam ran things, it wasn't complicated. You knew what you were going to do every day. He had the respect of guys. And it was fun. You knew you were going to practice hard and you're going to get a bunch of shots up. Nothing crazy. We were always fresh for games. Sam was a solid coach." This worked just fine for Ford. So did Mitchell's directness, which fit Ford's own philosophy: "Be honest, be straightforward, and don't bullshit me."

Even still, with the Raptors struggling to start the 2006–07 season, all eyes were on Mitchell. As Ford remembers it, "I came into that situation where the expectation was that we were supposed to get a new coach. I think everybody knew that. Everybody felt that. In Canada, I think everybody *wanted* that." During that early-season losing streak, the rumblings started again. "We were hearing rumors that Sam could get fired."

Their early losing record also pointed, at least according to some outsiders, to problems on the court. At the center of it: the supposed conflict between Toronto's two point guards, Calderón and Ford. At the time, Ford knew it was just noise. "I was trying to understand why people thought we couldn't play together if we were both getting eight assists a night. We were both efficient in different ways. We were both putting up crazy numbers in a short span."

Put together, Ford felt, the two guards were complementary rather than redundant, even offering a glimpse of the small-ball future Colangelo was helping to build. "I was able to play at a high level and José was able to play at a high level. If you put that team in today's game, it would be amazing. People wouldn't be afraid to keep us on the court at the same time." In the end, despite all the chatter around the supposed José–TJ battle, it was watching Calderón grow that still resonates with Ford today. "Being able to watch a guy like José, being a backup, being able to elevate his game to a whole other level? I just felt proud. Me and José, we performed at a high level."

As the season chugged along, it seemed like the Raptors, despite their locker room bonhomie, just couldn't catch a break. In December, with the team 7-12, Bosh went down with a bone bruise in his left knee, pulling him out of the lineup for 11 games. It was up to the

(Left) Matt Bonner and Cory Joseph, both as San Antonio Spurs, posing with a charity T-shirt designed by Eric, November 2012.
COURTESY OF MATT BONNER

(Right) Jonas Valančiuñas with Eric's son, Jackson, December 2014.

Fellow Raptors Amir Johnson and Greivis Vásquez watch Tyler Hansbrough go up for the layup against the 76ers at Wells Fargo Center in Philadelphia, January 23, 2015. COPYRIGHT © 2015 NBAE (PHOTO BY JESSE D. GARRABRANT / NBAE VIA GETTY IMAGES)

Kyle Lowry and Steph Curry joking around pregame at the NBA All-Star Game in New York City, February 2015.

(Above) Eric interviewing DeMar DeRozan and Kyle Lowry for Sportsnet, February 2016.

(Left) Patrick Patterson modeling the newly unveiled Raptors uniform, September 2015.

Bismack Biyombo answers questions during an off-day press conference, May 2016.

Eric with Vince Carter at the NBA Finals in Cleveland, June 2016.

Raptor Cory Joseph signing autographs while in San Antonio to play against his old team, the Spurs, January 23, 2017.

remaining Raptors, including Ford, to eke out some wins. Mitchell, too, was once again on the hot seat. On January 3, the team dropped another game, this one a tight 100–98 contest in Toronto to Colangelo's old team, the Suns.

Then, with the Raptors a troubling 13-19, the seemingly impossible happened. After four losing seasons, the team started to win. A lot. In Ford's words, "We went on a hell of a run!" By the close of the 2006–07 season, the team had reeled off 34 wins in their final 50 games, good for a record of 47-35, for which Mitchell was named Coach of the Year. Ford started 71 games that season, putting up 20 double-doubles. Perhaps most shocking of all, they finished first in the Atlantic Division. "*That* changed the culture," Ford says. "That changed everything."

It was a mixed blessing, however. The Raptors might have secured their first playoff berth since 2002, but there was also a downside: In the first round they had to face a stacked New Jersey Nets team featuring Jason Kidd, Richard Jefferson, and none other than Vince Carter. During the series, Toronto squandered the first game at home, before winning the second. Back in East Rutherford, the Nets took two more wins with Vince putting a hurting on his old team, including a 37-point game-three performance. Toronto took game five, only to lose a sixth and decisive matchup back at Continental Airlines Arena, a close-fought 98–97 loss that came down to the final possession.

Behind the scoring power of Bosh and Parker, Ford played well throughout the series. He even drained 21 points in the opening matchup and put up a team-best 27 points in the team's game-three loss. But his defensive assignments were tough in the series, whether he was facing a 6'4" Kidd at point or Carter at shooting guard. Throughout the series, Mitchell shuttled players in and out of the starting lineup, looking for an advantage. In the final game, Ford came off the bench for the first time in the series, going 7-10 from the field for 19 points.

During Ford's second season with the team, the injury bug reared its ugly head. In December, the Raptors were in Atlanta for a game against the Hawks. Ford had been playing well. Well, maybe better than well. "I was *killing* that game," Ford deservedly recalls, having finished the contest with 8 assists and 26 points on an efficient 11-of-15 from the field. With 1:32 left in the fourth and the Raptors up 92–84, Ford had leaked out on a fast break only to be hit by Al Horford with a hard foul. Eric still remembers the eerie quiet of the arena as Ford lay motionless on the court. "The pain was brutal," Ford says. "You always think, *That's it,* when you're lying there. The first thing that came to mind, right then and there, was that I wanted to retire."

Ford was rushed to the hospital but had to wait to be examined. "For three or four hours, I was in the hallway lying on a gurney. I was just lying there, waiting for a technician to do an MRI." Strapped to the gurney, unable to move, Ford had no idea what was next, thinking, "I don't know if I can walk."

After the game, Eric went with the team to the hospital, where they waited hours to hear more about their injured guard. Eventually the players were told that they had to go, with a matchup the following evening back in Toronto, though the team was unsurprisingly loath to leave Ford behind. For his part, Horford was ejected from the contest with a flagrant-two foul and suspended an additional game. But the guilt was overwhelming, and the young Hawks center also visited Ford in the hospital that same night, staying with him for a few hours. "TJ was real cool," Horford told the *Atlanta Journal-Constitution* the next day. "Thank God he's doing better. He told me that he understood I didn't do it intentionally or anything like that. It was a really good visit."

When Ford was finally released from the hospital the following day, he knew that, once again, he had a lengthy rehab ahead. He was uncertain whether he wanted to continue on. "It was fear not knowing how I would recover. I got talked out of retiring by family and friends. One of my mentors was like, 'I'm fifty years old. My fucking knees hurt too.'" *Fair enough,* Ford thought. "When you land there paralyzed, it takes a lot to be able to come back from that and play. That's damn near saying you are willing to die for the game of basketball. I don't think people understood. Why would a person come back and play? That's the only reason: for the love of the game. I wanted to be able to express and show that."

His passion for the sport and willingness to endure another major recovery was one thing. But so, too, was the money. Though he was only in the first year of a four-year deal, Ford's contract came with a heavy stipulation about time missed due to injury. "My contract was set up that I had to give back fifty-two percent of my money if I got hurt. With my spinal injuries, it was part of my deal that people didn't know about." That clause changed everything. "If my contract was one hundred percent guaranteed, I probably would have never suited up again that season."

In the end, Ford was knocked out of the lineup for eight weeks. His return to the team was momentous. He had mostly been away from the Raptors while rehabilitating, finally meeting the team on the road against the Heat in early February. "I wasn't supposed to play in Miami. I was just coming to practice so they could see what I looked like. I practiced with the team when I got there and I dominated. I was the same guy that left. People saw that, like, 'Damn, he's back.'"

Ford's return to the court also led to a lasting image in Raptors history. Despite all the noise around who ought to start for the Raptors at point guard, Calderón was the first player to greet Ford when he subbed in against Miami. "I checked in the game and everybody's excited. I think even the Heat fans. I got a cheer and José meets me at halfcourt as he's checking me out and he gives me an awesome hug." In the end, it was a great return to the court. "I get in that game and I make a hell of a behind-the-back pass. I also dunked that game." His 17 minutes off the bench, with 4 points, 4 assists, and a couple of steals, offered positive signs that Ford might once again be able to marshal the team.

Still, the effects of Ford's run-in with Horford lingered. "Multiple times in Toronto I was playing games with full-blown stingers in both of my hands and my arm. Just imagine that feeling from your waist all the way up to your neck all the way to your hands. I'm used to psychologically dealing with the pain and minimizing how brutal it really was."

Only in the final weeks of the 2008 season did Ford regain his starting position, in part thanks to his strong play and in part thanks to Calderón, who directly approached Coach Mitchell, requesting a return to the bench. The Raptors finished the season 41-41 and managed to make the playoffs again, only to lose in five in the first round to Stan Van Gundy's 52-30 Orlando Magic, led by Dwight Howard, Hedo Türkoğlu, and Jameer Nelson.

Sadly, that series also ended the Raptors' short-lived string of playoff appearances, with Toronto faithful having to wait another six seasons, until 2014, for the Raptors to become postseason regulars again. It was also the end of Ford's run in Toronto. "Everybody knew I was getting traded, even at the damn end-of-season press conference. That's all we talked about at my exit meeting." True to expectation, during the summer Ford was shipped to Indiana, where he played three more seasons, before a brief stint in San Antonio. In 2012, after eight years in the NBA, Ford decided to retire, after being traded to and then waived by the Warriors.

Looking back, Ford runs through the what-ifs that define the endings of so many Raptors seasons during the Vince and Bosh eras. His own journey is more personal, however. What if he stayed healthy? What if the Raptors had kept Calderón and him together? "We all knew that they were going to choose either me or José. At that time, I knew I was the one out because I got hurt. If I didn't get hurt and we finished the season, then I think the conversation would have been different. I think it makes it a little more challenging." At the very least, Ford conjectures, "I probably would have had more opportunities with more teams." Even still, he doesn't look back with any anger or resentment. "I feel good about my career. I had my best two years of basketball with the Raptors. I loved the environment. I loved the culture. Toronto was one of the best experiences for me that I still cherish."

Raptors Moment

January 22, 2006: The Untold History of Kobe's 81

Imagine this scene: The Raptors are facing the Lakers. Toronto is playing well, up 63–49 at the half. But then the Lakers heat up in the second, eventually beating the Raptors, 122–104. It's hardly anything to write home about: You win some, you lose some, and it's never easy playing in LA. That's one story you could tell.

But that's not how the game is remembered.

Instead, it's rightly known as the night Kobe Bryant dropped 81 on the Raptors—the second-most points by a player in a game in NBA history—a story that has simply eclipsed the other one, about the Raptors' strong start followed by a cold second half.

That story has largely been forgotten, though not by everybody.

"Kobe was getting his," Charlie Villanueva admits with a shrug. "But we didn't know it was gonna get to that *point*. He was playing well, but *we* were winning." Matt Bonner also remembers the team's worry-free strategy. "Coach Mitchell said, 'Let him score all the points he wants. We're winning the game.' It was the ultimate backfire."

Even still, when the final buzzer rang, many of the Raptors had no idea just how well Kobe had played. "It was a quiet eighty-one," Villanueva said, disbelieving that such a thing could even exist. "I remember the locker room at the end of the game. We looked at the stat sheet. 'Yo, this dude just had *eighty-one*.'" Thinking about their squandered lead, the Raptors' guard Mike James kicks himself now. "At halftime, I came out real passive. That's my only disappointment." The Raptors were helpless to stop the second-half onslaught.

"We were doing box-and-one, throwing two guys at him, three guys at him," Villanueva recalls. "But at that point, it's videogame mode: He *NBA Jams* all over again."

The team was on the wrong side of history, but they also saw history happen. "Everybody took it as a bad thing," José Calderón told us. "I'm not saying I was happy that we lost the game, but it's a historic moment and I was sitting front row most of the night."

For many of the Raptors players today, the game—commemorated by the Lakers in 2024 with a nineteen-foot-tall statue of Kobe walking off the court—is not an embarrassment. "My name is on the Kobe statue, too, because they had it engraved with the box score," Villanueva laughs, shaking his head. "I'll go to LA, take my kids, like, 'Hey, look!'" Bonner is only grateful that he played well, with 12 points and a couple of clutch threes. "I'm so glad I had a decent enough night, because otherwise I would have been immortalized with a crappy game."

For Eric, the 81-point performance was also a special moment. In nearly three decades of covering the league, he has never gotten an autograph from a player.

Except once.

Eric and his broadcast partner Paul Jones kept two box scores from the game. Years later, in 2016, when Kobe was in Toronto for his 18th and final All-Star appearance, they all ended up in a room together, and Kobe offered to sign their mementos.

After signing the first one, Kobe handed it back to Eric, who thanked him, and then took a look: "Kobe Bryant 24."

"Kobe," Eric said with an apology, "you were in number *eight* at the time."

"Goddammit." Kobe laughed, and signed the second box score, correcting the error: "Kobe Bryant 8."

Today, that showdown in LA is deservedly remembered as a historic moment for Kobe. But for the Raptors franchise, Kobe's 81 is also a significant moment—a metaphor, even, for the Raptors' struggles across the Bosh era: of good but not great teams that faced the pleasant surprise of performing well only to founder, whether it was in the second half against Kobe's onslaught or in the first round against stacked competitors.

For the Raptors who faced the Lakers that night, it was also a bittersweet memory: when one of the game's leading players single-handedly beat a flat-footed Toronto squad. But for those same players, it is also a memory, strangely enough, worth relishing, when they all had a front-row seat to one of the NBA's greatest-ever players making history.

14

Anthony Parker (2006–2009)

It's the summer of 2005. The Raptors are hosting Maccabi Tel Aviv for a preseason game at Air Canada Centre. Everything has come down to the fourth quarter. With the teams tied at 103 and 11.7 seconds left on the clock, Maccabi are inbounding near center court. Everyone has their eyes on one player: Anthony Parker, the so-called "Michael Jordan of the EuroLeague," who has been putting a hurting on the Raptors all game with 22 points on deadly shooting.

As a college prospect, Parker had once seemed destined for NBA greatness. He was a star at Bradley University, a D1 program in Illinois just two and a half hours by car from Naperville, the Chicago suburb where he grew up. He spent four years at Bradley, eventually winning MVP for the Missouri Valley Conference and earning All-MVC first-team honors.

In the 1997 draft, he was selected 21st overall by the Nets before being traded to the 76ers. In Philadelphia, Parker struggled with his health, never finding meaningful minutes. Two seasons later, in the summer of 1999, he was sent to Orlando, but then was released by the Magic in January 2000 and finished the season with the Quad City Thunder of the Continental Basketball Association.

From hometown star and a first-round pick to out of the league by twenty-five, Parker began to look overseas. Maybe a strong season in the EuroLeague, he reasoned, with increased on-court responsibilities and a chance to show off what he could do with the ball in his hands rather than his butt on the bench, might be his ticket back to the NBA. For Parker, Maccabi Tel Aviv offered the perfect opportunity, one he remains grateful for to this day. In Israel, basketball is "a way of life," he said years later. "You're not just playing basketball; you're playing for the pride of the people."

Early on, Parker kept his NBA dreams alive. "When I first got overseas, my whole thing was to come back to the NBA as quickly as possible after one year." Before long, though, Parker was reimagining his future. "Once I got over there, everything changed. I was happy and it became more about playing the game that I love at a high level. I was at peace with that."

In his first season with Maccabi, the team won the Israeli domestic championship, the Israeli National Cup, and the FIBA Supro-League Cup. Parker then spent a season in Rome before returning to Tel Aviv, where he was named EuroLeague MVP in 2004 and 2005. Winning and personal success quickly changed his outlook on his supposed gap year abroad. "I got over there after really not playing for three years in the NBA and was a part of something that was really cool. We had a really good team, a lot of support, and it was just a lot of fun to play at a high level."

Life on the balmy shores of the Mediterranean was also not so bad. "I tell everyone the basketball experience and the off-the-court experience I had in Tel Aviv was amazing." Case in point: His family was growing as Parker and his wife, Tamaria—or Tamy, as he calls her—made a home for themselves in Israel. At first it was just the two of them. By the time they had left Israel, Parker and Tamy had two children: Alonso and Julian.

Soon Parker had a new reputation—as the best player *not* in the NBA. After his years with Maccabi, he was a different athlete, both physically and psychologically. He had an enhanced on-court role and he had learned to think about the game through the team-oriented, skills-and-fundamentals outlook that dominated European basketball.

Parker was also getting scouted again. But rejoining the NBA was no easy decision. He was hesitant to spend another season sitting on the bench, for less money and less job security, just to say he was back in the NBA. "There were teams that had contacted me, but they were for minimum contracts or make-the-team situations. I didn't want to go back to a situation where I wasn't playing again." For Parker, it was his own tree-falling-in-a-forest problem: If you spend all of your time sitting on the bench, are you even an NBA player?

Even after six years in the EuroLeague, though, that old itch never went away. "We had success as a team and I had accomplished all I could. It got to the point where I wanted the next challenge." The NBA seemed a natural next step. "If the opportunity to go to the NBA ever came, I would certainly jump at it. But if I never got to the NBA again, that was fine." Whether he succeeded or not, Parker knew that the NBA was the obvious jump. "I knew I wasn't a superstar, so there was no identity crisis, but I wanted to see where I fit in. I wanted to see what I could do as a player. And I knew after I played against Toronto that I fit in the NBA. I just didn't know where."

Back in Toronto in the summer of 2005, with only 11.7 seconds left in a tied game, Maccabi is inbounding the ball against the Raptors, and Parker is finally getting his proof-of-concept moment. The ball makes its way to Parker, who catches it in front of Toronto's bench with his back to the net. Morris Peterson tucks in close to Parker, who's clearly mapping out his shot. He pulls back out to the three-point line, then drives hard to the baseline in one dribble, stopping on a dime and rising up over Mo Pete, who reaches out helplessly as Parker fades away in his best Kobe imitation. Everyone in Air Canada Centre watches as the arcing jumper falls cleanly through the hoop, snapping the net. Maccabi 105–103. Eight-tenths of a second left on the clock. Parker calls game.

That exhibition matchup in Toronto—as well as a second game that fall in Orlando—was an opportunity for Parker to test himself. The results felt like confirmation. "It was a chance to play against NBA players and I came away feeling like I could be an NBA player. I just didn't know if that meant a starting or rotation player."

The rest of the story is perhaps no surprise, at least to Raptors fans. A year later, the NBA came knocking again. "There were a couple of teams that reached out. The two last teams were Cleveland and Toronto. I just didn't know what my role was going to look like with the Cavs. I felt like there was a better fit and a better opportunity for me as a player in Toronto. I had played Toronto and it just felt right, and I'd always loved Toronto as a city." He asked Tamy, who felt the same. "It was not a difficult decision. It was like, 'This is a great opportunity.'"

On July 13, 2006, Parker signed with the Raptors on a three-year, $12 million contract. Even less of a surprise? By the start of that 2006–07 season, Parker was in Toronto's opening-day lineup. Suddenly "the best player not in the NBA" was back in the big time.

Parker's journey to Toronto and the NBA was as much a shock to him as anyone else, but he finally had the maturity and mindset to take on the professional challenges that had proved so daunting just years earlier. "I came back when I was like thirty, going on thirty-one. I had a family, I had experiences, I had been all over the world, I had met people from all these different places. I grew as a player and knew who I was and what I could do on the court."

But the return to the league was no easy task, and the switch in playing style required Parker to rethink some of his in-game choices. "There is an adjustment from Europe to the NBA, the same way when people go from the NBA or college to Europe," he explained.

"One of the biggest adjustments was shot selection. What was a bad shot in Europe was a good shot in the NBA, because of players' defense, length, and athleticism. The windows close up so fast in the NBA and it's hard to generate those opportunities."

There was also the grind of the 82-game schedule, something that took a toll on the newly resettled Parker family. "My first year in Toronto, we had two West Coast trips *before* Christmas," he recalls. "Our travel schedule was crazy. Julian was close to ten months and Alonso was going on four when we got to Toronto, and both of my kids were awful sleepers. Tamy was really struggling with the adjustment, being in a new city, not knowing anybody, the kids, all of those things." At the same time, Parker faced equal pressure to perform on court. "You feel that strain: 'I'm back on an NBA team and I'm trying to make an impression and do as well as I can.'"

Eventually, the Parker clan found a rhythm. Tamy was increasingly folded into the larger Raptors family, especially with the team's Spanish players and fellow EuroLeague vets, José Calderón and Jorge Garbajosa. "The cool thing was, once we found a babysitter that we trusted, game nights in Toronto were kind of like date nights. Afterwards, Tamy and I would go to dinner with Jorge, José, and José's wife, Ana. My wife is from Puerto Rico and speaks Spanish, and obviously they all spoke Spanish, so she enjoyed that."

The Raptors acquired a variety of players from all over the world during Parker's three seasons in Toronto, and the team's international flavor was something he could appreciate after his many years overseas. "We had players from all these different places and countries. You had Jorge and José from Spain, Andrea Bargnani from Italy, Uroš Slokar and Rasho Nesterović from Slovenia, Carlos Delfino from Argentina."

That diversity could be infectious—even among young Americans who had never played overseas. "I remember Chris Bosh being like, 'Wow, you're speaking all these languages. I want to learn some.' He got a private tutor and then, years later, Tamy and I were lying in bed watching a Latin American talk show and Chris was on there, doing the entire interview in Spanish. I thought that was amazing. I always use him as an example whenever I talk about basketball players being more than just basketball players."

In a strange way, thanks to his time overseas, Parker was viewed to some degree as a foreign player. "There was an event celebrating the international flavor of our team and there were all these tables set up with a flag for each country that the players belong to. I had a table with the Israeli flag on it. I was like, 'Guys, I'm American.'" Parker could only laugh at the confusion, but he also appreciated what the mistake meant. "It illustrates a little bit the bond that I had with the country, with the team, and with the fans. It's crazy, because Israel is such a small country, but anywhere I travel, I'll run into not just Jewish people but Israelis, and there's always that immediate recognition, that bond, even twenty years later."

That recognition is understandable. Parker had cultivated a special relationship with his Jewish and Israeli fans, something that was subtly expressed in his jersey number. "My whole time in Israel, I wore the number eight. But when I went to Toronto, José had number eight. Along the way, I discovered *chai,* which is the number eighteen and the symbol of life and good fortune. A lot of times in Israel and in the Jewish faith, people attach eighteen to whatever it is they're doing as a blessing. My choosing number eighteen was my way of bringing everything that had happened to me in Israel with Maccabi Tel Aviv—all the memories, all the fans—with me to the next stop."

That synergy between fans and players was also apparent in the ACC, where the multiculturalism of the city and country were often on full display—even during Maccabi's exhibition game in 2005, where fans could be seen waving giant blue and white Israeli flags. "You could see the diversity in the crowd and when you walked around the city. At any home game, you would have a pocket of fans that were holding up a sign for Rasho or for Andrea or for whoever it was. I always say Toronto is the most diverse place I've ever been.

You walk around the city and you hear like all of these different languages, see all these different shops and restaurants representing wherever people are originally from and that's unique in Toronto. That to me is the coolest thing."

During Parker's three seasons with the Raptors, it was easy to like the wing's do-everything game, including his efficient three-point shooting and hard-nosed defense, qualities that led to a 47-35 regular-season record and the Raptors' first-ever Atlantic Division title in 2007. "We were trying to play a different style than most of the NBA was playing at that time," Parker recalls. "We were this three-point-shooting team, five out a little bit, and we would spread out and swing, swing, swing. And then it just started to click. The team was just ten years old when I got there. I think it's special to have a chapter in that."

In the first round of the playoffs, the Raptors faced the Nets and Vince Carter, who had been traded to New Jersey two seasons earlier, and Toronto fans still harbored hard feelings about the star's controversial exit. "You could certainly feel the edginess," Parker said, recalling how that intensity fueled the team. "What I remember is the playoff games at home and the crowd and the atmosphere. It was so fun to be a part of it—to have a run and the crowd just exploding. The Toronto fan base was incredible. *That's* what you do it for."

During the series, it fell to Parker to guard Carter, by then twenty-nine years old and at the height of his powers. "They played out of the post with Vince a lot, and he was so tough to defend, how talented he was and how easy and effortless it was at times. I got to play against some of the best to ever do it—D-Wade, Kobe, Tracy McGrady, Joe Johnson—and Vince had no weaknesses in this game. Talent-wise, he was up there with Kobe. I wouldn't say I held him in check that series—you just try to make it as tough as possible—but I'd say he probably didn't make shots that sometimes he made. But in the end, if

Vince was going and he was at the top of his game, there was nothing I could do," Parker says with a laugh. "I was not *that* defender."

Eventually the Nets took down the Raptors in six games. "New Jersey had more experience," Parker said. "We were still finding our way. It was just disappointing that we couldn't get it for the fans." The team regrouped the following season, but things never came fully together. Parker suffered a bad ankle sprain and he, and the team, limped to a 41-41 finish, only to be bounced from the playoffs from the first round once again.

During Parker's third season, the Raptors went 33-49 and even fired Sam Mitchell, who had been named Coach of the Year in 2007, after an 8-9 start. After missing the playoffs and assessing the lay of the land, Parker, by then thirty-four, decided to move on. "There needed to be changes. I thought Toronto was going to go in a different direction and they had drafted DeMar DeRozan. Bryan Colangelo was still interested in bringing me back. But I needed a change, and I felt Cleveland was probably a good situation in terms of playing off LeBron."

Parker would play three seasons for the Cavaliers, before retiring in 2012. He then became a scout for the Orlando Magic, eventually working his way up to general manager of the Lakeland Magic, Orlando's development team, before becoming an assistant general manager for the Orlando Magic and being promoted to general manager in 2023.

Just as his time in Tel Aviv had prepared him for his return to the NBA, so too did his time in Toronto under Colangelo prepare him for his new role as an exec in Orlando. "One thing I'll give Bryan credit for is he had the guts to pull the trigger on things when maybe other people would be a little more hesitant. You learn really quickly how incredibly difficult it is to build a roster. There's a level of luck. You put together something and something clicks and you're like, 'Wow, that worked!' It's like this experiment that, when it works, everybody thinks you're the smartest guy ever. And when it doesn't, it's like, 'What are you doing?'"

Looking back, Parker views his three years in Canada as a true high point in his NBA career. Toronto, like Tel Aviv, still holds a special place for him. "In your career, you play in a place or two that feels like home. That's the feeling I get when I go to Tel Aviv or Toronto. It feels like going back home. Toronto was that place for me. I love it."

A decade and a half later, he still retains that connection to Toronto, especially when he runs into Raptors fans. "I get stopped by so many people from Toronto, even today, and it's just a cool experience, the love that the fans show me. I wasn't a *great* player, you know what I mean? I wasn't Chris Bosh. I wasn't any of those guys." But those shout-outs are representative of the connection the fans felt and that he in turn felt with the fans, the city, and the country. "I don't know how many other places you could go and get that experience. You felt that you represented a country. It was unique."

15

Jorge Garbajosa (2006–2008)

By the age of twenty-eight, Jorge Garbajosa had accomplished almost every major goal he had set out for himself as a member of the Spanish national team and as a pro in Spain and Italy.

Then, in 2006, the Raptors came knocking.

It wasn't Garbajosa's first flirtation with the NBA. Years earlier in Italy, he had been approached by the Phoenix Suns. "I was twenty-three," Garbajosa told us. "I was playing for Treviso and my coach was Mike D'Antoni. It was an amazing year, probably one of the first years in my career where I felt like a leader with all the responsibilities and all the confidence of the coach, and we won the league in Italy. At the end of the year, Coach D'Antoni told me, 'I've been talking with Phoenix and they are interested in you.'"

It was news to Garbajosa. But it was also not quite reality. "Honestly, I understood it not as a joke but as nothing serious. I said, 'Come on, coach, what the hell am I going to do in the NBA?' I thought my place was in Europe. My level was in Europe and my idea was to go back to Spain to play. I saw the NBA at that time as an almost unachievable goal."

By the time the Raptors came to the Spaniard in 2006, things had started to change—both in the NBA and in Garbajosa's thinking. Most notably, the league was becoming more diverse, with players from all over the world, including Spain, and even Garbajosa's teammates from the national squad. "When you see that José Calderón is playing in the NBA and he is having a great experience, and Pau Gasol is having a great NBA career, you think, *We are teammates, we have played together, and we are different players, but our level is similar.*"

Still, it was hard to know what to do. At the time, Garbajosa was in the middle of leading his own team, Unicaja, in the Finals. During the playoffs, his agent called, explaining that Maurizio Gherardini, who had managed Garbajosa in Italy before becoming vice president and assistant general manager of the Raptors, wanted him in Toronto the next season. "My team had never won the league, so it was not an easy role, but we had a great feeling and we had a great team. I said, 'It's not the right moment. Let's wait until the season ends and then we will see.' When we won the league, it was very emotional for me, because we won against Vitoria, where I played when I was in the grassroots program with TAU Cerámica. I remember sitting in the locker room afterward and this thought came to my mind—the idea to go to Toronto."

Garbajosa's own situation had simply evolved, and with it his view of himself as a player. "It was a goal for me right in that moment, not before. We won the league in Italy, I won the league in Spain, I played in the final four of EuroLeague, we became world champions. I needed a new challenge." The selfless star could also already glimpse the end of his playing days. "It was my moment. I was twenty-eight years old, turning twenty-nine. It was my last chance, my last train. I had to try. I decided that in the locker room."

Toronto, moreover, offered the ideal landing pad. "There are two main reasons why I decided to go to Toronto without hearing any other options," Garbajosa explained. "First of all, I'm a very personable guy and it was a very familiar environment for me. Not only Maurizio, but also José and Andrea Bargnani. I talked to José many times before I signed the contract. Maurizio was also crucial for me. We had a very close relationship and he convinced me to go."

There was also a second reason, one that helped to assuage the big man's fears about adjusting to the NBA. "Even if I knew that this was my opportunity," he said, "it's a big step in your career and life to go to the NBA and to move to Canada to play in the league that you have been watching on TV." That, again, is where his former GM—and new assistant GM—stepped in. "When I was in Toronto to sign the contract, I asked Maurizio, 'There are a lot of good players in Europe. Why me?' He told me, 'Jorge, we will have a roster full of talent, but everyone is very young and they have never won before. You are older and you have won a lot and you have done everything you have to do for the chance to win.' It was the perfect answer. It made me feel so proud. I was able to put all of my experience at the disposal of the team to help them win."

Shortly after, on July 24, 2006, the Raptors signed the versatile big. Then they threw him in the deep end—something that Garbo actually thinks was a benefit for the paradoxically seasoned rookie. "The life of an NBA player doesn't allow you to think," he laughs today. "Practice, game, travel, practice, game, play—you don't have time to think. It's easy to get used to that life, because you just have to follow the team. I thought I had the time to get adapted to life in Toronto, to the league, to the new franchise, the new teammates, to a different way to play, but it was 'boom!'"

Luckily, he had great mentors. "I was like a guy from Mars who came to Earth, but from the first day, I felt at home because of the team, because of my teammates, and because of the coaches—Alex English, Jay Triano, and Sam Mitchell—but also training staff members, like Rory Mullin, Scott McCullough, and Ray Chow. As part of a team with so many European players, it was easy to connect from the very beginning, also with Chris Bosh, Darrick Martin, and Anthony Parker."

Acclimating to NBA life also meant doing things the NBA way. That was another learning experience for Garbajosa, but again one that he valued, having spent his entire career in Europe. "The most important tip was to be extremely respectful with all the people around you. Not only your teammates, obviously, but also your franchise, the media, and the fans. It was a huge improvement of my understanding of basketball. In the NBA, they respect the fans. I was lucky because Bosh, as a franchise player, was a great example for us. How he practiced, how he behaved with his teammates, how he behaved with the fans and with the media. I spent the whole day with my eyes open like this"—Garbajosa laughs, wide-eyed like a surprised child—"trying to learn from him, from Darrick, from Anthony, and from Rasho Nesterović."

His head-down work ethic quickly garnered the respect of his new teammates. "One day T. J. Ford was joking in the locker room and told me, 'I think that in Europe you're a gangster.' I said, '*I'm* a gangster? Why?' 'Because you never talk,' Ford explained. 'You are always watching. You look dangerous, man.'" Garbajosa couldn't help but laugh at Ford's insight. "It's true. That first month, I never talked, because I wanted to learn, I wanted to earn respect, and I didn't want to show them that I was there to be the man. I just wanted to practice hard and show them that I'm there to help the team. Then, step by step, I gained confidence. But I will never forget that conversation with TJ. I said to him, 'No, I'm not dangerous.'"

With the breakneck speed of his adaptation—playing in sunny southern Spain one month to practicing with his new Canadian squad the next—it took a while for the reality to set in: Garbajosa was actually playing in the NBA, something he had thought was truly impossible just a few years earlier. "The Raptors would play at home during Eastern time. Then you go home and watch the West Coast games. My feeling was like, 'The *real* NBA is what I'm watching on TV.' I never fully realized, seriously, that I was in the league. It was an amazing feeling, but at the same time it helped me not to lose control of myself."

Despite his celebrated career overseas, Garbajosa also knew that, as an unknown rookie, he needed to find his role on the team. "We were at training camp, and Coach Mitchell told me, 'I want you to be tough and I want you to be ready, but you have to wait for your moment. I don't know you, but everybody told me good things about you. I want to see you bust your ass, work hard every single day, and raise the level of the intensity of the practices.' So that's what I did."

Eventually, that willingness to grind paid off. "I didn't start for the first seven games. In the seventh game, we were playing in Oakland against Golden State. We were losing and Sam had tried everybody on the bench but me. So at the end of the game, he said, 'Okay, you, the European kid, go try.' I played some decent minutes, and the next game, we were playing back to back in LA. Sam said, 'Today, maybe you will play some minutes as a guard.' And I said, 'Sam, I'm a four.' 'Yeah, but I need you as a guard.' And in the same game, I played guard, small forward, power forward, and center against Andrew Bynum, Lamar Odom, and Kobe Bryant. *In the same game.*"

His willingness to shapeshift into whatever Coach Mitchell needed was immediately acknowledged. "Sam said, 'You are in the starting five. You earned it in the last game because you did what I asked you to do.'" Earning the role and understanding the role were, however, two different things. "Right after those back-to-back games, we went back to Toronto. As a rookie, I went very early the next morning to practice, shoot, and work out. Sam came up to me and asked, 'What the hell are you doing here?' 'I'm a rookie, coach. I'm practicing.' 'No, you are now a starter. So relax, get some treatment, get up some shots, and go home, because tomorrow you have to play thirty minutes.' From then on, I played thirty-plus minutes a game."

On court, the gifted big man made an immediate splash not only with his coach but also with his teammates. "I don't know how much people remember," Anthony Parker recalled, "but Jorge was such a glue guy to our team. He was just this high-IQ, winning player and he knew what to do and where to be. He was a versatile four that could make decisions and could shoot." Thanks to his gritty and intelligent play, the Spaniard also became a fan favorite. He was known for his do-everything-at-all-costs bravura and willingness to get his nose scuffed in the wrestle for a rebound. But Garbajosa was also capable of extending out to the three-point line, even as the center, while orchestrating plays from the elbow, controlling the offense, and executing finesse finishes around the cup.

So much of what Garbajosa did on court, though, hardly translated into easy counting stats. "My mentality was: Bust your ass on defense, try to be the toughest guy in the league, and be ready to take your shots. That's why in some games I had zero points. Some of them I got fifteen or sixteen. When the game is over, you look at the stats and maybe you went zero-for-six, but you feel that you were useful for the team to win. Sometimes you score twenty points, but lose, or I was not helpful enough for my team to win. As a player, you can lie to everyone: to the media, to the fans, even to your family. But you cannot lie to yourself; you know how useful you are to your team."

Garbajosa and the Raptors soon found a rhythm on court, offering glimpses of the positionless basketball so familiar in the NBA today. "We cannot compare ourselves to the San Antonio Spurs of Tim Duncan, Tony Parker, and Manu Ginóbili, and I was no Tim and José was no TP," he recalls today, waving away the heresy. "But we played with the same mentality: to share the ball, to create from the one-on-one and from the pick and roll, to look for the shooter in the corner, and to give the ball to our franchise guy, Chris, so that he can create not only for himself, but also for his teammates. You had to be ready, because the ball would come to you. It was fun to play together."

He also saw the newfound love of the fans reflected in the stands, even if it was in part borne along by simmering resentments. "Assistant general manager Marc Eversley asked me, 'What number do you prefer?' I had worn the number fifteen my whole career, so I said, 'Fifteen.' He looked at me, like, 'But it was Vince's number.' I said, 'Yeah, but now it's mine.' He said, 'Okay, I like that.' I could have chosen another number, but honestly I wanted to show that I was not afraid."

The number's former owner soon met its new one during a preseason game. Carter approached Garbajosa and lovingly patted the 15 on the Spaniard's chest. "That's a great memory because it's Vince Carter," Garbajosa recalls. "*Vince Carter.* He could have come up to me and said, 'What the hell are you doing wearing my number? Blah, blah, blah.' Instead, he said, 'Take care of this.' I said, 'I will respect it.'"

That moment only solidified the feelings Garbajosa already had for Carter. "I never expected to play in the league. When I was a kid, Vince and Tracy McGrady made the Raptors global. I never thought that I could even come close to their level. They were icons and idols. So to play for the same franchise, on the same team that they played before, it was a tremendous honor."

As far as the Spanish big was concerned, there was only one step left in the reconciliation. "The Raptors should retire fifteen," Garbajosa argued during our interview, just months before news leaked that the Raptors would retire Carter's number in late 2024. "At the beginning of his career, Vince was a spectacular player. As soon as he was becoming a veteran, he became a shooter, a three-hundred-sixty-degree player doing *everything* on the court. It's not easy to adjust your body and your age to the game. But he did it with a great attitude. He also became an icon because he was always smiling on the court. He's the kind of player that I really admire."

Garbajosa's first season with the Raptors, at least initially, could not have gone better. After a fumbling start, the team began to gel around its crop of new players, including not only Garbo but also Bargnani, the team's first-overall pick from the 2006 draft; Parker, a two-time EuroLeague MVP; Ford, who had been acquired from the Bucks; and Nesterović, who had come to the Raptors in a trade with the Spurs. Most importantly, Bosh, by then in his fourth season, was coming into his own as the face of the team. For the first time in a long time, it felt like the Raptors were not only winning but also had real potential to make a playoff run.

Then, tragedy struck. Late in the season, the 38-31 Raptors visited the Boston Celtics. It was a classic Garbo performance: 5 points, 5 rebounds, a couple of assists, and a steal in 38 minutes on the floor, with the Spaniard doing all the little things that endeared him to his coach, his teammates, and the fans.

Then, with just over four and a half minutes left in the game and the Raptors down 75–66, Garbajosa trailed a streaking Al Jefferson, who had caught an outlet pass behind the Toronto defense. The chase-down was also classic Garbo: a hustle play late in a losing game, as the team struggled to generate offense. For Parker it was also standard-issue Garbo, the embodiment of the mentality he brought to every game: "We're not giving up layups."

It's what happened next that came to define Garbajosa's prematurely short career in the NBA. As he went up to block the shot, he came down awkwardly, breaking his fibula and dislocating his ankle.

At first, Garbajosa had no idea the extent of the injury. "When I fell, I was like, *Oh, that hurts.* But I didn't realize how bad it was. I put my leg up—and I can joke about it now—and the ankle felt like, boom, no control. I said, 'What the fuck is this?'"

Luckily, one of the first players on the scene was his fellow countryman. "It's one of those things you never want to see on the court," Calderón told us, still visibly shaken more than a decade and a half later. "That's a friend that I have had a long relationship with. You see the position he's in. You just react, try to help."

"I remember José putting a towel over my ankle, so nobody could see or get pictures, which I really appreciated," Garbajosa recalls. "I remember him saying, '*Tranquilo, tranquilo,* you're gonna be okay,' and hugging me. In that moment, having my brother close to me made it less difficult. Also, my wife was alone at home watching the game on TV. I remember that José's wife went right to my apartment to be with my wife at that moment."

Garbajosa was rushed to the hospital, but even after surgery, he had no idea how devastating the break was. "I gave an interview on Spanish radio and they asked me. I said, 'It's going to take a while, but I'm going to be okay.' I didn't realize at that moment how difficult, how tough, or how bad the injury was."

Even still, he was committed to getting back on the court, so that he could play in EuroBasket that same summer. "I fought to recover on time to play. After a few big discussions, I came to an agreement with Toronto, Bryan Colangelo, and Maurizio that I would rehab in Spain with my physiotherapist and my doctor and with Ray Chow in charge."

Chow, who was the Raptors' massage therapist and assistant athletic trainer, proved a godsend during the lowest moment of Garbajosa's career. "Ray and I were good friends, but during those four months almost living together—he was at lunch with my family and having dinner out with my friends—we became very good friends. I remember having a cigar with him when my dad passed away. He became a very important person in my life because, at that moment, I was so up and down. Ray was always on my side, trying to pull me up when I was too down. I will never forget, never in my life, how much he did for me, for my family, and for my career in such a difficult moment."

Despite his commitment, Garbajosa never regained his earlier form. The next season he managed to play a few minutes off the bench during the first few games. In his seventh and final appearance—with the Raptors and in the NBA—it was the Garbo show again: 8 points, 6 rebounds, a couple of assists, and a steal, all in an efficient 24 minutes. And then his NBA career was over. Following the game, an MRI revealed residual damage in his left leg and ankle, and Garbajosa opted for surgery.

Despite his rapid rise and fall in the NBA, Garbajosa is philosophical about his choice to chase down Jefferson and even about the injury itself. "I didn't think about it. It was just a reaction, which was to protect our basket. It's what you have to do. You have to respect the game, the fans, your teammates, even the opponent. I would do the same thing a hundred times. It happened. And I think it happened for a reason. It was my destiny to have that moment in Boston. I will never forget it, but I never watched it again. It's life. I cannot control it. I played pro for like fifteen years. Now I have a nice career as an executive in Europe, so I'm very happy. I'm blessed."

16

Jason Kapono (2007–2009)

In 2007, after four years in the NBA, Jason Kapono had finally found his footing. He had shot a league-best 51.4 percent from beyond the arc as a member of the Heat during the 2006–07 season and had even won the 2007 Three-Point Contest. Both had raised his profile in the association. It came as no surprise, then, that plenty of teams were eager to acquire his length and shooting in the summer of 2007.

The only question: Where did he want to play?

Kapono had not always been so spoiled for choice. Following a four-year stint at UCLA, where he had led the Bruins in scoring each season, the rangy wing was selected in the second round of the 2003 draft by the Cavaliers. During his rookie and sophomore seasons, first with the Cavs and then with the Charlotte Bobcats, who poached him during the 2004 expansion draft, Kapono struggled to find consistent minutes. Whenever on the floor, though, he seized the opportunity, offering glimpses of his deadly range, shooting 47.8 percent and then 41.2 percent from three in those first two seasons.

As a free agent in 2005, Kapono signed a two-year deal with the Heat, who eventually won the 2006 championship behind the unstoppable duo of Dwyane Wade and Shaquille O'Neal. Despite seeing limited floor time during the Finals run, Kapono broke out in his second year with Miami, playing in 67 contests, starting in 35 games, and averaging over 26 minutes and nearly 11 points. By the end of his contract, though, he knew it was time to move on.

"I had a good run in Miami," he told us. "Starting felt extremely good, but I knew that in terms of the salary cap and what they wanted to do, I wasn't a long-term fit there."

Among the teams seeking Kapono's services in the summer of 2007 were the Raptors. Toronto looked ready to take a leap behind Chris Bosh. By then the two-time All-Star was entering his fifth year, supported by a raft of talented and seasoned players—guys like T. J. Ford, Anthony Parker, José Calderón, Carlos Delfino, Jorge Garbajosa, and Rasho Nesterović—alongside high-upside draftees like sophomore center Andrea Bargnani and small forward Joey Graham, who was entering his third year with the team.

For Kapono, the Raptors were an obvious fit. "I was trying to catch a team on the rise, where you feel as a player that you can help them take the next step," he explained. "The most important thing was to find a team where I could bring value to them *and* achieve my own goals. I had a pretty prominent role with the Heat, but I was looking to take that next step, to be a starter, a fixture, playing twenty to twenty-five minutes a game."

Still, Kapono didn't quite know what to make of Toronto. He knew he liked the squad from the outside—"Toronto was always a fun team to play against and a fun team to watch"—but could he see himself as a Raptor? Could he see himself, more importantly, in Toronto?

Born in Long Beach, California, Kapono is, to put it mildly, a *dude,* who still looks today more like the world's tallest surfer, even in his mid-forties, than the player he became on court: a routine-driven, dead-eye wing. Yeah, why not play in Toronto, Kapono thought. He didn't mind going against the grain. "I've always been a risk taker.

It was a time to take a chance. As a player, you're always trying to achieve more, and sometimes it takes stepping outside of the box and your comfort zone and going to a new team in a new country."

Even still, he needed to be certain. Things *sounded* good. But was that all just smoke and mirrors? "Obviously, a GM and a coach, they can sell you on something. I didn't really care what Bryan Colangelo said or what Sam Mitchell said," he says today with a chuckle. "I didn't really want to hear the sales pitch."

Instead he turned to Arn Tellem, his agent, who connected him with two of his other clients, both former Raptors: Morris Peterson and Tracy McGrady. He also turned to his 2003 co-draftee T. J. Ford, who confirmed everything he had heard from Mo Pete and T-Mac. "He said it was a fun place, an awesome city, and a great team to play for."

In the end, all signs pointed to yes.

There was, perhaps, only one hitch—the broken-record refrain that has plagued the team for decades—but one Kapono was able to shrug off. "The only thing that I ever heard was that it was cold. Thank God I got dropped in Cleveland as a California boy. So I already crossed that bridge. Plus, if you care about weather, then you shouldn't be playing pro sports."

What *actually* mattered was much sunnier. "You want playing time. You want to have a good contract. You want good teammates. You want a good coach. You want to win." Check, check, check, check, and (hopefully) check.

Signing the three-point specialist was also a coup for Colangelo, who offered Kapono a four-year, $24 million deal, a huge bump over his two-year contract with the Heat. As far as the Raptors were concerned, it was money well spent. "Everyone was just so happy, just glad that you actually chose to come play for their team," Kapono recalls. He felt it in the streets too. "The pride of Toronto and the country was 'Wow, here's a player who actually *chose* to play for us.'"

For a player who spent most of the previous four seasons hunting for minutes, that reception felt good. But it also pointed to a dynamic peculiar to Toronto, something we heard again and again from former Raptors. "With a lot of teams, you feel like you are just the paid product. All they want is a good performance. They just want a picture. They want you to sign something for them. They want to say that you won. Versus in Toronto, I felt like family. Like, 'Hey, you're coming to our country, to our team, let's go all in.'"

Playing for Toronto also lived up to expectations. "Toronto fans care because they're actually genuine fans," Kapono explained. "Out of thirty teams, there's maybe eight to ten teams that have a true, loyal fan base. Toronto's is die-hard. They don't show up at the end of the first quarter. They actually sit at home and watch the games on the road. They had *all* the jerseys—even guys who are the fifteenth man—whereas in other cities, they don't even know who the new free agent is."

That passion was motivating, though it also came with increased scrutiny. During his second season with the Raptors, Kapono lived right next to Air Canada Centre. After games, he would often make the journey home by foot. Sometimes it was a hero's welcome. The fans would "high-five you and say nice things to you," Kapono recalled. At other times . . . well, not. "People are pulling out of the garage, they'd say, 'Kapono, you suck!'" He laughs about it today. "I'd think, *It's probably best not to walk anymore, unless I played well.*"

For Kapono, catching grief from fans was standard fare. "It's a part of playing pro basketball," he says with a shrug. But he also viewed it as a strange positive. Raptors fans actually *knew* who was performing well and who was not. "If a player gets cussed out, or they get anything said to them that's bad," he argues, then it's a sign that "the fans also actually know you and that they pay attention. I could feel the love. Even if someone did say anything negative or bad, it was because they truly cared about you and they were on your side—they wanted to help you win. Any not-so-nice things that were said were well deserved. I respected that. I *loved* that."

Despite the hype and optimism, Kapono's first season as a Raptor didn't quite go to plan—for him or the team.

Kapono started the first six contests, only to get sent to the bench for all but one game the remainder of the season. "I felt I should be the starter. I was extremely mad because I had a pretty decent training camp and I got named a starter. I don't think I played that bad!" His stat line also bears out his recollections. During those first six appearances, he was the portrait of offensive efficiency, averaging 24 minutes and 8.2 points on a .441/.500/.800 slash line.

Kapono's déjà vu struggles to secure minutes and a starting role were symptomatic of a larger problem the team was grappling with throughout his two seasons in Toronto: a hunt for consistency. The Raptors were on a fulcrum, having witnessed a rapid about-face just a season earlier. Colangelo had been hired late in the 2006 season and had aggressively taken the GM reins. There had been massive roster churn, some of which had clearly worked. The team went 47-35 the following season, tying a franchise-best record, with Colangelo being named 2007 Executive of the Year.

That refashioning of the Raptors seemingly put the team on a winning trajectory, but it also led to an embarrassment-of-riches problem: logjams at every position and widespread contract uncertainty by the time Kapono had arrived in Toronto. "We had a really good team on paper, but we also had a lot of guys who were in the same boat. Calderón and TJ both playing point guard. Then you got five or six wings. I was on a fresh contract. So you have all these guys who are hungry and, in terms of the mix and the ages and the contracts, it was so much of an inner battle going on."

In the locker room, there was no tension. But it was clear that the team was having trouble balancing individual goals with collective ambitions. "Cohesiveness and chemistry are hard to get," Kapono reflects, pointing to the consistency that has defined the most winning teams of the last fifteen years—the Death Lineup Warriors, the Double-J Celtics, the Heatles, even the Golden Era Raptors. As Kapono and his teammates knew, stability, steadiness, and predictability were part of the not-so-secret sauce to winning, something he had witnessed firsthand as a member of the Heat. "Consistency is achieved by the consistency of minutes of roles over a long period of time. Unfortunately, I think we lacked that."

Despite those challenges, Kapono and his fellow Raptors never lost sight of the bigger picture. What mattered most to everyone on that roster was winning. "It's way better to be the eighth man on a really good team than to be the third man on a really bad team. I learned that quickly. There are not many players that put their personal goals ahead of the team. I played on nine teams, so with 150, 160, 170 players. Whether you're a role player or a roster player or a top-tier star, the most pressure that you feel is the pressure that you put on yourself. That's because every player wants to perform at their peak so that they can win. You don't get any street cred for saying, 'I was a baller on the worst team.' No one cares. The first thing is: How did your team do? Were you in the playoffs? Did you win?"

Eventually, during Kapono's first season, the Raptors found their groove, finishing 41-41, good for second in the Atlantic Division. It also meant a playoff berth against Stan Van Gundy's 52-30 Orlando Magic, led by Dwight Howard, Hedo Türkoğlu, and Rashard Lewis. On paper the Raptors were outmatched, but the vibe among fans was good. "As soon as we got to the playoffs, every fan in Toronto, whether it was in the media, on the streets, or at the grocery store, they were like, 'You guys will beat the Magic.'"

Kapono also liked the team's prospects. "I believed in our team. We matched up fairly well against them and we had a good chance to beat them." All those positional logjams also translated into critical playoff depth—a testament to Colangelo's master plan. "We had a lot of guards and we had a lot of guys who could guard the perimeter. We had a lot of shooters and they had shooters too. Pretty much it came down to rebounding. Could you keep Dwight out of the paint and away from easy putbacks or dunks?"

Kapono had tasted playoff basketball with the Heat—he knew what it meant to hold the Larry O'Brien Trophy—and he was eager to play a critical role. "I hadn't played in the playoffs since Miami, so I was personally driven." It also opened up another chance to contribute after his early-season return to the bench. "I was proud of myself, to hang in there, to go through the ups and downs. You deal with it. That's part of being a pro. You got to bounce back. I ended up coming off the bench, but I performed extremely well in the playoffs." Like, *really* well. Kapono was third in minutes played, behind Bosh and Parker, but second in points scored, averaging nearly 16 per contest, with the team's highest offensive rating. And he did it all efficiently, shooting 58.5 percent from the floor and 54.2 percent from three.

The Magic series proved a hard-fought affair. Kapono still believes that the Raptors could have pulled out the series, if only they had stuck to their game plan. The evidence was game three, which they won at home. "We played well. Stan Van Gundy's whole scheme was just go high screen and roll Dwight hard to the paint. Schematically, we thought, *Let's just settle for Dwight scoring sixty points, but we're staying home on Rashard and we're staying home on Türk.* We were closing out hard and we won that game. But then I think we got away from that. You can't give up dunks and layups at a high clip *and* also give up long threes at a high clip. We should have let Dwight get his sixty and the rest of the guys were going to shoot twenty or twenty-five percent on threes."

Game four again proved a neck-and-neck battle. Orlando only secured the lead in the final minutes of the fourth quarter, once again riding Howard, by then a fourth-year player who dominated the paint. "He was a *beast*," Kapono recalls, and Howard's stat line showed it: 22.6 points, 18.2 rebounds, and 3.8 blocks per game. Down 3–1 and heading back to Orlando, the Raptors could do little, but the team still showed up. They even captured the lead with a few minutes left in the third and managed to keep the contest within two in the final five minutes of the game. Despite those efforts, Orlando eked out the win, clinching the series.

The close-fought back-and-forth was discouraging, but the players all believed there was room to grow. "Everyone was down after the game," Kapono recalls, "but we were encouraged and extremely positive, thinking that we could go further in the playoffs. Everything was all about how to get better in the offseason. Throughout the summer, everyone was talking and trying to get back to Toronto a couple weeks early to work out and to play. The whole goal coming back into that year was that everyone wanted to get better and everyone wanted to contribute to a winning team that went to at least the second round."

Kapono's second season never fully panned out, despite that optimism in the locker room. The wing still performed well, again shooting efficiently off the bench and even garnering votes for Sixth Man of the Year. But he suspected that his time with the team was coming to an end as rumors circulated that he might be dealt. He tried to ignore the noise. "I'm a positive person. I'm an optimistic person. I'm a confident person. So if I do get traded, great. If I don't, great. I'm going to prepare and train no matter what. I'm ready to contribute if I get traded or not."

In the end, following the 2008–09 season, when the Raptors went 33-49 and missed the playoffs, Kapono was dealt to the 76ers for Reggie Evans. Kapono spent the next two seasons in Philadelphia, then signed a one-year deal with the Lakers in 2011, before being traded back to his rookie squad, the Cavs, in March 2012. That spelled the end of Kapono's NBA playing days. Following a brief stint overseas with Athens-based Panathinaikos of the EuroLeague and Greek League, Kapono retired in 2014.

In the end, not everything went to plan with the Raptors, but Kapono's time with the Raptors was filled with professional high points. In his first season with Toronto, he once again shot a league-best 48.3 percent from three and contributed massively in the playoffs. He also won the Three-Point Contest for a second time, in 2008, as a Raptor in New Orleans. It was extra special. "I felt more pressure because I was the defending champion in a new jersey on a new team. Going with Toronto and representing the country in my first year there, it meant a lot as a player." Even in the streets of the Big Easy, it felt like all of Canada was cheering for him. "Anytime I went out to eat, the fan base was so excited, to the point that it was like they had one of their own family members in the Three-Point Contest."

Part of what made his experience as a Raptor so satisfying was Toronto itself and the way the country was reflected in the team. Before arriving, Kapono says, "I never understood how multicultural the city was. I thought it was extremely cool too that you were playing in one country, but it basically felt like twenty-five countries. It was a global stage. It coincided with the Raptors having Americans, an Italian in Bargnani, an Argentinian in Delfino, a couple of Spanish guys (Garbajosa and Calderón), and a Slovenian in Rasho. It was cool."

Despite all those differences, despite all those guys, hungry for minutes and shots and contracts, and despite all those challenges, the team gelled. "It was fun. On some teams, if you have a big gap between ages, you may only get one or two guys as a small clique. But we were always hanging out. There were a lot of team meals with six guys, which is extremely rare. We did a ton of golf outings with four or five guys. There were a lot of road hangs. It was a really family-centric team, where everyone could straight-shoot each other. It was an awesome mix."

Kapono has only *one* regret, and it's one he shares with his fellow Raptors from those two seasons. "I just wish that we all could have contributed to a second round and beyond in the playoffs." Still, he remains unequivocal about his spell in Toronto. "That was a great time. Honestly, it was probably one of the best two years of my life and of my playing career."

PART IV

THE GOLDEN ERA AND BEYOND, 2013–2025

We could have called this the Masai Era, or the Casey–Nurse Era or the Kyle–DeMar–Kawhi Era. All those names point to the same thing: a period defined by both continuity *and* change. It was a team happy to stick with what was working but also unwilling to stand pat.

Those names also suggest something else: that the key to success is not one big move, but the right move after so many smaller ones. Take Nick Nurse, who replaced Dwane Casey, the reigning Coach of the Year, right before the championship season. It was something that raised eyebrows across the NBA, but Nurse, of course, had been there all along, first joining the coaching staff in 2013 as an assistant. He hardly wiped the board clean, instead erasing bits here and there, adding to the game plan Casey had already put in place.

You might even say the same about the Kawhi deal during the 2018 offseason. The trade was a high-risk, high-reward move for a top-five player. But acquiring Leonard, with only a year left on his deal, was a nail-biting affair. Nobody could doubt his talent or efficiency, but his recent injury history was reason for pause. Adding Leonard also meant trading away a franchise cornerstone in DeMar DeRozan. It was a bold gamble, but one Raptors president Masai Ujiri was willing to take, knowing that if Leonard could stay healthy, he might just prove the final piece in the Raptors' championship puzzle.

Like Nurse before him, Leonard built on the culture that had already been established. Its source was in part Kyle Lowry, who had been with the team since 2012, and in part DeRozan, whom the Raptors had drafted in 2009 and who had often led Toronto in scoring and had pushed the team to winning records and playoff runs again and again during the franchise's Golden Era. So when the Raptors traded for Leonard, it was hardly a break in team history. Leonard had been handed a baton. From the outside, it might have looked like the final sprint to the championship, but it was actually the last leg of a marathon that DeRozan and Lowry had been running for years.

Above all, though, the Golden Era was defined by winning. Starting in 2013, the team made seven straight playoff appearances, good for a cumulative regular-season record of 374-190. Between 2013 and 2020, the Raptors had the best overall record in the Eastern Conference and the second-best record in the entire NBA, behind only Steph Curry's Warriors.

Today, as the Raptors look ahead, there is good reason to be optimistic. At the head of the squad is Scottie Barnes, a do-everything All-Star. RJ Barrett also sees a promising future. "In a very short time, a couple of years, I think Toronto is going to be back where it needs to be to have a chance. With some time together, it'll click."

17

Jamaal Magloire (2011–2012)

The first time Toronto-born hooper Jamaal Magloire even went to a Raptors game, on November 20, 2000, he was a rookie on the Charlotte Hornets. The four-year collegiate player out of Kentucky had been drafted 19th overall by Charlotte. During his first season, Magloire came off the bench, checking into 74 games and earning the trust of his teammates and coaches through his steady play and tenacious work ethic. That homecoming in Toronto could not have gone better. The rookie played 22 minutes off the bench, scoring 16 points on 6-of-7 shooting and grabbing 8 rebounds alongside 3 blocks and an assist in a 36-point win.

The performance at the ACC was something he had fantasized about since the team's founding. "I've always been a Raptor fan," he told us. "Obviously, I was always rooting for the team that I was playing on, but the Raptors are my hometown team. I watched their games when I could when I was at Kentucky. There was a sense of pride having only one of two Canadian teams at that time."

As one of only three Canadian players in the league, Magloire also felt the pressure to succeed. "I was a big fish in the small pond of Canada. The challenge was to win, to do well, to get all the accolades." Still, Magloire could hardly believe his luck, suddenly playing against the pros he had once idolized. "Shaq and Chris Webber, guys that I had a poster of on my wall in my room as a kid. I wanted the same thing, so regardless of how, I was going to persevere."

Magloire's time with the Hornets would last five seasons—two in Charlotte, and then three in New Orleans after the team relocated in 2002. During his second season, he played in all 82 games, almost entirely off the bench. He started 82 games in his third season, and built on that iron-man streak the next year, even making his first and only All-Star Team in 2004.

Just before the start of the 2005–06 season, the Hornets sent Magloire to the Bucks, where he would again start all 82 games. The following summer, Milwaukee traded him to Portland, starting his journeyman career as a steady bench player who could provide both veteran leadership and a physical presence in the paint. During the offseason, he signed as a free agent with the New Jersey Nets, who waived Magloire just after the 2008 trade deadline. He signed almost immediately with Dallas, where he finished the season, before moving on to Miami in a series of one-year deals. During his three years in South Beach, he had the opportunity to play alongside Dwyane Wade and later LeBron James and Chris Bosh, garnering valuable playoff experience along the way, including a run to the 2011 NBA Finals.

Throughout his time in the league, Magloire always found a welcome home for his grit, leadership, and tenacity. His edge—a relentless work ethic combined with canny defense and a willingness to get banged up in the key—was something Magloire's hometown even helped to cultivate. "Toronto is blue-collar, full of hard workers and resilient fighters—don't-take-no-shit kind of people—especially in Scarborough," he explained, pointing to the hardscrabble East End of Toronto where he grew up with his parents, Garth, a welder, and Marion, an insurance worker, two Trinidadian immigrants to Canada who inspired him to persevere. "Growing up with two parents that immigrated to Canada had a lot to do with watching their work ethic and their core values. They instilled in me how to treat others. It was about more than just wanting to do well. I wanted to make them, my friends, and my family proud."

His hard-nosed approach was cultivated in the pickup games he played across Toronto. "You had all these community housing places that we would go to play each other in community centers, which really molded me. On our home court, if somebody would dunk on somebody, everybody on the sideline of the gym would take their plastic chairs and throw them on the court as a celebration. The referees eventually would clear all the chairs away. As soon as they put the last chair back, before the next play started, they just would take it and throw it again. That was the culture. I never did that Bob Knight thing of throwing chairs," he says with a laugh.

Rowdy celebrations were one thing. But playing on those same community-center courts could sometimes be tense. "I remember going to Regent Park one time to play. We were all thirteen, fourteen, or fifteen years old. In the gym, they had all their bigger brothers and all the gangsters standing around the perimeter of the gym, yelling and threatening us. 'You better not win or you're not going to leave here!' We ended up beating them, but they would chase us out of the neighborhood, so we put our shoes on quick and ran."

His own upbringing even prepared him for the challenges of the NCAA and the pros. "Those are the things that when you go into Kentucky, or in the NBA, and somebody tested you, you look at them and you slap them in the face. That's where that kind of mentality started from."

His most challenging experience, however, had nothing to do with basketball. In the summer of 2001, following Magloire's first season with the Hornets, his nineteen-year-old brother, Justin Sheppard, was shot and killed in the city's East End. Justin was a rising talent at Eastern Commerce Collegiate Institute, which Magloire had also attended, and had earned a scholarship to play at a Maryland prep school the following academic year. Despite Magloire offering a $50,000 reward for information about his brother's murder, no suspect was ever found.

It was a haunting and yet formative experience. "I was twenty-three and it was very difficult at the time," Magloire says, reflecting back. "That's not anything that anybody could plan for. But I had a great support system—people that encouraged me, people that have been with me through my trials and tribulations." It was that larger support system of his community that kept him motivated. "My family and my friends just propelled me to do even more," he said. "It's not just my own family. It's the Caribbean community and the city of Toronto and even Scarborough."

That web of support translated into his own on-court tenacity. He was simply willing to do whatever it took to gain an advantage. "A lot of basketball is psychological," he explains. "If you think you're going to get hurt, you're not going to play as well. As a player, I'd look at the injury reports to see who's injured and what's bothering them on the other team, so I could pull at it. That was my MO. It had nothing to do with malice. It's competition; we're trying to win. If it's within the confines of the rules, then it's all fair play."

All along he knew, however, that there were more important things than winning. "I'm a no-nonsense guy and very focused on keeping the reputation of this organization high. You can't be a jerk. You can't burn any bridges. You always try to do the right thing. Integrity is important to me. What kind of person are you when people are not watching you?"

Through his experiences, he developed his own role as a do-anything player, a natural fit for the big man, who had never prioritized scoring over winning. "That's the kind of player that you need—the ones that will go above and beyond the call of duty, not just the ones that are scoring thirty points a game. You need guys that are keeping everybody engaged, keeping the energy up, keeping the focus on the bench, and making sure that they're echoing the sentiments of the coach." That, in a nutshell, was Magloire.

During his first eleven seasons in the league, every visit to his hometown was sweet. "Even when we came to Toronto as an opponent, I got a standing ovation. I'm playing on the *other* team," he recalls, laughing. "The fans have always been good to me."

As his playing days drew to a close, Magloire had only one more thing to check off his NBA bucket list. "I had an offer from both the Miami Heat and the Toronto Raptors at the time. I had always wanted to play in Toronto at some point in my career, and I felt that, if I didn't take the opportunity to come back, then it might not happen. I wanted to come home."

By the start of the 2011–12 NBA season, the league was in a lockout, leading to a 66-game campaign when play finally resumed on December 25. Luckily enough, Magloire's Christmas present came a few weeks early when he inked a deal with Toronto. "I remember signing my Raptors contract in the locker room. It was a great day for me," he marvels. "Eleven years in the NBA and to come back home and finish where I started." The one-year deal also made history. It was the first time that a Canadian-born player would play for the Raptors.

Magloire only spent one season in Toronto but contributed to the shift in culture that was already happening in the organization. "I went with the attitude of winning. I was the captain of the team. My energy infiltrated the whole organization. I had come from Miami and I had that Heat Culture pedigree. There was nothing other than wanting to win. That was the tunnel vision I had coming here." Nonetheless, the season didn't pan out, with the Raptors going 23-43. Still hunting for success, the team waived Magloire just before the start of the 2012–13 season. Ultimately, he chose to retire.

Magloire walked away from his playing days without any regrets, and even later got to witness firsthand the Raptors' first and only championship as an assistant coach. "Being a Canadian and winning a world championship in your hometown doesn't happen to too many people. I'm very lucky that way. It has been part of the journey: of being a captain on the team, being the first Canadian to play on home soil, being the first Canadian coach to win one. There are so many things that go with this city and this great organization that I've been able to be a part of. This place is second to none. We all had a hand to play in the championship."

Today, Magloire can hardly believe how his life has played out, from his youth in Scarborough to his collegiate career at Kentucky, and from his time in the NBA to the many roles he has played for the Raptors. Magloire now serves as a community ambassador for the team and is president of the Toronto Revellers Cultural Association, a not-for-profit organization that celebrates the diverse culture and traditions of the Caribbean.

"It's surreal for me," Magloire says, reflecting on the twists and turns of his life. "I left Toronto at eighteen years old as a boy and went to Kentucky and came back as a thirty-five-year-old man. I've been able not only to play here as the first Canadian on home soil, but also to coach a championship team and now work in the front office for the Raptors. The feeling of winning the championship is probably one of the best days of my life. There's only a few. There's my son being born. There's being drafted into the NBA. There's being an All-Star. And there's being a world champion and being able to come back and share that championship with my city. It is a dream come true."

Over his two and a half decades in the league, he can see the effects of his own era as one of only a few Canadian players. "There were Canadian players before me—Mike Smrek, Bill Wennington,

Rick Fox. In our time, it was the three of us: me, Steve Nash, and Todd MacCulloch. We did the best that we could. Todd had some injuries and wasn't able to finish his career the way he wanted to, but he was a great player. Steve Nash was obviously the best Canadian player of all time. We have a lot to be proud of and we set the precedent."

Since that handful of hoopers just a few decades ago, Magloire has witnessed a rapid change. "We started from humble beginnings, but we've come a long way." Today, Canadian players like the 2025 NBA MVP Shai Gilgeous-Alexander, Jamal Murray, Andrew Wiggins, Dillon Brooks, Nickeil Alexander-Walker, Luguentz Dort, Bennedict Mathurin, Dwight Powell, Zach Edey, and Andrew Nembhard, among many others, fill NBA locker rooms—and have even, in the case of RJ Barrett, Kelly Olynyk, and Chris Boucher, featured prominently in Raptors rosters in recent years. The WNBA has seen similar growth, with Kia Nurse, Bridget Carleton, and Aaliyah Edwards, to name only a few, making their mark on the league. "We're not finished yet," Magloire argues with a smile. "I dream of a world where we have just as many Canadian as American players."

Just as important as the Canadian players, Magloire argues, were the organization and so many American-born Raptors who embraced the city. And one above all. "Vince Carter had a great deal to do with the growth of Canadian basketball. He was the start of what you see today. It's not limited to only Canadian people. Every Raptor that has come through Toronto has probably had an influence on our young people."

The city and the fans also played a reciprocal role in ensuring the success of professional basketball in Toronto. For Magloire, that's no surprise. "What really stands out for me is the culture that we have here—how good we really have it. I've played on a lot of teams, and we have the best fans in the league; they come to our games regardless of if we're winning or not. Plus, the energy in the arena. The University of Kentucky arena holds more than ours, about twenty-four thousand, and we have nineteen thousand in our arena. Kentucky has great fans as well who follow them everywhere—the Big Blue Nation—but Toronto is a lot louder. We have something special here and the leadership that we have now is pretty damn strong. It's just a great place."

Today he remains as dedicated to the Raptors as any die-hard fan. "I don't have any motives other than to help the Raptors win." Eric still remembers Magloire coaching during the 2019 championship run, when he trash-talked the opposition and used a Gatorade cup as a mini-megaphone to bark from the sidelines at guys coming onto the floor, even in pregame warm-ups. He wasn't messing around—and the fans loved it. "It's psychological warfare," Magloire says with a shrug. "I remember things that people used to do to me as a player that had me thinking twice, like somebody hissing at me when I was at the free-throw line and it totally rattled my nerves. It may be unorthodox, but winning is the bottom line, and it's a valuable tool. Every time I would clap my hands if somebody was about to shoot a free throw or something like that, and he would miss, Fred VanVleet or Kyle Lowry, if they were sitting on the bench, would turn around to the second row and give me a high five, because they understand the importance of winning. They understand the value in what I was doing."

Despite his win-at-all-costs mentality, Magloire has gained a reputation among staff and players for his enthusiasm and positivity. As Boucher remarked, Magloire is a "light in a dark room." Magloire responds, "I understand the players, having been one myself. I feel for them when they don't play or when they feel like they should have an opportunity and they don't. I've seen guys that I've played with for many years and you know right off the bat that they're uncoachable jerks. The kind of passion that I have is something totally different. I'm obsessed with success and watching these guys develop. I have worked out every day with Boucher, Kawhi Leonard, Jonas Valančiūnas, Bismack Biyombo, and on and on. I'm very proud of what I've done both as a player and a coach, but it's only the beginning."

Magloire also has massive optimism for the Raptors' future. "These guys in Toronto are obsessed, though I think 'obsessed' is too modest. They are *obsessed* with success and winning. It's only a matter of time. We've done it before; we'll do it again."

He looks forward to reliving the joy of winning in Toronto a second time. Back in 2019, he joined thousands of fans in Toronto following the Raptors' game-six win at Golden State. "After the game, when we won, they were out there singing 'O Canada' and I sang with them. We have the best fans, but that's Canadians: They bleed red and white."

To this day, he still celebrates with his fellow Raptor fans. "I don't wear my championship ring very often, but when I do for appearances, I'll make sure that the fans put it on too. The ring doesn't have any magic power, but it gives people an opportunity to see something very special, to celebrate something special and know that you could hope and you could plan and you could try and execute your dreams. It *was* a dream for us. We wanted to win, but there was no guarantee that we were going to be world champions in 2019. We had to work for that. So the fans putting on the ring and taking a picture is something that I do with Torontonians specifically. It was a championship for us all; it's their championship too."

18

Amir Johnson (2009–2015)

By the time Amir Johnson arrived in Toronto in 2009, he was ready to turn a new page in his career—and his life. Drafted 56th overall by the Pistons in 2005, Johnson remained with Detroit his first four seasons. Early on, floor minutes were hard to come by, and he spent much of his first two seasons shuttling between the Motor City and the team's D-League affiliates, the Fayetteville Patriots and then the Sioux Falls Skyforce.

Despite his limited on-court time, Johnson viewed Detroit as a positive learning experience, something needed for a talented yet raw player who was only eighteen when he entered the league. "It was the era when guys were getting drafted out of high school," he told us. "I'd seen guys ahead of me in the 2003 and 2004 drafts—LeBron James and Dwight Howard—committing to the draft and playing well in the NBA. By the time my year came up, in 2005, I wanted to give it a try. I made it to the McDonald's All-American Game and played alongside Lou Will, CJ Miles, Gerald Green, Andrew Bynum, and Tyler Hansbrough. I played well in the game, so I put my name in for the draft in 2005."

The choice was a risk. Johnson was forgoing both a free college education at the University of Louisville and the chance to play under Rick Pitino. In the end, Detroit turned out to be his own learning experience. Everywhere he turned, he found mentors on a 54-28 team that had just gone to the Finals. "Everybody pretty much took me under their wing. That team was Chauncey Billups, Rip Hamilton, Rasheed Wallace, Ben Wallace, Lindsey Hunter, Tony Delk, Kelvin Cato, and Dale Davis. The old-school guys sent me in the right direction."

Johnson in turn proved an eager mentee. "They were a contending team, so I really didn't get to jump in the fire right away. I was a young kid, but I was all open ears. My vets told me what to do and I did everything to a T." That eagerness to learn, and willingness to play whatever role was asked of him, never went away. "That was a big key to me lasting in this league for fifteen years."

There were only two problems with Detroit. "Coming from California, I'd never gone to the East Coast. It was my first time ever seeing snow," he says today, laughing at the memory. Second: "Being from Los Angeles, I was a big Laker fan. I'd watched the three-peat Kobe and Shaq Lakers. And then I get drafted to the Pistons team that beat my Lakers in 2004," he recalls, half jokingly. "I was just excited to be in the league."

Johnson eventually carved out a role for himself on a talented team that went deep in the playoffs seven straight seasons. "By my fourth year, my last year in Detroit, I ended up starting twenty-four games. Then everything got discombobulated. They weren't winning, and when they realized they couldn't win another championship, that's when all the trades started."

Johnson was stunned by the league's cavalier treatment of even franchise players. "Chauncey was like, 'Bro, this is a business. They could trade *me*.' That gave me a little shock, like, *For real, they ain't gonna get rid of Chauncey, who set the foundation and was basically already a Hall of Famer in Detroit?* Then they traded Chauncey to Denver for Allen Iverson and we ended up getting Chris Webber."

When Johnson's own trade to the Raptors happened—he was sent to the Bucks in June and then rerouted to Toronto in August with Sonny Weems—he was ready for it. "It wasn't really a shock. I had great vets in Detroit that ran everything down for me and prepared me for it." Entering his fifth season, it was time to hit reset.

Johnson immediately embraced his new life in Canada. "It was a fresh start," he recalls. "It was like, 'Let's rip the Band-Aid off and see what I can do on my own.' I was this young kid, in my twenties, living in Toronto, in a country I didn't know nothing about. I was excited and wanted to know everything about the city, so I basically just started walking around."

Johnson immediately recognized, and appreciated, Canada's multiculturalism—and the food that came with it. "I was just so surprised by how diverse it was. Like you go to an area in the city that's fully Irish over here, or you go to a Spanish spot over there, or you go to a Jamaican spot. Like, 'Let me see what this culture is like. Let me try this food that I've never tried before.' I had some *good* food—like festival, a sweet Island bread; it was fire. I tried some Indian food; it was banging. I had everything, from poutine and shawarmas to a lot of Island food, which I wasn't familiar with, like oxtail. I loved the food and I loved the culture. I just wanted more."

He was also surprised by how welcome he felt. "In some areas in LA, you feel like you got to look over your shoulder. I didn't feel that in Canada. You walked into a place in Toronto and it felt like you belong right away. It was 'Hey buddy!' We were all vibin'. Toronto is a big place, but at the same time it's a small city. I felt so comfortable there."

Johnson even did the unthinkable—at least according to NBA standards. Rather than jetting back to LA as soon as the final buzzer rang out, Johnson spent his offseasons in his new city. "I stayed all six years in Toronto. Every summer. I was driving around, going to Caribana, hanging out with friends that I met during the season and just kickin' it. I just loved the atmosphere. It was all new and I embraced it—every bit of Toronto. It definitely has a piece of my heart."

Johnson was increasingly eager to give back to Toronto and to all the Raptor fans he had met throughout his adventures in the city. It all began with his buddy, Corvaughn "Veezy" Cornelius. "I started to realize that some fans couldn't get to the games. I thought it would be cool to help fans get tickets through my social media. We did an Easter egg hunt. Veezy would drive around Toronto and leave hints or clues for tickets or whatever. He even dressed up in a bunny outfit."

The Raptors, in turn, fully embraced Johnson's efforts in the community. "I brought it to the organization," Johnson said. "We would only get three or four tickets to a game. I asked, 'Will you guys be able to put in more tickets so we can have more fans from different areas in Toronto come to the game?' They said sure, and then we just made it a big thing." Nike also stepped in, making "I Roll with Amir" T-shirts in support of Johnson and Veezy's antics.

That support encouraged Johnson to remain engaged in the community. "Veezy and I used to just ponder doing more stuff. We were like, 'What can we do for the fans and people that show support for the game and for a city that we love so much? Maybe we can take the fans to the game or take them out to eat; maybe they ain't experienced a good restaurant.' We were freestyling and I was able to take twenty or thirty fans to a game and to Ruth's Chris Steak House. Another time, we took them to Medieval Times for a game and dinner; another time we went to Benihana's. It became a cult almost."

The most cultlike event was also his most famous: his "Zombie Walk" along Yonge Street in downtown Toronto with hundreds of participants around Halloween 2013, which culminated with 6'9" Johnson, in full zombie makeup, reenacting Michael Jackson's "Thriller" video. "I wanted to do the *whole* dance routine with our dancers, the Dance Pak. I talked to the head dancer, Amberley Caroli.

She said, 'Come in to dance classes and we can rehearse it.' I was also able to find a good makeup artist to turn everybody into zombies."

Doing a massive dance routine was surprisingly difficult for Johnson. "We practiced for a week. It was not easy. I had never taken a dance class or dance lessons. It actually helped me with footwork, too, in the game. I was a little shaky, but the Dance Pak definitely took over on the day and fans showed up. I always said I wanted to be in a zombie movie, and I got to dance right in the middle of Yonge Street in front of everybody. People were really into walking like zombies. They loved it."

All of those events allowed Johnson to connect with the fans in new and unexpected ways. "I actually still talk to some of those fans who were able to come to the game. I know their kids, too, and have seen some of them grow up and go to high school." He also met some of the Raptors' more famous fans. "I got a call from one of Drake's partners that I used to just hang out with. He said, 'Drake wants to play some late-night hoops.' I used to go late at night, open up the practice facility on the third floor at the arena. He'd have his crew and we would play full-court. Then Justin Bieber came along and he had his crew and we made it this thing, late-night basketball." Besides Drake and Bieber, there was one more famous attendee, one of the Raptors' youngest players and the future face of the team. "DeMar was always in the gym late at night, just working on his game."

Johnson also embraced the chance to get to know the fans through social media. "Back in the day, we couldn't text Jordan or reach out to Kobe or Shaq. Now you can do that. I thought, If I was a kid, I would be wondering like, *Yo, what's Jordan doing? You sleeping, man? You working out?* It's cool that I can connect with fans and see what they're actually thinking. I wanted to go out and talk to people. I was an open book."

For his efforts, Johnson won a Community MVP award in 2015. "The team definitely supported me," Johnson recalls. "They loved it. Anything I did they posted on their social media. It was bringing more light to the team and we were doing positive stuff in the community and getting fans excited about the games."

Johnson was a Raptor, through and through—even shaving the team's logo into his hair and dying it red in 2012. "I remember telling Coach Casey that I was going to dye my hair," Johnson recalls. "He was like, 'Please don't do nothing.' I was like, 'Man, I'm doing it.' I had the barber the next day come in and he did the logo to a T and I dyed it red. It was really just the love I had for the city and the team."

During his first season in Toronto, the optimism was high, but so too was the pressure. The team was coming off an underwhelming 2008–09 campaign. They now had a new coach, Jay Triano, and a superstar in Chris Bosh who was entering his seventh season. "We were a young/vet team," Johnson said. "I was just ready to work and had a good vet in Bosh; I learned a lot from him. We also had Rasho Nesterović, Andrea Bargnani, José Calderón, Jarrett Jack, Hedo Türkoğlu, Sonny Weems, and a young rook in DeMar, who was a super workhorse. We had some good assets."

Johnson saw exactly how he could contribute. "I was ready for any challenge and to use what I learned from Detroit and bring it to Toronto. If this is my situation, let me refocus my mind and make the best out of it. I got that from my parents, my mother, and my grandmother. I was ready to work, like, 'What's next? Let's do it.'"

That first season, the team went 40-42, missing the playoffs, with Bosh leaving in the offseason to play for the Heat. "Everybody was devastated," Johnson says. "We were like, 'Dang, what are we going to do now?' When everything blew up, it was just the young guys, rebuilding. It was like starting all over."

Eventually, they did start to figure it out. "We went through some ups and downs and we had some tough teams to get through. We lost a couple of series and just couldn't get over the hump, with those top teams in the East. We were one of them, but we were still young. It was an accomplishment, just winning our division and moving forward from when we were a young group and had lost most of our vets. We were very proud of that."

Even still, the losses stung. "We really wanted to win so bad for our fans, not only for ourselves. I remember being on the road and our coaches showing us back in Toronto, like, 'Look at the fans outside supporting us.' We fought our hearts out, but we came up short."

Along the way, Amir became a fan favorite, not only for his off-court exploits but also for his on-court play. He did a little bit of everything: scoring efficiently in the post, gobbling up rebounds, and taking on challenging defensive assignments. Whether coming off the bench or starting, Johnson was the quintessential team player, always willing to do the dirty work while sacrificing personal stats.

Despite that lunchpail attitude, Johnson could also be thrilling on the court, especially as a member of the so-called Young Gunz lineup with DeRozan, Weems, Jack, and Ed Davis. Young Gunz T-shirts, in allusion to the N.W.A album, soon began to appear in the stands of Air Canada Centre, with all five players lined up above the tagline "The World's Most Dangerous Group/Full Court Highlight Reel Material." As with any viral phenomenon in Toronto during that period, Johnson of course had a hand in it. "It all came up when I challenged DeMar and Sonny to a dunk contest on YouTube. After that, for a few games, we were just a highlight reel, going in transition and just soaring and dunking. DeMar would come down and dunk or Sonny would fly in transition or I would get a lob from Jack and Davis was a flying dunker too. I was like, 'These guys are some young guns, man.' The people I was working with on social media made the graphic and some T-shirts. It was pretty cool when people started ordering them."

It wasn't his first time being branded. Back in Detroit, he was part of a young bench unit, with Jason Maxiell, Rodney Stuckey, Arron Afflalo, and Jarvis Hayes, known as the Zoo Crew. "They called us the Zoo Crew because when we got in there, we used to just cause *havoc*. Either it's a foul or a dunk on somebody." Both the Zoo Crew and Young Gunz are testament to the type of player Amir was: not merely someone to watch on court, but an ideal cog in any lineup looking to run the floor.

In 2015, after six seasons, Johnson's time as a Raptor came to an end. "I definitely wanted to come back to Toronto. No question. But the organization wanted to go in a different direction. Boston was one of the first teams that called me during free agency." It was Danny Ainge, Boston's executive director of basketball operations, who made the overture. "He said, 'We love what you do out here. We want to sign you.' They threw down an offer, so I ended up signing with Boston."

It was hard to leave his adopted home, but Johnson had seen similar moves in Detroit, after the team had shipped out Billups. He saw it again in Masai Ujiri's continual tinkering, something that would pay off, of course, in 2019. "Masai was steady making moves; some worked out, some didn't. That's the job of the GM."

When the Raptors finally hoisted the Larry O'Brien Trophy, Johnson got to witness it both firsthand and from afar as a member of the Philadelphia 76ers, whom the Raptors beat in the Eastern Conference Semifinals. It was a tough loss for Johnson, but also an opportunity to sit back for the remainder of the playoffs as a former Raptor. "We the North in Jurassic Park was epic. I've never seen nothing like that. I wish I was there for that. It was nuts. I was pissed that we lost because I was on the opposite team," he can admit now. "But I was just really happy for Toronto. They really deserved it." It was the perfect long-distance conclusion to what he had helped to start so many years earlier.

Unsurprisingly, Johnson only has good things to say about his time in Canada. "I have a daughter, Amelia, who was born in Mississauga. I'm in and out of Toronto a lot, because she's still going to school out there." For Johnson, it's an easy journey that he's always happy to make. "Toronto is dope and a top-three city to play for sure. Toronto is family all day."

19

Tyler Hansbrough (2013–2015)

The adage goes that a professional athlete dies twice: once in life and once when they retire. For Tyler Hansbrough, it is more like three times.

Merely calling him an accomplished college athlete would be a gross understatement. In his four years at the University of North Carolina, Hansbrough won seemingly every award and honor imaginable. To take a small smattering: ACC All-Freshman, ACC Rookie of the Year, USBWA Freshman of the Year, First-Team All-ACC Tournament, Consensus Second-Team All-America, and First-Team All-ACC. And that's from his *first* season. A steady stream of awards would follow in the succeeding years, with Hansbrough routinely earning conference, NCAA, and All-America first-team honors.

Hansbrough's skill set fit ideally in the NCAA, and his particular gifts—his relentless motor combined with a smashmouth post game—were maximized under Coach Roy Williams's Tar Heel system. Year after year, Hansbrough improved at Chapel Hill, gaining strength and new tricks that he could leverage against the steady crop of eighteen- and nineteen-year-old hopefuls that populated the first division of the NCAA. At 6'9", he was big, strong, and aggressive, and generally able to outmuscle and outhustle everyone else on the court. He was hell in the post, a vacuum on the glass.

After winning the national championship with UNC—the collective cherry on top of a never-ending sundae of personal accomplishments—Hansbrough decamped to the NBA, where he was selected 13th overall by the Indiana Pacers in 2009. There he seemingly found another sport. "Honestly, they're two different games," he told us. "It's very hard to compare college and NBA basketball."

Suddenly, 6'9" wasn't so tall. Suddenly, 250 pounds wasn't so big. Suddenly, everything was just a bit faster, all the players just a bit more athletic. And suddenly—but above all most importantly—the post was no longer the hub of the offense. By 2009, it was a change already long underway in the NBA with its newfangled pace-and-space philosophies, up-tempo offenses, and no-kidding realization that three points were worth more than two. It hardly helped that Steph Curry, drafted just six spots before UNC's most celebrated big man, was ready to shoot from seemingly any daub of paint on the court, becoming in the process the face of the league's three-point revolution.

For Hansbrough, the world beyond the arc was largely terra incognita. During his first three seasons as a Tar Heel, some 108 games, Hansbrough attempted just 15 three-pointers, hitting only three, though he would show surprising range from the NCAA arc in his senior year, shooting 39.1 percent from outside, while still only averaging less than one per game. Still, it was a foreign land to the post monster, who in his seven-season NBA career attempted only 22 three-pointers. It was also a rough turn of events for the former college star, who had never needed the outside game to play in the NCAA, even if it was slowly colonizing every position in the NBA.

That was his first death. Leaving the NCAA meant retiring the player he once was in a league that offered, at best, a funhouse mirror of the NBA. For good reason, Hansbrough's name is still often listed among college basketball's all-time greats, including Kareem

Abdul-Jabbar, Bill Walton, Pete Maravich, and Christian Laettner. But after being drafted by Indiana, Hansbrough never saw his career in the NBA match anything close to his glory days in Chapel Hill. NCAA Tyler and NBA Hansbrough were like two different species caught between two different ecosystems: a single player, with a single game, divided by two leagues with competing, and seemingly irreconcilable, versions of the same sport.

Life in the pros wasn't all bad, of course, and during his four years in Indiana, Hansbrough offered glimpses of himself as the NBA had come to view him: as a reliable power forward. Even still, Hansbrough watched his minutes dip during his third and fourth years, after Indiana brought in David West just before the foreshortened 2011–12 lockout season began. "David West was a much better pro than me and a much better player. I was backing him up. I knew that if they re-signed him, their intentions for me were to come off the bench."

Bench time was something Hansbrough could accept, so long as it came with real playing time on court. "I just wanted the opportunity to be a bigger piece of a team—I was young and really hungry—whether that's more minutes or having a chance at a starting role."

After entering free agency in the summer of 2013, Hansbrough began to look around. The Toronto Raptors presented a ripe opportunity on a team that needed a dose of those gritty intangibles that had made Hansbrough so unstoppable in the NCAA. Dwane Casey was on the hunt specifically for defensive-minded players, guys who live up to his "pound the rock" mentality. "Every time a stonecutter hits a rock," Casey explained back in 2011, "it may not break. You may have to hit it a hundred times, but on that hundred-and-first time you hit it, now you crack the rock." Pound the Rock: you could find the phrase emblazoned on walls and printed on banners in various Raptors' practice facilities—and even manifested in an actual boulder in the team's locker room.

Hansbrough was willing to pound the rock. "In Indiana, we were a very good defensive team and I was part of that defensive rotation. My hard-nose playing was appealing to Toronto. When I hit the free agency market, Toronto was a team that initially reached out to my agent, Jeff Schwartz."

The decision was made: Hansbrough was going north, with a chance to showcase his skills alongside increased responsibilities. "Toronto was the best opportunity for me to get heavy minutes and be a big part of the team. I remember Casey specifically saying that he was excited about signing me, and I was really happy to be part of a team where the coach wanted me on the team. I was pumped up to go there—the pound-the-rock thing fed into the direction he was trying to go."

Despite the opportunity, and his enthusiasm, Hansbrough didn't fully know what to expect with his move north. "Initially, in full transparency," Hansbrough admitted to us, "I was a little nervous about going there and I wasn't excited about Toronto, because I didn't know much about it. A lot of people view Toronto, as part of Canada, as being secluded, and I had no idea how great of a city and how great the fan base was before I got there."

In the end, Hansbrough's role on the Raptors never fully blossomed. "I don't really think it panned out the way I expected. But I got my opportunities. I had a lot of games where I started and played well at times, but every time I started to get a little bit of momentum, there was a speed bump like an injury." In addition, despite Casey's commitment to the defensive end, coach and player alike could see the league's pace-and-space future. "The style of play in modern basketball limited my play during my time in Toronto. My position—as a six-foot-nine bruiser inside—was an awkward fit in modern-day basketball and was not at the time the most appealing position to any NBA team."

As the league went smaller and smaller, fewer and fewer minutes were available for interior big men, even skilled bigs with a feathery touch around the rim like Jonas Valančiūnas. "It had more to do with the style of play in the NBA," Hansbrough explains. "Jonas was a heck of a young player and such a good dude and great teammate. I knew that Toronto had a lot invested in him. I was not big enough, and Jonas was a better player and had a brighter future. So I knew I probably wasn't going to take minutes from him."

Instead, Hansbrough was left battling for minutes off the bench, first against Amir Johnson and later against Patrick Patterson, both of whom he respected and worked with for the sake of the team, even in the heat of competition for minutes. It was hard for Hansbrough to sit happily on the bench, though. He wanted to play and he wanted to contribute to the team's newfound winning ways. Today, he can see what he did wrong. "I was young. I wish, looking back, that I would have been a little more mature handling some of those situations. Coach Casey is a great coach. I wish I would have just walked into his office and asked, 'How can I be better for this team and get more minutes?' I never did that."

At the same time, his college days hung over him, always mentioned not as an accomplishment in themselves but as a burden: a set of expectations that he could never fulfill in the NBA. It drove him on, the criticism, but it also made it hard for him to accept a diminished role, with his NCAA accomplishments hung like an albatross around his neck. "I love UNC and I love the Tar Heels. I love being part of that family. Growing up in a small town in Missouri, and putting work in on the basketball court, it just seemed unattainable when I was a twelve-year-old. It was just a dream, all the success I had with UNC. But I'll always be viewed for what I did in North Carolina."

The impossible standard of his NCAA run led to both external and internal pressures. "I felt early on in my career the expectations—probably perfection—that I put on myself heading into the NBA. I don't think I would have ever met those expectations. That I was a good college player was a piece of criticism that I heard a lot. I played the game at times to prove people wrong. That backfired on me. I love the game of basketball and I love studying and playing it, but I didn't play for the love of the game; I played to prove people wrong. If I would have looked at it through a different lens, it would have been maybe a little bit of a different outcome for me personally. I valued way too many people's opinions that had no impact on my life. It hurt me, and as I've gotten older I've realized that it does not matter—I'm over it—but at the time, it bothered me a lot."

Despite those struggles, Hansbrough could recognize that he was once again playing inside a winning system. It was hard not to get caught up in the enthusiasm. "When I first got to Toronto, we weren't that good, but the fans showed up and the atmosphere was crazy. The energy in the building. The music was on point. The fans were passionate and hungry and really into it. It's not like you went to a Raptors game and you just sat in the front row, on your phone, not really paying attention. *Everyone's* locked in and pulling. When the refs made a bad call, everyone's yelling. I love stuff like that. That's how it was at Air Canada Centre, and it was easy to get motivated for those games."

He saw the fans' passion firsthand—and repeatedly. In his first year with Toronto, the Raptors made the playoffs, ending a five-year drought, where they faced the Brooklyn Nets. "I don't care how they describe the energy in the arena before game one of that playoff series, nothing will ever do it justice. The Raptors in a way represent all of Canada. I could feel the whole country behind that team. It's hard for me to describe the energy, man."

The gravity of the moment was not lost on Hansbrough. "One of my favorite memories in all of my playing days is when we first made the playoffs. Right before the first game in Toronto, the crowd started singing the national anthem of Canada. All of a sudden, the whole arena was singing it. The singer just stopped and let the crowd do it. The fans were so into it. The energy in the arena was unlike anything I've ever felt. It was beautiful. I almost started crying. And then you could see all the fans in Jurassic Park out there, the support at that time, it really showed how hungry those fans were and how they wanted to be part of that team. I've never seen anything in sport come close to what I felt that day. Untouchable," he recalls, shaking his head.

Despite that rush of enthusiasm, the Raptors couldn't get past the Nets, falling in seven games. "It was a gut punch," Hansbrough said. "Everybody really wanted to win, and not only for themselves. Hell, the franchise was hungry to win a playoff series. It was tough, but the energy after losing that game to a talented-ass super team, you could feel what direction we're heading. We had young and emerging guys that were hungry." Ujiri also saw the promise of the group and ran it back, adding Landry Fields and Lou Williams, who even bagged Sixth Man of the Year with the Raptors that season.

That 2014–15 season was more of the same, both good and bad. On the upside, the team was winning, going 49-33, and on a personal level, Hansbrough finally got his moment of glory in a Raptors uniform. The team was at home, losing badly to Steph Curry's Warriors, who were en route to their first championship. "We were getting our ass kicked by Golden State," Hansbrough recalls. "They came in and they were just handing it to us."

With a few seconds left in the third quarter, and the Raptors down 96–57, Hansbrough got tangled up with Festus Ezeli in the paint, which led to a pushing match. "Everyone in the crowd started chanting—like roaring, standing up and clapping. I absolutely loved it. It was just like a hockey game when two people get in a fight." The atmosphere meant something extra to Hansbrough, who had played street hockey with his brother growing up and attended Maple Leafs games while living in Toronto. "We used to play all the time. We probably sucked," he recalls today, laughing at the image of him and his brother ripping around on Rollerblades in the backyard of their parents' Missouri home, "but we loved hockey." In Toronto, hockey

(Left) DeMarre Carroll in a postgame interview, wearing the Toronto Huskies jersey, January 2017.

(Right) Eric and former Raptor John Thomas in Minnesota, January 2018.

Matt Bonner catches up with Eric at a Raptors game in Toronto, October 23, 2017.

Eric interviews former Raptor Chris Bosh, December 5, 2018.

Jonas Valančiuņas gives Eric an involuntary thumbs up after surgery, December 13, 2018.

(Left) CJ Miles checks in the game, January 22, 2019.

(Right) Kawhi Leonard, Pascal Siakam, and Fred VanVleet celebrate the championship, June 13, 2019.

Paul Jones and Eric at the Raptors' championship parade in Toronto, June 17, 2019.

(Left) RJ Barrett preparing for his first game in a Raptors uniform, January 1, 2024.

(Right) Garrett Temple shares a laugh with former Raptor Vince Carter during Toronto's preseason game against the Washington Wizards in Montreal, October 2024.

(Left) RJ Barrett with fellow Canadian and Cavaliers forward Tristan Thompson on Opening Night, October 2024.

(Right) Scottie Barnes checks in for a postgame interview, January 1, 2025.

(Left) Danny Green in Toronto prior to the Raptors taking on the Los Angeles Clippers, February 2, 2025.

(Right) Eric with Norm Powell—as a member of the Los Angeles Clippers—back in Toronto to take on the Raptors, February 2, 2025.

(Left) Tracy Murray, back in Toronto for '90s Night, poses for a photo on the court, February 5, 2025.

(Right) José Calderón and Jamaal Magloire, Raptors teammates during the 2011–12 season, reunite in Toronto, March 7, 2025.

(Left) Two former Raptors, Alvin Williams and Jason Kapono (with one of his sons), catch up in Toronto, March 7, 2025.

(Right) Former Raptors Jerome Williams and T. J. Ford pose on the court at Scotiabank Arena, March 23, 2025.

fisticuffs with Ezeli played well. "You could tell that they really liked that someone went out there and mixed it up and was showing a little fight till the end. It says a lot about those fans: that they were still engaged, regardless of how bad we were getting our ass kicked."

It was a photo-perfect moment for Hansbrough, the embodiment of a synergy that emerged between Toronto faithful and the hard-nosed kid from Missouri. "The fans resonated with the way I played. I was out there grinding, chipping away, and working. Toronto is a blue-collar city and the fans really embraced that mentality as well. That's also the way I was brought up and how I've been my whole life. I'm a worker; I'm a blue-collar guy. I was just happy to be part of that."

Going into the playoffs a second time, hopes were high, but Toronto once again fell short, when the team was bounced from the playoffs by the Washington Wizards. It was a stunning loss, and Ujiri wasn't about to stand pat. "We got swept, and that game four, that was just an old-fashioned ass-kicking," Hansbrough recalls. "I knew there was going to be an adjustment after we lost to Washington."

Among those players shuttled in and out was Hansbrough. Even after two seasons on the bench, all the lineup changes, and a growing focus on playing smaller and faster, Hansbrough still wanted to be a Raptor. "I would have loved to come back. But I knew that, with the role I had in Toronto, I wasn't going to sustain a spot in the league if I didn't have more of an impact." In the end, Hansbrough's agent ended up rerouting him to Charlotte, where he played his final season in the NBA, before stints in the G League, the Chinese Basketball Association, and the Baloncesto Superior Nacional in Puerto Rico. He finally retired in 2022, the pro athlete's first death, and Hansbrough's second following his miraculous run at UNC.

Today, Hansbrough has some regrets about his time in Toronto—about how he handled himself and his situation—but he has no regrets about his decision to go north. "I was hungry and I wanted to stay in the league, so I fell victim sometimes, when I got minutes, to trying to be Superman instead of just finding my rhythm and flow in the game. I felt like I had to make an instant impact because I didn't know when I was going to get minutes." Still, his time in Toronto was gratifying, not least in his role as a cog in the eventual championship machine Ujiri was building. "I felt pretty good about my time in Toronto. I had a little bit of influence on the direction that the program was going. That meant a lot."

Plus, once a Raptor, always a Raptor. Years later, during the team's championship run, Hansbrough was locked to his screen, cheering for his old squad. "Hell, you would have thought I was from Toronto the way I was yelling at my TV and pulling for them. I was extremely happy for Toronto. I knew how passionate the fans were and how connected they were to the Raptors. It was a program that was so hungry and finally they made the right moves. I was so happy for the franchise."

20

Patrick Patterson (2013–2017)

In December 2013—smack dab in the frosty heart of an Ontario winter—Patrick Patterson suddenly found himself a Raptor. Along with Chuck Hayes, John Salmons, and Greivis Vásquez, the Sacramento Kings had sent Patterson to Toronto in exchange for Quincy Acy, Aaron Gray, and the team's go-to scorer, Rudy Gay. "I just got traded in a blizzard," he recalled to us, laughing at the bad meteorological timing. "The worst time for a guy from nice, beautiful, warm California to come to a new team. There was snow everywhere, and none of us had winter coats."

Patterson had good reason to be down. It was the second time the spread-the-floor power forward had been traded, without warning, in less than ten months. It was all part of a start-and-stop career. Patterson had been drafted by the Houston Rockets 14th overall in 2010 but had struggled to find a reliable spot on the floor. During his first two seasons, he shuttled between Houston and the team's G League affiliate, the Rio Grande Valley Vipers. Even when he was in a Rockets uniform, he came mostly off the bench. In his third season, Patterson began to see regular minutes on the floor and even started 38 of 47 games. Finally, some consistency, he thought. Even better, they were winning behind the new face of the team, James Harden, and were on the way to a 45-37 finish.

Then, a day before the 2013 trade deadline, Houston dealt Patterson to the Kings without warning. It was a drop-everything moment. Time to pack a bag and head to Sac Town, but that's it. In the meantime, he watched his role regress—he was back on the bench with fewer minutes and fewer touches—and the Kings finished the season a woeful 28-54. There was only so much Patterson could do to help, especially in an organization building for the future around two talented but largely unproven chips: the big man DeMarcus Cousins, Patterson's old teammate at Kentucky, who was in his third year, and the score-first point guard Isaiah Thomas, who was only a second-year player.

Patterson had the summer to pull his new Cali life together, but then, just ten months later, he was caught off guard a second time. "My agent had absolutely no idea that my name was involved in any type of trade," he recalled to us. "The next thing, it's 'Hey, you're traded. Thanks for your services.' I had ultimately no idea of any type of trade whatsoever in Houston *or* Sacramento. I didn't think it would happen again."

It hardly helped the way he found out. In a cinematic motif that would define both his time with the Raptors and his post-basketball career, news of the trade came while he was at the movies with his mother, Tywanna, watching *The Hunger Games: Catching Fire*. "I'm in the movie theater with my moms and my phone is blowing up nonstop. My agent reached out, and I'm like, 'With all due respect, Moms is in town right now, so my focus is on her.' But her phone is blowing up too. Her friends are contacting her, doing the exact same thing that they're doing to me."

By the time Patterson finally touched down in Toronto in the middle of that frosty winter, he had a laundry list of complaints.

He wasn't happy with the weather.

He wasn't happy with the city.

He wasn't happy with the country.

And he wasn't happy with the team.

At the time, the Raptors were an underperforming squad, and here Patterson was, being asked to drop everything, again, and head north from California? Sheesh. He was hardly alone (even if his teammate, Vásquez, told us that the move to Toronto represented for him a massive opportunity). "Honestly, when we started, the guys who got traded there, me included, didn't want to be there. We were calling our agents, saying, 'Yo, do whatever you got to do to get us out of here.' I was in my head. I was frustrated. I was like, 'Why am I here? How did this happen again? How am I going to thrive here? How am I going to see my family? I gotta get them passports, yada yada yada'—all of that was flowing through my brain. I was ready to get up out of there."

Despite having the trade to the Raptors revealed mid-movie, being with his mother proved a stroke of luck. She put it all in context. "We get out the movie theater and we had a little moment. We hugged and she said, 'Make the best of the situation. You did this once before. Just do well and enjoy it.'"

Okay, he thought, not savoring the prospect of having to start all over in Toronto. Maybe he would play for the Raptors for just a few months. Maybe his new agent would come through and reroute him somewhere better. Maybe he would even be back in the US, perhaps somewhere sunny, playing on a winning team. Maybe.

In early December 2013, Toronto was struggling, off to a 6-11 start. It didn't get much better after Patterson joined the team, which had gone a disappointing 11-15 by Christmas.

Then something clicked for the Raptors. Patterson saw it, too, and above all in the leadership of the team's star players. "Number one, it was Kyle and DeMar. There was no more Rudy, so they realized it was their time and their team. That gave DeMar an opportunity to be the ultimate scorer on the team. He was a guy we went to when we needed a bucket."

Across the lineup, Patterson also witnessed an emerging chemistry. "Coach Casey had a new mindset," Patterson recalls. "He had a team now that was a bunch of guys he could shape and develop into a system. Everyone was hungry for the new opportunity. That caused us to compete more in the gym and, thankfully, everyone was on the same page as one collective unit. The rest of the guys were slowly finding their niches on the team and how to contribute. All of us were buying in."

The results showed on the court. The team started winning, going 37-20 after Christmas, and finished 48-34. Suddenly, attitudes also started to change. "Once we started winning, guys started buying in because we had never gone on a winning streak before. It was fun. The guys just enjoyed being with each other. That's what catapulted it. Just genuinely having fun, finally, and enjoying being out there on the court, whether it was practice or it was the game, and rooting for each other."

In practice, that hunger for playing time and success led to a healthy camaraderie, with teammates pushing each other to perform. "We were competing for this opportunity because none of us necessarily had an opportunity to play that much." Amir Johnson had established himself as the starting power forward while Jonas Valančiūnas was slotted in at center. "I was competing with Tyler Hansbrough for the backup four or five. It was literally me and Tyler competing every single day, but there was a respect. I had always admired Tyler since his university days, him being arguably one of the best college basketball players of all time. It was fun and never disrespectful. Never someone being jealous or envious. We would always root for one another, whether he played more one day or whether I played more one game. It was all of us collectively laying down our egos, finding our roles, and buying into what Case had created."

The organization also showed its appreciation for Patterson. That too felt like a first, something he had rarely witnessed after being unceremoniously traded again and again. "Having literally Masai and Case and later Nick Nurse tell me how much they appreciate me and how much they believe in me and how thankful they were that this trade had happened and what they envisioned, how they saw me being a part of it. It was someone finally believing in me and finally wanting me to be a part of something and having a home."

With a newfound investment in the team, even life in Canada started to look sunnier—literally. "That short amount of time spent in Toronto opened my eyes to the opportunity. Toronto completely changes when the weather gets warm. Next thing you know, there's patio furniture and chairs being put in the streets and people walking up and down Queen Street and King Street. It came alive and was totally different. I was like, *Where has this city been the past three, four months?*"

Those positive changes kept coming, not only on the court but also off it. "I was enjoying myself and developing relationships with Kyle, DeMar, and Terrence Ross, embracing the city, going out and meeting people in Toronto, and developing friendships that I still have today. One of my good friends, Joel Reilly, had a shop over in Parkdale." By coincidence, the store was called Community 54, named after the address of its New York location, 54 Clinton Street, on the Lower East Side. That number was also Patterson's. "We did a collab for clothing called Team 54. That sold out in two days."

Slowly but surely, Patterson was starting to enjoy his time in Toronto, and not least the fans and their enthusiasm. One thing he noticed: "Whenever the Canadian national anthem is being played, you're supposed to sing it loud and proud. It's every single game: the Canadian national anthem happens, and the Canadians are singing it. I always found that interesting. The same thing doesn't happen in America. The American national anthem? No one's singing it." He found the singing infectious. "Probably by the fifteenth game after I got traded to Toronto, I was singing 'O Canada' in my head. I knew it word for word. By the playoffs, I was literally singing along with the crowd. You feel the energy whenever the Canadian national anthem is played. It always hyped me up and made me proud to wear that jersey. I'm singing it to this day. If I'm watching a game and 'O Canada' is playing, I'm literally singing it."

Before long, his entire outlook on being a Raptor had shifted. "I thought, This is where I'm meant to be. Everything that led up to this was unfortunate, but it was supposed to happen and it led me to this opportunity. I am a hundred percent buying in. I'm going to embrace Toronto. I'm going to embrace the fans. I'm going to embrace the situation. I'm going to ride with it and see how long it lasts and see what we can make happen and for how long."

And all that talk about getting out of Toronto, just a few months earlier? "My teammates and I ultimately changed our minds in that short frame from 'Get me out of here' to 'Let's ride this out.' Our agents were like, 'We got these teams lined up. They're interested.' And we're like, 'You know what? Hold on. There's something going on here. We don't know what it is, but we can see that there's something happening with this team. Let's just see what happens.'"

It was a predictable-enough turn. "Winning cures all," Patterson says with a shrug. "It doesn't matter where you are, it doesn't matter what team you play for, it doesn't matter what the city is. If you win, the city comes alive. Your energy totally changes, your mindset totally alters, and you thoroughly start enjoying yourself, and the city will enjoy that sport and team even more."

Suddenly, being a Raptor—and living in Toronto—didn't seem so bad. From wanting out half a year earlier to feeling at home, Patterson eventually signed a three-year deal with the Raptors in the summer of 2014. He would get a chance to sing 'O Canada' a few hundred times more.

After things had clicked into place during Patterson's first half-season in Toronto, the Raptors headed to the playoffs for the first time since 2008, where they fell to a veteran-laden Brooklyn Nets team in a hard-fought seven-game series.

The loss stung, but the group remained optimistic. "We were all confident going off of that game seven. We felt like we should have won. We had gotten that far and lost to a team full of champions and Hall of Famers. We were confident that what we were building was going to carry into the next season. That was the mindset all summer: Stay focused and work our asses off. Our workouts, meeting up together, linking back in Toronto, training camp—that was our mindset."

The team had also improved. Valančiūnas was going into his third season. In the summer of 2014, Ujiri signed Landry Fields and traded for Lou Williams. The team went 49-33 during the 2014–15 campaign, besting the previous season's record, but again fell short in the playoffs in a four-game, first-round sweep by the Washington Wizards.

Despite the loss, Patterson still believed in the team, but Ujiri was not yet done moving pieces. The starting lineup revolved around Lowry and DeRozan, with Ross at the wing and Valančiūnas in the frontcourt, and with Patterson and James Johnson off the bench. Ujiri brought in a raft of talent behind them: DeMarre Carroll, Cory Joseph, Bismack Biyombo, and Luis Scola—all quasi-interchangeable pieces that could start any given night—and added two rookies through the draft: Delon Wright and Norman Powell via the Milwaukee Bucks in exchange for Vásquez.

Patterson was surprised by all the moves but loved the new-look squad. "They did a great job of bringing in pieces that could help the team as well as still keeping the core guys. It was all guys who didn't have egos, who never fought, who all wanted to win, and who all got along. True professionals. We all played well on the court collectively. All those guys brought something different to the team that we hadn't had the previous two years."

The result was massive optimism—and, thanks to the NBA All-Star Weekend being hosted in Toronto, healthy pressure—going into the 2015–16 season. "The city was so alive, because they knew

All-Star was coming," Patterson said. "All of that energy shook us and motivated us. Like, we can't be a shitty team when the All-Stars are coming here." On the court, Ujiri's canny moves soon translated into wins—the most wins, in fact, in team history, with the Raptors finishing the season 56-26. "That season was by far the most fun I've ever had."

Once again Toronto was playoff bound, taking out, in two seven-game series, Paul George's Pacers and Dwyane Wade's Heat. The team could breathe a temporary sigh of relief. By the 2016 playoffs, twenty years into the franchise, Toronto had only ever won one playoff series. Now they were in the Conference Finals for the first time ever, where they would face LeBron James's Cavaliers, though they ultimately lost that series in six games. "Being so close to advancing to the Finals and then losing to arguably the GOAT, just falling short," Patterson recalls. "It hurts, but we lost to the champions. We had a great year and a great opportunity, but you don't get awards for losing."

Despite the exit from the playoffs, the fans recognized the Raptors' massive growth, applauding the team as they walked off the ACC floor after game six. In the moment, though, it was hard to be satisfied. "We were so pissed," Patterson recalls. "Once we came off our frustration, we appreciated what we had always known: that the Raptors, Toronto, and Canada have arguably the best fans in the world for any sports program and any professional team anywhere in the world. We've always known that the Raps and their fans are elite."

It was those fans that Patterson tried to connect with during his time in Toronto. What better way than through his love of film? "I was always a huge movie guy," Patterson explained. "It started in summer 2015. While I was out in LA, I did an internship at Open Road Films. Coming back to Canada, I went to the Toronto International Film Festival for the first time. I was like, 'Yo, what's a movie festival?' That's when I knew that I want to do something for fans where we do screenings for movies and we all hang out. I wanted to give back to the community in my own way: 'How can I incorporate this on a smaller scale in Toronto?' That's when 'Pat Presents' came alive. We would reach out to studios, they would give us an early release of a film, and we would hold a screening and do Q-and-As."

Those screening events often started with some kind of trivia or challenge on social media as a chance to interact with players and see them for who they really are: very tall but otherwise normal people. "It was an opportunity for fans and my teammates to be in a theater, hang out, and take some photos. Even though we're on the court and you see us on TV, we're normal people. We sit down to watch movies with popcorn. We drive in our cars to and from work. We have families." In turn, the Raptors faithful embraced "Pat Presents." "They loved it. It was such a great experience because it allowed us to engage with the fans on a personal level. I was so thankful whenever the guys at the top of the totem pole, the superstars like DeMar and Kyle, showed up, because they were always doing a million things. I'm still thankful."

Patterson would play one more season in Toronto. There were more new faces—Ujiri was, as always, tinkering—including Pascal Siakam and Fred VanVleet. The team would compete throughout the season, going 51-31, only to be once again knocked out by LeBron and the Cavs in the Conference Semifinals. That loss spelled the end of Patterson's playing days for the Raptors, though going into the offseason he was eager to re-sign. "I was thinking I was going to return. But with the success of Pascal and Fred and Norm and Delon, I was seeing their development." That offseason, Patterson signed with the Thunder for two years, before joining the Clippers for two more.

Even still, Patterson bore no ill will to the Raptors or Ujiri, eventually recognizing the endless cycle of regeneration that defines the most successful teams. "Although I was mad and upset about not coming back, because I love the city so much and I love the team and the organization so much, ultimately I understood. A change did need to happen. It was time for something new. Those guys just needed an opportunity to grow. When the trade initially happened with me and the rest of the guys from Sacramento, we just needed an opportunity. The same thing happened with Pascal and Fred and all those guys. And it worked. It was all appreciation and love at the end of the day."

Patterson is still grateful for his time as a Raptor and for all that Toronto and Canada had to offer. "Outside of family, religion, and basketball, Canada is probably one of the most important things to ever happen to me. It gave me access to the movies and it's where I met my business partner"—Joel Reilly, his friend from Community 54, with whom he started a production company called Undisputed Pictures. "The most important thing Canada gave me is my wife, Sarah, who's French Canadian, and my wife has given me my child, who's going to have a Canadian and an American passport. Because of Canada, I am where I am today, which is why I'm always so eternally grateful that things did work out that first year after that trade—that I didn't beat the nail with the hammer, saying, 'Get me out of here.' This was kismet. It was supposed to happen. It's crazy."

21

Greivis Vásquez (2013–2015)

By the start of the 2013–14 season, Greivis Vásquez had established himself as a promising fourth-year point guard. Born and raised in Caracas, Venezuela, he moved to the US at age seventeen to play for Montrose Christian School, a top high school program in Rockville, Maryland. He then spent four years at the University of Maryland before being selected 28th overall by the Memphis Grizzlies in the 2010 NBA Draft. During his second season in Memphis, he was traded to the New Orleans Hornets, where he started 78 games, before being rerouted, in the summer of 2013, to the Kings in a three-team deal with the Trail Blazers. After arriving in Sacramento, he took over at point, starting all 18 games of his short career in Kings purple.

Just five months later, in December 2013, Vásquez became a Raptor, traded alongside Chuck Hayes, John Salmons, and Patrick Patterson in exchange for Rudy Gay, Quincy Acy, and Aaron Gray. For many onlookers, Vásquez was the most promising asset in the deal and the key return for the Raptors: a young and talented point guard on a team-friendly $2.1 million expiring contract who offered the organization both financial and roster flexibility.

But with the Gay trade, Masai Ujiri wasn't done dealing yet. If you believed the rumors at the time, then next on the chopping block was Kyle Lowry. Whispers suggested (which were later confirmed) that he was headed to the Knicks. Vásquez remembers that period of limbo well. "The rumors were like, Kyle's going to get traded to New York," he told us. The potential trade, at least at first, sounded good—not only to the critics, but also to Vásquez. *"If Kyle gets traded to New York,"* he recalls thinking, *"then I'm going to be a starting point guard for the Toronto Raptors.* That was a tremendous opportunity for me."

Opportunity was all he longed for. The trade to Toronto, in fact, was a fresh start for Vásquez. "Honestly, my situation in Sacramento was awful. I wasn't really comfortable there. It was a young team and I didn't want to go through what I went through in New Orleans again. DeMarcus Cousins was too young at that time. Isaiah Thomas was basically my backup. We used to play together, but there was no chemistry, even though we respected each other. We still have a good relationship today, but it just didn't work."

The prospect of starting anew in Toronto proved a seasonal gift, plopped down unexpectedly in his lap. "Two weeks before Christmas, I got traded to Toronto," Vásquez said. "I was buying toys for my kids and I got a phone call from my agent. 'You just got traded to Toronto.' Honestly, I was the happiest kid in the world. That was one of the best days."

Then, in the midst of so many rumors and so much alleged uncertainty, the unexpected happened. The Raptors started winning. "It just clicked," Vásquez recalls. "My first couple games, I just wanted to play together with DeMar. My chemistry with him was, from the get-go, unbelievable." The change of scenery also helped Patterson, and the two began to work well together on the second unit. As Vásquez told us with pride, "We were one of the best pick-and-roll duos." By the beginning of January, the team had finally found its winning form and was on its way to a franchise-best finish of 48-34 and the team's first playoff berth in six seasons. Suddenly the Raptors weren't just rebuilding. They were actually *good*. It was hard not to get caught up in the excitement. "I remember us talking in the locker room,"

Vásquez recalls, as the team came together. "It was like, 'Fuck no, let's not trade Kyle. I love winning. I'd rather come off the bench.'"

For Vásquez, the Sacramento trade was more than just an accidental rebuild. It was day one of the new-look Raptors—the precise moment at which the team started to become one of the most-feared teams in the league. "The trade really worked," Vásquez argues. "Toronto won the 2019 championship the moment Masai made the Sacramento trade. From that moment on, we were building a winning foundation and culture."

Vásquez could see that culture shift not only in the locker room and on the court, but also in the city. "It was so cool to walk from my apartment to the arena and see everyone outside waiting for the game. The whole gym was always packed. It was a tremendous experience and I will never forget the chemistry that we built. That was the base that later on produced a lot of fruits."

Throughout his first season in Toronto, Vásquez played an important role, backing up Lowry and consistently putting up 10 points, a few assists, and a couple of rebounds in his 22 minutes off the bench. "I give myself credit, but we also gotta give Masai a lot of credit—him, his staff, and the front office. I don't know if they were expecting it to click the way it did. I don't think *anyone* thought, *This is going to be it.* But we did something amazing: We created a winning foundation and we did it together. It was a 'we.' *We* made great things happen."

On the personal side, the move from Sacramento also proved a welcome change. "I got to Toronto and, honestly, I fell in love with every single thing. My years in Toronto were probably the best years that I had in the NBA just because of how I acclimated myself to the city, to all my teammates, to the front office—to everything that was going on in the city. It was amazing." It was hard not to get caught up in the vibe. "The Raptors have the best fans in the NBA."

The city and its multicultural landscape also appealed to Vásquez. "I'm an international player but people never looked at me as an international player, because I went to the United States and I went through the same American process—high school, then college, and I ended up getting drafted. Masai got guys that really cared and understood their role and embraced the city and embraced the culture. We represented a country."

Bringing in players from around the world was one thing. But bringing in the *right* guys was key—not only hoopers who could fill the box score, but those who would happily play their assigned role on the team, no matter how small or unglamorous. Take Chuck Hayes, traded alongside Vásquez to the Raptors. He proved a critical veteran head for a team now led by DeRozan and Lowry. "Chuck was huge for the trade. He was in Kyle's ear. He was talking to DeMar. He was the glue guy. He only played a few minutes, but he had a lot of experience in the NBA and was a voice in the locker room. That's intangible. He was doing a job more important than him getting twenty rebounds and twenty points. He was doing the job to give the other guys that were playing the confidence to win basketball games."

Hayes's role in Toronto was symptomatic of the Raptors' own approach to complementary players. "The Raptors, the city, and the country simply appreciate the job of the role players. That's why they get the most out of them." Moreover, in Vásquez's view, almost *everybody* is a role player. "How many superstars are there? Forget about scoring and being the best player and walking around like your shit don't stink. Ninety percent of the players in the NBA are role players."

Vásquez also saw firsthand how an organizational culture of attending to the little things brought the entire team closer together. "I wanted to sell my own Under Armour shoes in Toronto—and they sold out the first day. All my teammates went and some of my teammates bought Under Armour shoes even though they wore Nikes. And I was a *role* player." That appreciation for everyone on the team kept even those guys with smaller roles engaged and productive. "You play the game of basketball to be respected. You don't play to be a millionaire. Any NBA player that tells you, 'I play the game just to make money,' he's lying. We play the game of basketball to be respected. To walk around and hear people say, 'That motherfucker was a badass. He was a pro. He was the best passer. He was a lockdown defender. He was a great locker room guy. He was the guy that was doing the right thing when nobody was watching.' That's respect."

That newly forged unity paid off during Vásquez's first year in Toronto. After several losing seasons, the team was headed to the playoffs, where they would face the Nets. Before the series, during a rally in Jurassic Park, Ujiri infamously yelled, "Fuck Brooklyn!" He was eventually dinged for it, paying a $25,000 fine and apologizing. But in Toronto, and especially among the Raptors players, it was a boss move. Vásquez's teammate at the time, Tyler Hansbrough, thought it was worth it. "He knew that wasn't the right thing to say and knew he was probably going to get some punishment," Hansbrough recalled to us. "But he didn't care. I loved when Masai did that." It was just more evidence of the confidence Ujiri had in his guys. It was also a clarion call to the fans that the Raptors had arrived. "That, to me," Vásquez recalls, "*that* was leadership. Masai knows how to inspire. He knows how to squeeze that lemon. Everything he does, it's with a purpose."

Unfortunately, the Raptors were knocked out in the first round, after a closely fought seven-game series. But the team's growth felt real and sustainable, and Vásquez was excited to re-sign. Ujiri, too, was eager to retain an important offensive cog in the bench rotation. "When I signed my two-year deal with Toronto, Masai led the whole negotiation. Coach Casey was there with me. They signed Kyle and Patrick first, then Patrick called me, 'Yo, now we're only missing you!' I was like, 'Bro, no worries. I'm signing.' I wanted to go back, so we got a deal done." Ujiri, in fact, was even willing to table a long-term contract for Vásquez, but the point guard declined, betting on his future. 'Masai offered me a four-year deal, but I was playing so well, and my agent was telling me, 'Let's just sign a two-year deal because, by the time you become a free agent, your worth's going to be higher.'" That might be his only regret as a Raptor. "I'm a risk-taker. I was thinking long-term when I signed that deal. Now, looking back, I should have signed that four-year deal."

In his second season as a Raptor, Vásquez once again performed well. He played in all 82 games, starting 29 of them, reliably averaging 9.5 points, 3.7 assists, and 2.6 rebounds. The Raptors also had a strong regular season, improving to 49-33, another franchise best, but were once again being bounced from the playoffs in the first round, this time by the Wizards.

That would spell the end of Vásquez's time in a Raptors uniform. During the offseason, Ujiri would send him to the Bucks. "I was in my apartment in Caracas, watching the draft, and I got a call from Masai. 'We're going to trade you to Milwaukee. Thank you for everything. I love you, but this is the business.'" Vásquez was not entirely surprised. "I always thought they were going to make a move," he recalled at the time, "but I never thought it was going to be me, because of my connection with the city and because I was an asset in the locker room. I was caught off guard."

Well reasoned or not, it still stung. "It hurt me a lot, mentally and emotionally, when I got traded," he admits today. "I was disappointed and really confused. I was excited about my future in Toronto." His reaction was understandable. "If you're a competitor, if you care, you get upset. If you don't care, then you don't want to be there. But I wanted to be in Toronto. I wanted to play for the city."

Not only did he love playing for the Raptors and the fans. He had also made a home in Toronto. "I thought I was going to retire from basketball as a Toronto Raptor. I was living a dream. At that moment, I took it personally." Still, Vásquez could see the upside. The Bucks clearly wanted him, and the move to Milwaukee represented an opportunity to mentor two up-and-coming prospects. "They wanted me because, at that moment, Giannis Antetokounmpo needed a vet to run the point. Michael Carter-Williams was the starting point guard for the Bucks, so they wanted a mentor for him as well."

Unfortunately, Vásquez played only 16 games off the bench in Milwaukee, struggling with an ankle injury that would eventually require surgery in December. He managed to play short stints in the last few games of the season, but found himself once again a free agent, with his two-year Raptors contract having come to an end. He signed a deal with the Nets that summer, only to be waived in November, with his ankle still causing him difficulties. That would spell the end of his NBA playing career.

With time, he has been able to rethink not only the trade that brought him to the Raptors, ushering in years of winning, but also the trade that sent him to Milwaukee. "Now that I'm older, I understand. I think if I ever become a GM, I'm going to have a lot of players being upset at me. But it's not about that type of relationship. It's about my club. It's about the franchise." The Milwaukee deal, moreover, was classic Ujiri. In exchange for Vásquez, the Bucks sent to Toronto Norman Powell, the Bucks' 2015 second-round pick, and a 2017 first-round pick that would become OG Anunoby. "Even now I get emotional. I got traded, but even though he traded me, Masai added value to his team. I was always a tremendous asset in the NBA. I'm proud of that."

Today, he has only fond memories of his two years as a Raptor. "People showed me a good time. The city was always great to me and is still great to me. The biggest thing, and probably what makes it different, is the fact that it was the national team in a way, so you have the whole country behind you. I was just living the dream, man. Every time I go back, people remember me. Toronto is one of the best cities to play for with the best fans in the NBA. I still feel a part of Toronto. I will be thankful forever."

22

Bismack Biyombo (2015–2016)

By the summer of 2015, Bismack Biyombo knew it was time for a change. His first NBA contract had finally run out after four seasons in Charlotte, and the only question remaining was where the high-energy big man would land. "My agent, B. J. Armstrong, was talking to most of the teams," Biyombo told us. "He said, 'As soon as free agency opens, you will start receiving calls.'"

Soon enough, his phone started to ring. In the end, about five teams were in the running for his services, including the Raptors. "I was in Belgium running a camp, and the first person who called me was Masai Ujiri." Talking to Ujiri had special meaning for Biyombo. "I've always admired Masai from afar for the work he has done across the globe and the impact it has had on the youth in Africa. There are some GMs and presidents that say, 'I want this player to play one day on my team.' From a player perspective, though, you also go around and start thinking, 'I want to play for this guy someday.'"

Biyombo was hardly alone in his regard for the Raptors executive. Since joining the NBA in 2002, Ujiri had again and again proven his worth, first as a scout for the Magic and the Nuggets, before joining the backroom staff of the Raptors in 2008. Ujiri was named general manager and executive vice president of the Nuggets in 2010 and won NBA Executive of the Year in 2013. He returned to the Raptors as general manager and executive vice president of basketball operations in 2014, eventually becoming president of basketball operations in 2016, until he and the team cut ties in 2025. Along the way, Biyombo had kept tabs on Ujiri, rooting for his success. "I wanted to be in an environment to be able to say, 'I play for the only African GM and I was part of the success that he had, small or big,' because as an African player I wanted to see him succeed."

Ujiri was one thing. But the Raptors also looked like a good fit for his skill set, and the team represented a real chance not only to contribute but also to win. The second person to call him, right after Ujiri, was Dwane Casey, who spent an hour and a half laying out Biyombo's potential role with the Raptors. "Choosing teams, I was just able to sit back and look at the rosters and how I can play around them and help them perform to the best of their abilities."

Back home in Africa, after some hasty intercontinental back-and-forth between Belgium and Canada, Biyombo signed with the Raptors, a choice that had a special resonance. "I was in Congo, in a park visiting the gorillas. It is the only contract I signed in Congo. It was probably one of the most fulfilling." It was also a special moment for him, as a player from Africa. Just a couple of weeks later, in fact, he was able to see the culmination of so many years of important developmental work on the continent at the 2015 NBA Africa Game—"the first NBA game in Africa!" Biyombo recalled with pride, remembering the exhibition match. The showdown took place in Johannesburg, South Africa, between NBA players with African roots, including a young Giannis Antetokounmpo and future Raptor Serge Ibaka, against NBA players from the United States, Spain, and Montenegro, led by Bradley Beal and Chris Paul. "Dikembe Mutombo and Hakeem Olajuwon got to play as well," Biyombo said, marveling at the veteran African ambassadors to the sport, who even logged court time in the game as retired NBA alumni. "It was pretty cool."

It was hard not to be giddy about his good fortune, but in signing with Toronto, Biyombo knew he was taking a risk. He had grown up in the Democratic Republic of the Congo (known as Zaire until 1997), before playing professionally in Spain as a teenager. In 2011, he was drafted seventh overall by the Kings before being immediately dealt to the Charlotte Bobcats in a three team deal with the Bucks. In his first four seasons, he mixed starting and bench duties, often using his high motor and defensive prowess to gobble up rebounds and block shots. His offensive game was limited, however, with Biyombo typically pulling down more boards than points each night. In his last two seasons with Charlotte, he saw his minutes dip, and the team ultimately decided not to extend or re-sign him, making him an unrestricted free agent.

As a result, by the summer of 2015, Biyombo knew he was at a crossroads, but he remained optimistic about the coming season. "I assumed it was going to be one of my best years, just from the feeling I had. That summer I was working hard. It was just about me getting better, stronger, and faster. When I did focus on that, the rest just fell in place, and there was no pressure whatsoever."

Ujiri also recognized in Biyombo a special talent and tabled a flexible contract. The deal—a two-year, $5.75 million offer—allowed Biyombo to showcase his talents in a new context and in a complementary role on a stacked roster. The contract also allowed him to bet on himself. The second year had a player option, meaning that he could reenter the market after just one season (something he did the following season, when he signed a massive four-year, $72 million contract with the Magic). It was a bet he was willing to take. "Of course this was a no-brainer, because I knew this year was going to be *the* year. It was just about being a kid and playing free in an environment and in a system that I fit into. I could tell this was gonna be a great year from the get-go."

Throughout the 2015–16 season, Biyombo played well for the Raptors, filling in gaps in the defense, gobbling up rebounds, complementing his teammates, and even starting a couple of stretches when Jonas Valančiūnas was injured. Slowly but surely, the team came together. "In preseason training camp, you could see everybody coming along," Biyombo said. "Everyone was putting ego aside. That year Kyle and DeMar really accepted each other's presence without one overshadowing the other one or one taking over the team."

Across the lineup, he also saw the growing chemistry. "Cory Joseph, DeMarre Carroll, Patrick Patterson, Norman Powell—they were good dudes to be around." Even players on the bench had a critical role. "James Johnson was a pro on that team. As a competitor, he would come in knowing that he could play, but was able to take a back seat and say, 'Even if I'm not playing, I'm still going to push all these other guys.' It became a family thing where everybody was connected: We moved as one and we supported each other. To this day, I talk to everybody on that team. It's a relationship that goes beyond basketball."

His teammates in turn came to appreciate Biyombo's skill set, especially his relentless motor, which would wreak havoc against opponents. "DeMar and I joked about this a little while back. He was like, 'Man, I used to hate you every time I played you.' But then as we got the ball rolling from training camp and then a few weeks into the season, it was like, 'Yo, this is one of the best dudes I've ever been around.'"

The same held true for Lowry. "Kyle and I were not close early on. I was like, 'I'm here to do my job and I'm going home.' Then we started building a relationship. I think Kyle and DeMar realized that I could protect them more than anything," he recalled, laughing. But there were also things that Biyombo could do defensively that patched up leaks. "We had a fair trade in a way that was fun for me—you know, 'I'm gonna protect the basket for you guys.' Kyle would have a blow by and then be like, 'Please go get that.' Then I'd chase the player down for him, and he would be like, 'I'll get you an assist.' It just clicked naturally."

At the head of the snake was Casey, who expertly managed all the personalities on the team. "He made it clear what he expected from everybody. He constantly communicated with us. Going into each and every game, I knew what I needed to bring to the table for the team. He simplified everybody's life."

What Casey communicated was also simple: Win. But the larger goal was more forbidding. Not simply win, but also go further in the playoffs, an issue for a team that had been sidelined in the first round in back-to-back postseasons. "The goal every night was: What can we do to win? And what can we do not to have the same experience as the year before, which was like, 'Oh, Toronto, here we go: another first-round loss.'" Biz, though, was cool as a cucumber. "I'm sitting there, 'You guys got to be out of your mind, because we have more than enough not to be a first-round team.'" And Biyombo, again, knew the role he could play. "My mentality when coming into Toronto was 'I'm going to bring just what is missing and we're going to flip this building upside down,' which we did. It was fun."

The season was a massive success, with the team going a franchise-best 56-26. It was in the playoffs, though, that Biyombo truly shone.

In the first round, the Raptors faced Paul George's Pacers, whom they took down in seven games. It was a massive relief for a team that had been summarily bounced two straight postseasons in the opening series. The players breathed a sigh of relief, but so, too, did Toronto. "I remember leaving the arena—we had just won the game and closed out Indiana—and I stopped by a gas station. This old man walked up to me. He asked me, 'Can I hug you?' I was like, 'Yeah, sure.' Then he gave me this hug and he had tears in his eyes. I asked, 'Why are you crying?' He said, 'We've been hoping to get past the first round, and we can finally say we're not a first-round-exit team no more.' You think when you play the game, it's just about the teammates and the organization, but there is more to it than that. It's about the fans. I could sense he had so much appreciation in him. Going into the next series, I thought, *Now we really got a bigger fish to fry.*"

In the Conference Semifinals against the Heat, the Raptors once again took the series in a seven-game slog. "When we lost game six, I was outside, and Paul Jones from the broadcasting team walked by me like, 'Man, it's game *seven*.' I was like, 'Don't even worry about it. We're going to close out by like twenty.'" Biz was not only good to his word but better, with the Raptors beating the Heat 116–89. He also delivered on court, starting in place of an injured Valančiūnas, playing nearly 41 minutes, scoring 17 points on 6-of-8 shooting, and grabbing 16 rebounds—with 2 blocks and an assist thrown in for good measure.

Going into Cleveland, to play LeBron James, Kyrie Irving, and Kevin Love, the Raptors knew they were facing their hardest challenge yet. It was also another first for the team: the Eastern Conference Finals. Expectations—and tensions—were high. "The stress was not just on the players. The stress was more so on the organization, the city—everybody. How do you absorb that? Dwane Casey did an incredible job of managing it for us."

At the same time, Biyombo had trouble treating it as anything more than healthy expectations. "The pressure of playing basketball is not pressure. Real pressure is growing up with no food. Playing basketball is fun." As he put it then, contemplating the formidable hill that stood in Toronto's way, in a quote that later went viral: "People were like, 'Are you guys afraid of LeBron?' Guys, we've got to stop this nonsense. Why would I be afraid of LeBron? I'm not afraid of a human being. I don't think there's one human where I'm like, 'Holy shit!' I'm afraid of *a lion*. We're not afraid of LeBron."

Even after Toronto dropped the opening two games in Cleveland, Biyombo retained his equilibrium. "They punched us, really, really hard, but I was never concerned about being down two games." For him it was an obvious consequence of the situation. Not only of playing James on his home court, but of having already fought through two draining, high-stakes series. "There was the exhaustion of the first series: game seven; the second series: game seven. It takes a toll mentally." Still, he kept his faith going into game three, back in the ACC. "I called my trainer. I'm like, 'Let's go to the gym.' We worked out maybe for an hour, and I was telling him, 'Brother, I don't know how we're going to pull out this win tomorrow, but I bet everything I got that we're winning.'"

Good to his word, the Raptors stormed back, taking game three 99–84, with Biyombo putting his stamp on the contest in a performance that defined the postseason for the Raptors. It was signature Biz: 39 minutes and 26 rebounds, including 8 offensive boards, setting a Raptors postseason single-game record, alongside 4 blocks and a true-to-form 7 points. "My only focus that game was getting as many rebounds as possible. They're not going to get no second chances. I came out that game swinging, like, 'I'm going to pour everything I have into the first quarter.' I just wanted to see how they would respond. By half, you could see they had started folding."

In the fourth game, Biyombo continued to exert his influence. With only three minutes left and the Raptors up 14, and the win seemingly locked up, Biyombo found himself guarding James on a defensive switch. James drove to the hoop and pump-faked. Biyombo, caught flat-footed, tied up James, sending him to the floor, for which he received a flagrant foul. (Not everyone agreed with the call. As Jeff Van Gundy remarked after the play on the US broadcast, "I thought James sold it pretty good. That's nothing. That's not a flagrant foul.")

Even if the game was in the bag, Biyombo was trying to make a point. "For me, it was like, 'Look, we came to your house and you punched us in the mouth. You're not about to drive into our house and dunk the ball. I'll take a flagrant foul, but what I'm not going to allow is for you to drive to the basket.' Yes, we were up, but at the same time, we're also focusing on the next game. All you need is a guy to catch a little rhythm. You leave a little door open: 'I can drive to the basket and go dunk the ball.' So I'd rather stop that thought process. For me, it was back to accepting my role. My job, in each and every game, is to protect these guys and to make sure that our paint is not a playground."

Biyombo's confidence and commitment spread throughout the locker room with the series evened up 2–2. "All of a sudden, everybody changed from 'Is this going to be a series?' to 'This is *anybody's* series.' What's crazy is that we had something where I don't think you could have explained it—where guys could just put their arms around each other and then you'd feel an energy like, 'We got something cooking here.'"

Cleveland recognized Biyombo's disruptive energy in the post and the Cavs' coach, Tyronn Lue, adjusted the team's plan going into game five. "I spoke to Channing Frye at some point later. He was like, 'Our scouting report was not on Kyle or DeMar. Our scouting report was: How can we stop that guy from grabbing a rebound?'" For Biyombo, it was an honor to be targeted. But it was also a symptom of the role he was playing—the way his game facilitated the play of others. "It took pressure away from DeMar, so he could do his thing." In turn, Cleveland sought to isolate Biyombo, dragging him away from the paint. "That one lineup they had would put me either in the corner or at the elbow with Kevin Love or Channing Frye, so now when they're rolling to the basket, I can't really tag that much, otherwise Love or Frye is hitting a three. They figured out a way to pull me completely away from the basket, which is what LeBron does. He is a smart basketball player and he figures out how to win."

In the end, the Cavs ultimately proved too much, with the Raptors falling in a fifth game on the road and a sixth at home. It was a painful loss after having come so far, but the fans still clearly appreciated everything the team had done, rising in the ACC to applaud the Raptors at the close of game six. Biyombo was physically and mentally exhausted. "When we finished the last game, I told my manager, 'I'm going to stay in the house for at least a few days.' I just wanted to eat and sleep. My body was hurting."

Eventually, cabin fever set in. "On the third day, I had to get out of the house for a little bit. We decided to go to dinner at the Cactus Club Cafe in Toronto. While we were at dinner, you could feel the appreciation of the fans. When we finished dinner, the manager was like, 'The bill's already taken care of. What you did for us, we can't let you pay.'" That appreciation and recognition gave Biyombo pause, allowing him to reflect on the hard work of the season and what their run truly meant to Raptors fans. "That year was just basketball. Nothing else mattered. All this sacrifice. It was just me, the ball, my trainer, and the gym, and watching game after game, studying film. That's it. So I think in the end, when things happened like that, I honestly just wanted to see the fans win. It was a beautiful journey and I am grateful for it."

23

Jonas Valančiūnas (2012–2019)

At just eighteen years old, Jonas Valančiūnas was riding high. He was already a rising star for Rytas Vilnius, his hometown club in the Lithuanian capital. Along the way, he had also collected trophy after trophy, including the 2011 FIBA Europe Young Men's Player of the Year and the Under-22 EuroCup Rising Star Trophy. That same year, he led Lithuania to gold in the U-19 World Championships, earning MVP honors in the process. As Valančiūnas told us, "I was living my dream, playing for my hometown, being successful, and scoring baskets with four thousand people coming to see us. It was amazing."

Play domestically, compete at the top European levels, win a few cups, lead the national team, maybe even become one of Lithuania's all-time greats—that was all the big man wanted. "I was eighteen years old and I had never thought about the NBA," he recalled. "It was too far away. Then my agent, Šarūnas Broga, told me, 'There's a chance you can go to the NBA.' I was like, 'Stop kidding.'" Before long, scouts and GMs were showing up in Vilnius, including Maurizio Gherardini, then vice president of basketball operations and assistant general manager for the Raptors. That attention had

Valančiūnas thinking twice about his goals. "*Maybe something* could *happen*, I thought. My agent asked about putting my name in the draft, and I said, 'Let's do it. I'm not gonna lose anything. My dream has already come true.'"

On draft night, on June 23, 2011, in Newark, New Jersey, Valančiūnas was a bundle of nerves, but optimistic about his chances of being selected early on. "It was a very stressful day for me, not speaking English that well and being away from home. I had a lot of feelings going through my body and my mind. And then: number five, Toronto picked me." Suddenly, Valančiūnas was a Raptor—and with it, he faced the dizzying prospect of a dozen changes. "I had another wave of *different* feelings coming," he recalled. "Now it's Toronto, it's Canada, a new life and a new start. It will be different from Europe—the lifestyle, city, culture—everything. And the basketball too. You've been taught to play one way, and now you're playing in the best league in the world."

One day later he was in Toronto, meeting general manager Bryan Colangelo, Dwane Casey, and Alex McKechnie, today vice president of player health and performance for the Raptors. And the next day? Back in Vilnius, where he was still under contract. Thanks to a significant buyout clause and the looming NBA lockout, the Raptors and Valančiūnas's representatives decided it would be best for him to remain in Vilnius for one more year. There he could play regularly, mature, and develop before joining the Raptors the next season. He made the most of his last year playing in front of his hometown crowd and for Lithuania in the 2012 Summer Olympics. "My mentality was *I'm going to ball out and enjoy playing.* I wanted to be the best I could be—work on my skills, get stronger, and be ready for the NBA."

The following summer, in July 2012, Valančiūnas officially signed with the Raptors. It was only when he landed at Pearson Airport for the team's training camp that he realized the challenges that lay ahead. "I didn't know *anything*. I knew I was going to struggle. My Lithuanian phone wasn't even working, and I wanted to call my mom so she wouldn't worry—you know, moms gonna be moms." He laughs. "'Mom, I made the flight. I'm good. I'm alive. Don't worry!'"

Valančiūnas felt overwhelmed, suddenly aware of all that had changed in one short year. He was only nineteen and had never lived abroad before. Now he was calling Toronto home, a city he had known nothing about until his first brief visit one summer earlier. All those changes hit home at dinner the night before camp started. "Everybody's talking in English in the restaurant, chatting. I remember the sound at the bar. Like, '*This* is Canada. *This* is life overseas.' I was shocked."

That anxiety carried over to the night—the day—before his first practice as a Raptor. "I woke up at like three thirty in the morning because I was jet-lagged and anxious. I was sitting there, at seven in the morning, waiting for two and a half hours, just watching TV, and it was fifteen hundred channels. We had five channels in Lithuania. It was a culture shock." All those channels started to feel like a metaphor for life in North America: everything was going to be three hundred times more complicated. "I just didn't know the basic stuff," Valančiūnas recalled with a smile. "I didn't even know the names of the stores. I went to Home Depot, asking, 'Hello, I need a sour cream.' 'Oh this is the wrong store.'" He laughs, shaking his head. "I didn't know!"

Some of the challenges were beyond his control, including negative stereotypes about foreign big men. In 2012, the word most readily associated with *European* in the NBA was the adjective *soft*. "I had to make adjustments," he explained. "I had never played anywhere except Lithuania." Staff and his teammates—including Jamaal Magloire, a thirty-three-year-old vet known for his edge—took it upon themselves to season the Lithuanian rookie. "They were teaching me physicality and toughness. They wanted me to be the best version I could be—a strong dude who could dominate."

In the Raptors, Valančiūnas also found an organization eager to make him feel at home. "I had Linas Kleiza in the locker room," he says, referring to another Lithuanian player on the team between 2010 and 2013. "Linas helped me a lot with the language barrier and learning stuff, always explaining to me how to deal with certain situations and how to make life decisions. José Calderón, too—he understood what I was going through." Valančiūnas's adaptation was also a two-way street. "I had to make everybody comfortable with me in the locker room. It's about fourteen other guys. How are they going to look at me? Are they going to accept me? It was not just about me."

Early on, the team even found Valančiūnas welcome connections to home. "I went to Bryan's office one day," he recalled. "There's a dude in a room and he says, '*Labas!*' I thought, 'Okay, some guy learned one word in Lithuanian and he's trying to make me happy.' But it was Stasys Kuliavas, like the father of the Lithuanian community in Toronto. 'I'm going to help you adjust!' The Raptors really cared about me feeling comfortable. They wanted me to be successful. They were not just doing their job."

During his first season, Valančiūnas proved his NBA worth. Despite missing a block of games with a broken finger, he played consistently and well, appearing in 62 games and starting 57 of them, averaging 9 points, 6 rebounds, and 1.3 blocks over 24 minutes on efficient shooting.

The Raptors struggled, though, to put up wins, going 34-48. On paper it was nothing to write home about, but Valančiūnas was optimistic about the team's direction. "My first season was rough," he admits. "But there was all this excitement. I was learning so much that there was no time for thinking, just doing. Sometimes I even forgot that we lost a game, because I learned so many new things."

The Raptors' fortunes eventually turned during Valančiūnas's second season, though not right away. In December 2013, Toronto sent

Quincy Acy, Aaron Gray, and Rudy Gay to Sacramento in exchange for Patrick Patterson, Chuck Hayes, John Salmons, and Greivis Vásquez. The trade proved prescient. "They were talking about rebuilding," Valančiūnas recalled, "but then things clicked."

The Raptors finished 48-34 and made the playoffs for the first time in six seasons, but the trade also introduced Valančiūnas to the cutthroat world of the NBA. It was a critical lesson, one that he would come to know personally years later: No player, not even a team's top scorer, is ever safe. The deal also hit the locker room hard, with Valančiūnas losing one mentor while gaining another. "Aaron was my veteran, but Chuck is a super sweet guy. I *hated* to play against him. He is such a strong dude. But when he got to the Raptors, he was always in my corner."

Valančiūnas's education kept coming during the team's 2014 postseason. "Everybody was saying that the playoffs are a different animal. It's a different crowd, a different physicality, a different speed." The challenges started right away. The Raptors faced the Brooklyn Nets in the opening round and Valančiūnas was tasked with guarding Kevin Garnett. "KG is not the easiest to go against," he said. "*And* he talks a lot. I remember the media asking me, 'How do you deal with the trash talk?' The good thing was that I was not understanding shit. I said, 'Sorry, I don't understand what KG's saying!' So it was easier for me."

The Raptors were eventually sent packing into the offseason, but the team's strong finish after the Sacramento trade had given Valančiūnas and his teammates a newfound ambition. "I had a taste for the playoffs and I knew Jurassic Park was outside behind us. It was to die for, playing with that kind of energy. I was finding my comfort zone, getting more experience and feeling more relaxed. You get into that rhythm a little bit more; you find the areas you need to work on and get better at." Toronto's fairytale season, though, also came with a brighter spotlight. "I felt the pressure a little bit more. Now it's year three and there are expectations: you're not expected to rebuild anymore; you are expected to get to the playoffs—and you have to fulfill those expectations."

Over the next few seasons, Valančiūnas did exactly that, becoming a full-time starter and regular workhorse, putting up a near double-double each game and playing in almost 80 contests a season, except in his fourth year, when a fractured left hand took him out of the lineup for 17 games.

The team also continued to grow but always seemed to run into a wall during the postseason, including a sweep by the Wizards in 2015. "I remember the Washington year," Valančiūnas said, still smarting from the loss. "It was a bad feeling. We didn't even want to go out in Toronto afterwards. We had one playoff run where nobody expected anything and we made it. Now we have another playoff series where everybody expected us to go further and we should have."

After two straight first-round exits, the Raptors regrouped going into the 2015–16 season. There was good reason for hope. "We had the core: DeMar, Kyle, Patrick, Terrence Ross, and Greivis, and then Cory Joseph. Plus, we had experience." In the first round, the team managed to down the Pacers. The twenty-three-year-old Valančiūnas played well in the seven-game series, logging consistent minutes and routinely bagging double-doubles, including a 23-point and 15-rebound game-two win at home.

He kept it up in the following series against Dwyane Wade's Heat, until an errant footfall took him out. "I remember in the first three quarters of game three I had sixteen points and twelve rebounds and we were winning, and then I stepped on D-Wade's foot and my whole ankle went out. I went back to the locker room. I said, 'Tape it up.' I was trying to run, but the foot kept giving out. I put a step down, and it almost folded over. I said, 'It's okay! Let's just go run in the corridor.' I started to run but I was limping. They did an MRI and I had two torn ligaments."

Toronto managed to eke out the win that night, but Valančiūnas missed the remainder of the series. In the meantime, he began rehabbing, hoping to return in the next series. In Valančiūnas's stead, Dwane Casey promoted Bismack Biyombo to starting center. He proved a menace on the defensive end and a key cog in the next series against Cleveland. Valančiūnas was able to come off the bench for a couple of games at the end of the series, but his ankle just wouldn't respond. "Coach asked, 'Do you want to go?' I'm like, 'I *want* to go, but *can* I go?' So I was trying to run it off, play on it for like fifteen minutes. I had a couple buckets, all middies, but my ankle was really limiting me. I didn't have two feet; I had one and a half feet."

Casey rode Biyombo for the rest of the series with Valančiūnas's support. "Biz started playing really well. I told him, 'Go do your thing. Give me some rest, please.' I still joke with Biz sometimes," Valančiūnas told us, recalling Biyombo's massive deal after his lone season in Toronto. "'I suffered with my ankle, but you got paid. You're welcome.'"

Ultimately the Cavs would pull out the series in six games and would bounce the Raptors from the playoffs again in both 2017 and 2018. Even still, Valančiūnas looks back on those seasons with few regrets, thanks in large measure to the Raptors faithful. "It was tough, but that was probably my best basketball experience. It was a great run. Toronto playoffs were always special because the crowd was going to go nuts. The last game we lost, everybody—players, coaches—was in tears because of the fans. They supported us throughout all the ups and downs. They were real fans and they showed the real face of Toronto."

During his first six seasons in the NBA, Valančiūnas was the portrait of reliability—and durability, averaging more than 72 games per season alongside 11.7 points on efficient shooting (.558/.785) and 8.5 rebounds per game. At the same time, he always faced a larger challenge, one entirely out of his control. A big man bred to bang in the post, Valančiūnas was in a battle with his body and how a center should play in the middle of the NBA's pace-and-space revolution. "My weight was always a topic of discussion. When I came to the league, I needed to get bigger and stronger, so I lifted a lot. Then, my third year, every big guy started to get light and run. I remember, in the middle of one of my lifting sessions, the trainers came into the weight room and said, 'Now you're gonna cut.' I had become a bigger guy, but now, it's *boom*: I'm running."

Those fluctuations in weight also shaped how he performed on court. "One season I was almost down to 245 pounds—even lighter than I was in my rookie year. I was really skinny, but then I had to gain it back, because I couldn't even push in the post. Over those years, I was trying to find my sweet spot, where I could run *and* be able to push."

Going into the 2018–19 season, the team was also about to undergo a series of radical cuts and additions. "I was in Lithuania, just chilling, during the offseason. I heard something might happen, but I was not paying much attention. A week later, DeMar got traded." In exchange for DeRozan and Jakob Poeltl, the Raptors received Kawhi Leonard and Danny Green. The deal hit the team—and Lowry, in particular, who was DeRozan's coleader and close friend—hard. For Valančiūnas, who recalled the Rudy Gay trade that had jump-started the Raptors' Golden Era years earlier, the DeRozan deal represented the precarity of life in the NBA, even for those who had spent years as the face of a team. "DeMar was a hardworking leader with unbelievable character. It was sad, but it's a business. I realized we could all get traded tomorrow."

Not quite. But then, half a year later, with the Raptors 39-16 and in Atlanta for a matchup against the Hawks, Valančiūnas found his name being batted around in rumors. "I had asked my agent, Leon Rose, what was going on. He said, 'Nothing. Don't worry.' And then, after the morning shootaround in Atlanta, I went back to my hotel room, and Leon called me. 'Something is going down.' There were two hours left till the trade deadline, when they showed the trade on ESPN." Valančiūnas had been sent to the Grizzlies with CJ Miles and Delon Wright in exchange for Marc Gasol. Despite the DeRozan trade and the rumblings, the deal still caught Valančiūnas off guard. It also hurt. "I didn't want to go. I didn't want to leave the team. I was happy with what I had. I'd seen it all, from the days when we were shit to the days we were up top in the East. And now I gotta leave. I thought, *Memphis? What am I going to do now? How am I going to deal with this?* I had a family now, too, and two kids."

A pro since the age of sixteen, Valančiūnas nonetheless knew exactly how to regroup. In Memphis he was immediately slotted into the starting lineup, ever the figure of frontcourt reliability, and never relinquished his position during his two and a half seasons with the Grizzlies.

Whether it was Memphis—or, later, New Orleans, Washington, Sacramento, and more—Valančiūnas never relinquished his ties to Toronto. It was something on ample display just months after he had been traded to the Grizzlies, when he returned to Toronto to root for his old team during the Raptors' first game of the 2019 playoffs against the Magic. It was a homecoming of sorts for Valančiūnas, who had quietly amassed a raft of team records during his years in Toronto: second all-time for double-doubles, rebounds, and field-goal percentage; third for two-pointers and blocks; and top ten in points, free throws, and games and minutes played. Unsurprisingly, he was greeted with a standing ovation.

Asked why he would return to the team that traded him away en route to the Finals that year, Valančiūnas doesn't hesitate. "I wanted to see and feel that Toronto playoff vibe for the last time for two reasons: the city and my teammates. I was with those guys two months earlier, and they were still my guys. It's about more than basketball. As the fans were cheering for me, I had a great moment. I was really sad to leave, and I was like, 'Okay, I'll miss you motherfuckers.' That was the city where I grew up. I was a boy when I came to Toronto, and I became a man there. I became a husband there. I became a father there. It's about more than basketball, more than the court, more than hoops. It's a city, it's a country, it's a lifestyle. It's where I started."

24

Cory Joseph (2015–2017)

When the final buzzer rang out on April 16, 2016, Cory Joseph could only look helplessly up to the scoreboard at Air Canada Centre. There stood the ugly truth. Indiana Pacers: 100. Toronto Raptors: 90.

It was only the first game of the Raptors' 2016 postseason, but it was a particularly tough loss, one that bore the added weight of franchise history. The team had reached the playoffs in each of the two previous seasons but had again and again hit a first-round wall. In 2014, it was the Nets. Then, in 2015, it was the Wizards. 2016 was supposed to be different. The Raptors had just gone 56-26—a franchise-best record at the time—and had seemed even better prepared to overcome their postseason hurdles.

But the loss to Indiana, at least for the Toronto-born Joseph, only in his first season with the Raptors, had started to feel like some horrible déjà vu. "When I was playing for the Spurs, I would always keep track of how things were going with other teams, especially Toronto," he told us. "I remember the whole stigma of the first-round situation, whether it was against Brooklyn or Washington." Some critics doubted whether Toronto could compete with the league's top squads. "Throughout the year that was in the back of our minds,"

Joseph recalls. "After we lost the first game to Indiana, you could hear a pin drop in our locker room, Like, 'Nah, not this again.'"

The Raptors regrouped and ultimately downed the Pacers, in the process shaking off the postseason albatross of 2014 and 2015. "After we won the first round, everybody's shoulders dropped. It was a big sigh of relief, like, 'Okay, we figured it out. Now let's get to the second round and then to the Conference Finals.'" The team did just that, first taking down the Heat, before facing the Cavaliers.

Today, almost ten years later, Joseph can finally put the closing minutes of that series into perspective. "When I first got to the Raptors, they had been getting stuck in the first round," he explains. "Then, we made the Eastern Conference Finals. Even though we lost to the Cavs, it was a bittersweet moment, because we knew the direction that the organization and the players were going. And that led, all those years later, to the championship. I knew it was a good team. We just needed to piece it all together."

Joseph, who was born in Scarborough in the city's East End and who grew up around Pickering, just east of the city, is a Toronto product through and through. But his connection to basketball, and especially basketball in Canada, extends even further back. Both of his parents, David and Connie Joseph, were collegiate hoopers in Alberta in the early 1980s. After their playing days, the Josephs moved to Toronto, where Cory was born in 1991.

Basketball, unsurprisingly, was everywhere for Joseph and his siblings, including his two sisters, Chantal and Danielle, and his older brother, Devoe. Hoops at home was one thing. But there was also the local inspiration. The Raptors' inaugural season began when Joseph was only four years old. "Having the Raptors there pushed the envelope. Being able to see the game up close, knowing that this is happening not too far down the street from you, was huge."

The NBA felt tangible to the young Joseph, especially when he spotted his hardwood heroes on the street. "Sometimes you might see a fancy car downtown or see somebody walking down the street and everybody was hovering around them. And you'd be like, 'That's Alvin Williams!'" To see so many Raptors up close, and especially the fellow guard, was inspiring. "Alvin was definitely one of my guys. There were a bunch of Raptors that I looked up to. Obviously, besides stars like the T-Macs and the Vince Carters—like, Vince was *that* guy—those guys definitely kept my dreams intact. 'Skip to My Lou' Rafer Alston, Donyell Marshall hitting all those threes, Dell Curry, Marcus Camby who could block anything. I even had a collectible doll of Damon Stoudamire that I *still* got. Seeing them definitely puts you in that realm. It's like, *Man, I want to be* that *guy one of these days.*"

The inspiration he drew from his hometown team is also part of the organization's legacy in Canada. "It was night and day. Once the Raptors came to town, I think that directly correlates to why you see so many guys in the NBA from Canada right now." During that era, in fact, basketball in the country witnessed massive growth. "I started playing Rep Ball for the Scarborough Blues, when I was seven or eight years old, and was playing with Kelly Olynyk, who was a little bit older."

By the time Joseph was playing at the high school level, in the mid-aughts, the level of basketball in the Greater Toronto Area was at an all-time high. "My brother Devoe, Tristan Thompson, Dwight Powell, and Myck Kabongo—that was Canada basketball at that point, and the competition was pretty good." In turn, Joseph's team gained more and more opportunities to compete south of the border, where, after racking up wins against top-flight US schools, his team had also garnered a reputation. "First they were writing us off, but as we showed them how good we were, they started inviting us to more tournaments. We played an NBA schedule—like eighty games. For real, we had an A team and a B team, and we would go to tournaments and sometimes the A *and* the B team would each win a tournament."

Ultimately, at the age of sixteen, Joseph decided to study and play in the US. "It was still a little bit of a struggle to find enough gym time in Toronto," he explains. "So I decided to go down to the States, because at the time the exposure in Canada wasn't so high." But that choice to play in the US was circumstantial, according to Joseph, and hardly a reflection of the competition in Canada. "Don't get it twisted." He laughs. "The top teams in Toronto could compete with *anybody* during that time. But after those top-ten teams, there was a drop-off. Now a lot of players go stateside. But before, nobody was leaving, so all of the talent was in Toronto."

The newly founded Findlay Prep, a high school basketball program located in Henderson, Nevada, just southeast of Las Vegas, offered an obvious destination. "Michael Peck, the coach of Findlay Prep at the time, saw me play. My mom wanted to see the school, obviously, because Las Vegas is a long way from Toronto. My brother had also signed to Minnesota and was already leaving to go to college at that time. Tristan was already down in St. Benedict's in Jersey and Myck was at Findlay. So we made the decision. We trusted Michael Peck and his vision for the program."

In Nevada, Joseph got an immediate taste of the school's competitive spirit. "I was probably the sixth or seventh person to arrive. Nobody knew nobody, so everybody was testing you at this point. You had to go to the gym right away, lace them up, and see what you got. Thankfully I played well. Avery Bradley came, too, and then halfway through that year Tristan came."

At the same time, Joseph retained his connections to basketball back home through Grassroots Canada, a nonprofit youth development and educational organization in Toronto. "The lines are a little bit more blurred now because you could have an AAU team and prep school all in one. Back then, it was separate: You have your school team and then you have your summer team, so I even played for Grassroots when I was living in America." With each passing year, Joseph could see the growth in Canadian basketball. "By that point, they were flying *us* to tournaments and putting *us* up in hotels."

Along the way, Joseph remained committed to the Canadian national team, something that continued throughout his NBA career. "I played for Team Canada for twelve or thirteen straight summers," he recalled. "I think that the only year I didn't was leading up to the draft. Even when I didn't have an NBA contract, I still prioritized Team Canada." For him, it was a chance to participate in a larger tradition. "I remember Rick Fox, Steve Nash, and Rowan Barrett. It intertwines really. It's the best basketball, the best competition, and the best opportunity to grow. But not only that. You're also representing so many people, and I love the guys that I played with. We have that brotherhood."

After his time at Findlay Prep, Joseph decided to attend the University of Texas alongside Tristan Thompson and Myck Kabongo. After just a year, Joseph and Thompson declared for the 2011 draft. "At the time, it was a big thing," Joseph explains. "You couldn't put your name in the draft and then pull out and go back to college."

Thompson was selected fourth overall by the Cavs. Joseph was taken 29th by the Spurs. The Thompson selection even made history: It was the highest Canadian pick ever in the NBA. It was also the first time since 1983, when Leo Rautins and Stewart Granger were drafted, that two Canadian players had been selected in the first round. Already the Toronto-area boys were offering a glimpse of the league's Canadian future.

During his first couple of seasons with the Spurs, Joseph didn't see much action, but he was learning, day in and day out, especially during the team's run to the 2012 Conference Finals and then to the 2013 Finals, where they faced LeBron James's Heatles. Even bench time was a gift. Joseph was in effect going to R. C. Buford's NBA University, where he played under Gregg Popovich and alongside three future Hall of Famers in Tim Duncan, Tony Parker, and Manu Ginóbili. "I was a kid when I got drafted. You get a lot thrown at you, not only on the court, but off the court, too, as a young guy. The reason I'm still in the league today is because of my time in San Antonio." By his third season, his patience and those lessons had paid off. Joseph was getting consistent minutes off the bench and even starting on occasion, en route to a rematch with James and the Heat in the 2014 Finals, which the Spurs won.

After San Antonio was knocked out of the 2015 playoffs, Joseph knew that his days as a Spur were numbered. He was a free agent, and with Duncan turning thirty-nine, Ginóbili thirty-eight, and Parker thirty-three, the Spurs were going hard after LaMarcus Aldridge, a costly signing that would mean cuts elsewhere in the lineup. Nonetheless, Popovich was always clear with Joseph during that period of uncertainty, something he still appreciates today. "Pop was keeping me in the loop. They wanted LaMarcus from Portland. Pop said, 'We love you and we hope you get the best deal you can possibly get.' That's what Pop was great at. He was so real with you. That's just how he is."

Joseph didn't sweat the details, however. "In my career, I've always let Rich Paul, my agent, do his job. So when I was a free agent, I didn't ask too many questions. I was involved, but I tried not to micromanage him. Rich knew that I'm from Toronto, he knew that I grew up there, and he knew how much it would mean to me to play there." Finally, during the summer, Paul delivered the good news: His hometown team had extended an offer. "I was in Toronto at my brother's condo," Joseph remembers. "I called my mom and my dad. We were just so ecstatic about it. You're gonna play for the city where you grew up. It's what you dream about as a kid. It was a next-to-none feeling."

Playing in front of his hometown immediately lived up to the expectations. "My parents were at every game while I was in Toronto. It felt almost like I was back in high school. I remember those times before games when I'd look up and see like thirty people I know, and then, during the national anthem, I'd be in my mind sometimes like, *Damn, this is crazy.*"

As a former role player in San Antonio, though, Joseph was overwhelmed—and blown away—by his newly elevated stature in Toronto. All of a sudden, as the hometown boy made good, he was being swarmed from all sides, pulled one way to do commercials, another to sign endless autographs. "It was super wild. You realize, oh shoot, this is *a lot*. But it was coming out of love, their love for the city, their love for me."

Joseph's reciprocal love was clearest on his back and chest, an allusion to Toronto itself, branded the 6ix by Drake in 2016 in reference to the city's area code (416) and former division into six regions. "I wasn't going to wear the number six at first," Joseph explained. "But then talking to people, my friends, and so many people that I respect, like, 'Man, you gotta wear number six. Number six is the move.' Then I saw the vision. From the 6ix, playing for the 6ix. And it worked out. In my whole career, I've never seen so many of my jerseys in the stands."

Like the Spurs before, the Raptors proved a top-flight organization, ready to support Joseph in his new role. "There were so many things that I needed or that were required of me while I was there. The organization did a tremendous job in terms of helping me with the community. They made a point of it: 'We have a Canadian here, playing in Canada. We know it's going to be a little different for him.'"

One favor he had to call in again and again was for friends and family. "I required a bunch of tickets, brother." Joseph laughs. "It was a bunch of tickets that year, because we went to the Eastern Conference Finals. I'd been to the Conference Finals with the Spurs three times, and you get a good little check from playing in each round. But that first year with the Raptors, when we went to the Eastern Conference Finals, I had to give them back the *whole* check and pay a little extra too," he says, recalling his shock. "*That's* how many tickets I was getting." Asked whether he regrets his largesse, Joseph is clear: "I wouldn't change it for a day."

Throughout the playoffs, Joseph felt his pride swell before each game, in gratitude to the country and for the reception he got. "You got to give it up to these fans. Even before the game, they were singing the national anthem. *Everybody.* They brought that hockey spirit into the gym. Everybody was standing, cheering. I always made it a point to get out there and make sure I stood tall for the Canadians. It was a little bit like playing for the national team. It's Canada's team. The outreach is bigger—the whole nation instead of just a state or a province. You get this sense of pride. You get that sense of how much they honor the anthem."

Life off the court was special during Joseph's two seasons back home. But on the court, too, the team performed well, even if the Raptors ran up against the same LeBron-shaped wall during each of Joseph's two playoff runs in Toronto. He saw the stress that those losses put on the team's leaders. "Kyle and DeMar were going through those struggles in the first round and I think they were extremely focused and determined to get over that hump. We just had to feed off that energy and, at the same time, bring our own energy. I was new and young, but I had the experience of going deep into the playoffs my first four years. In terms of camaraderie, we were super close as a team."

Eventually, though, his time with the Raptors came to an end, following the 2016–17 season. "I wanted to stay, but I knew that the organization was in a tough spot. We had drafted Delon Wright. Then Fred VanVleet signed with the team, and Kyle was an All-Star. We all loved each other and we all competed against each other. But I knew that, with four point guards, somebody was on the brink. I heard reports coming out that they didn't know if they wanted to keep Kyle or not. I was like, 'That's BS. He's an All-Star. He's one of the heads of the team. That's not happening.' Everybody wanted to keep Kyle, and Delon and Fred were on rookie deals. Fred and Delon also had glimpses of being really good players, so I understood."

His analysis proved prescient. In July 2017, the Raptors decided to send Joseph to the Pacers. It was a potentially controversial move—Ujiri was sending a hometown hero away—but Joseph could see the larger picture. For him, the trade to Indiana was symptomatic of Ujiri's willingness to take risks, popular or not. "He has to do whatever is best for the team," Joseph reasoned. "Masai was not afraid to shake it up. You have to be able to swing for the fences if you want to hit a home run. You got to give him kudos."

Just a couple of years later, Joseph got to watch his hometown team, and former employer, go to the Finals. "I was at my home in Toronto watching when they won the title. I also watched the parade on TV. I was like, 'Man, this is crazy. I can't even go outside right now because I won't be able to move.' At the time, I would have wanted *my* team to win," Joseph laughs. "But I was happy for the country and the city. The way I saw everybody come together, it really is Canada's team. I felt good about that part of it, and it was super inspiring for all the youth in Canada that play basketball and that love the game."

Being in Toronto that championship summer also had its perks. The fans and the organization had held out hope that Kawhi Leonard, Joseph's old teammate from San Antonio, might re-sign with the Raptors. A "Ka'Wine and Dine" promotion had emerged during the NBA playoffs, with restaurants across the city promising the Finals MVP free meals, if only he would stay in Toronto. The gambit didn't ultimately work—that summer Leonard signed in his own hometown with the Clippers—but Joseph was still able to reap the rewards. "I would take Kawhi out in Toronto and I'd get the 'Ka'Wine and Dine' discount too," Joseph says laughing. "I know he loved the city and he had a really good year there. He loved the people. But he's from LA, so it's like me going back to Toronto. I'm sure it was a hard decision for him."

Today, as a member of the Orlando Magic, Joseph is looking forward to basketball's future in Canada. But he's thinking not just about the Raptors or the national team. He imagines, in fact, a version of the country that would have been unimaginable just twenty years earlier. "Maybe one day people will be like, 'This is a basketball country and not only a hockey country.' That'd be dope."

25

DeMarre Carroll (2015–2017)

It had been a banner year for DeMarre Carroll. Already known as a defensive menace, the hard-nosed wing had added a little bit of everything to his game during the 2014–15 season, becoming in the process the Hawks' ultimate glue guy. Alongside a smattering of assists, rebounds, and steals, he had averaged just under 13 points and shot a career-high 39.5 percent from three. His selfless, all-round play had also translated into wins. Atlanta went a franchise-best 60-22 that season, en route to a showdown with LeBron's Cavs in the Eastern Conference Finals.

Going into free agency in the summer of 2015, Carroll was a predictably sought-after commodity: a versatile wing who could play without the ball, who could knock down threes, and who was big and athletic enough to guard up and down the lineup.

Unsurprisingly, the Raptors, like so many other teams, were vying for his services. Now it was decision time for Carroll, and the offer from Toronto was a good one: $60 million over four years. It was career-making and even life-changing money for Carroll, who was on the cusp of his twenty-ninth birthday. It was also a massive turn of fortune for the six-year player, who had spent most of his days as a pro shuttling around the NBA on one- and two-year deals.

That he was even in the NBA—let alone being wooed by multiple teams with gaudy offers—was a surprise, not only to once-skeptical scouts, but also to Carroll himself, who had again and again faced staggering challenges off court.

First, in the summer of 2007, while a star at the University of Missouri, Carroll had been shot in the ankle during a dispute. He and his teammates had attended a party, where another group of guys wanted to jaw with the Tigers stars. Looking to defuse the situation, Carroll tried to break up a verbal altercation, only to be shot while trying to pull his teammate away. As he recalled on Thanasis Antetokounmpo's podcast years later, "My brother and my teammates, they rushed me to the hospital. On my way to the hospital, in my head, I'm like, *My career is over with.*" By some stroke of luck, the bullet narrowly missed his Achilles. "The doctor said, 'You're the luckiest person on this planet at this moment.'"

Carroll would bounce back from the shooting, only to face new challenges as he prepared for the NBA. Just weeks before the 2009 draft, he was diagnosed with a serious liver disease—a lifelong condition that will likely require a liver transplant at some point in the future.

Ultimately, Carroll slid down the draft board to the 27th spot, where he was selected by the Grizzlies. Health concerns likely led to his going late in the first round, but in 2009, more than anything, teams just didn't know what to do with the defensive stopper, viewing him as a solid bench player with a limited offensive game.

Despite being a first-round pick, Carroll spent his first three seasons on the NBA fringe, hunting for court time in fits and starts. With the Grizzlies, he bounced between Memphis and the D-League, before being shipped to the Rockets during his second season. Only months later he was waived by Houston. It was more of the same the next season, when the Nuggets picked him up only to waive him after four games. That same season, the Jazz claimed Carroll off waivers. In Utah, his work ethic and defense were immediately rewarded, and the season-and-a-half stop proved a turning point in his career, despite his averaging less than 6 points per game and shooting 30.3 percent from the arc.

A free agent during the 2013 offseason, Carroll signed a two-year, $5 million deal with the Hawks. His evolution during his two seasons in Atlanta, between 2013 and 2015—from a reliable but mostly defensive-minded rotation guy to a starter-worthy two-way wing who could bolster any lineup—came as a shock. Less surprising? That numerous teams were suddenly soliciting his services at the end of the 2014–15 season.

Now it was day one of free agency in the summer of 2015, and Masai Ujiri, Dwane Casey, and Bobby Webster had flown down to Carroll's home in Atlanta to interview the three-and-D wing and make their case. "They presented me with their whole pitch," Carroll recalled to us. "They basically said they thought I was a key piece and was what the team needed. I went in the other room, talked to my agent, my dad, and my wife, and then they presented me with a number."

At four years and $60 million, Toronto's offer was seemingly impossible to turn down. But it came with a catch. Carroll had to decide immediately. As he recalled, "Masai said, 'If you leave this offer on the table, then we're going after Wesley Matthews,'" another talented wing who had also just entered free agency after averaging 16 points per game with the Trail Blazers.

Carroll was conflicted. He knew Toronto's offer was a massive pay bump and guarantee—with the team itself being a chance to keep winning—but it was the first time in his six years in the NBA that he had ever experienced such overtures. As he emphasized in an interview after joining the Raptors, putting the entire scene in context, "It's the first time in my life, after all I've done and all the obstacles I've been through in my life, I can finally see the reward."

Even still, Carroll had good reason to hesitate. He had other suitors waiting in the wings. The Hawks, for instance, wanted him back, but were facing cap difficulties. The team was looking to retain Paul

Millsap, whom they eventually re-signed to a three-year, $59 million deal. Carroll knew already that Atlanta couldn't match the Raptors' offer, but it was hard to abandon a squad known for its team-first mentality that had just gone to the Conference Finals.

Phoenix was also clamoring for his services, with Jeff Hornacek and Suns brass slated to visit Carroll. Then there were the Pistons. "I had Stan Van Gundy and Detroit coming in right after Toronto," Carroll recalled. "Detroit said, 'Can we at least get an interview?' Stan Van Gundy was saying, 'Can we please get ten minutes?' Then they presented a number to my agent, which was *more* than what the Raptors gave me. I was like, 'Wow, I have a decision to make. Do I take this offer?'"

Having spoken with his personal team, Carroll stepped back to assess the situation. "I had just come from touching the Eastern Conference Finals, so I had that winning taste in my mouth. I wanted to get there again, and I knew what Masai was putting together in Toronto. I knew it would have been beneficial for me to go to Toronto versus going to Detroit, which was trying to rebuild. The Raptors were a winning franchise and they were growing. They had competent pieces, like DeMar and Kyle and all those guys. I was like, 'I think I fit good over there.'"

The move to Canada also appealed to him and his family. "My wife, Iesha, weighed the decision about raising our kids in certain cities. She had heard a lot about Toronto and even wanted to go to Toronto. When she was on board, I think it was an easy decision. A lot of people can say, obviously, money also weighs into it, but at the end of the day, you gotta be comfortable."

Ultimately, Carroll picked winning and Toronto. "It was a hard decision, but I made it before they even walked out the house. I didn't take any other meetings. I felt like that was the best choice for me and my family. All of that combined made it a no-brainer."

Carroll settled in immediately in Toronto, in large measure thanks to Iesha, who went into executive mode. "I'm not even gonna lie," he explained with a laugh. "Throughout my whole NBA career, my wife was at the forefront. That's one thing I didn't have to worry about—finding a place, getting the kids in school—none of that. She basically just got to work and focused on that."

Carroll also flourished in Toronto. In part that was thanks to his charitable work around liver-health awareness, including numerous fundraising events in the city, such as a basketball camp whose proceeds directly benefited pediatric liver disease research. Most importantly for Carroll and Iesha, their family continued to grow. "I had my second child, Amare, when I got to Toronto. He's Canadian!"

Hopes were equally high in the city for their newest acquisition going into the 2015–16 season. Carroll was slotted into the starting lineup and immediately began to produce. During the Raptors' season opener—a 106–99 win against the Pacers at the ACC—Carroll drained 14 points and grabbed 8 rebounds, adding 4 assists and 2 steals.

It seemed like the Raptors had finally found the perfect complement to the team's All-Star duo of DeRozan and Lowry. But then a knee injury in early December pulled Carroll out of the starting lineup. After a short-lived return around New Year, he elected to have surgery and missed 41 straight games, returning for a few contests before the playoffs.

In the end, early-season Carroll never reappeared. His stats with the Raptors were solid—11 points per game on 39 percent from three, alongside nearly 5 rebounds and 2 steals per game—but his production flagged during the postseason. Over 20 games, he averaged only 8.9 points while shooting only 32.9 percent from deep. His still-swollen knee clearly hampered him, alongside a raft of nagging injuries, including a hyperextended elbow, sprained wrist, hip pointer, and twisted ankle—injuries that also made it nearly impossible to pester his punishing defensive assignments, which included

Paul George in the first round and LeBron James in the Conference Finals.

For the fans, the team, and the media alike, that first season was a disappointment. But nobody felt it quite so strongly as Carroll. "I wish I was healthy in Toronto like I was when I was in Atlanta," he recalled to us. "But you can't dictate when you're going to get injured. You gotta have a little bit of luck on your side. When I got injured, I felt that I wasn't performing at the level I needed to perform at. I felt the pressure at times, but that's when you stick to the people close to you—your family and your friends—and just try to block out all the naysayers."

Carroll, moreover, had the grit to gut it out, having faced so many challenges in his career, which had hardened him like a callus. "I've been through so much throughout my life—I've been through the *worst*—but at the end of the day, I just tried to go out there and be tough. Going through those things early in my career and in college, I think that's what gave me that mindset. On a small scale, it's, 'Okay, I got a knee injury. But that's nothing compared to what I've been through. If I can push through what I've been through, I'm sure I can push through a little knee injury.'"

That mentality helped Carroll get through his first year in Toronto. But it also impacted his second season with the Raptors. Despite starting 72 games in 2016–17, Carroll's production dipped even further. Today he can't help but second-guess his own approach. "Instead of trying to fight through injuries and play and guard the best person in the world—LeBron at that time—maybe I should have taken the first year to sit out and get all the way healthy and then come back the second year. Even though I was maybe sixty percent, I thought it would have done more justice if I fought through it and showed my passion and what I was trying to do to help the team. That was my thought process versus saying, 'I'm injured. Let me sit out and get healthy.'"

Such counterfactuals also force Carroll to ask larger questions about his time as a Raptor. "Maybe I could have had a long tenure in Toronto if I sat out," he conjectures. "But being young, being hungry, trying to not let people down, trying to live up to the contract—all those things, all that pressure—I was just like, 'I'm going to fight through it.' It probably wasn't the best decision, but that's how I built my career." It was also something his father had taught him, a lesson that had always served him well. "It's the thing that my dad instilled in me: Hard work is a talent. You might not be the most talented, but if you work hard, you'll get everything that you deserve and that you want in life."

It's easy to fixate today, almost a decade later, on the what-ifs. But at the time, Carroll was playing under a microscope in Toronto as both an important free-agent acquisition and, above all, a critical cog in the starting lineup, something he understood at the time. "At the end of the day, it's a lot of pressure," he admits. "The fans come to the game to see you perform at a high level and that's what you get paid to do. But you sign up for this and you get paid a lot of money."

Carroll's tenure in Toronto would end after only two seasons. Ujiri would trade away his prized acquisition in the 2017 offseason to Brooklyn. Two years later, Carroll was part of a three-team sign-and-trade between the Nets, Wizards, and Spurs that sent him to San Antonio. But his days in the NBA were numbered. After a few games with the Spurs, he was waived. He was picked up by the Rockets a couple of days later but saw limited court time during his second stint in Houston, playing only 9 games off the bench.

Since then, Carroll has had time to reflect, but he has few regrets about his time in a Raptors uniform. "Once I was done playing and I looked back on it, it wasn't as bad as I thought it was. I feel like, at that moment, I magnified it, versus taking a deep breath and just sitting back. I'm very thankful for the trials and tribulations I went through. If I didn't go through those things, I don't think I play eleven or twelve seasons in the NBA. I was in Toronto for only two years, but it helped me when I went to Brooklyn to lock in and move forward and really focus on trying to be the best. I probably squeezed another two or three years out of my career. I'm happy where I was at."

Those trials as a Raptor also prepared him for his postplaying career. Since 2022, he has served as an assistant coach for the Bucks, the Lakers, the Cavaliers, and his current squad, the Suns. "Even though it was hard at the time in Toronto, being injured and the criticism and all that, I think it molded me into who I am today. Hopefully it also helps me on my second career path as far as coaching: telling my story, getting guys ready. Now I can talk to other players and coaches and try to help them not to make similar mistakes. If it helps one guy or a million guys, I did my job."

In the end, Carroll remains grateful for his Raptors experience and for the time he got to spend in Toronto. "You always hear so many good things about the city. I'm not surprised about it. Toronto doesn't get enough credit. The people are friendly. You got a lot of diversity. The food is great. I think Drake helped y'all and put the city on the map, and people are finally catching on. I felt like it was a better decision to go to a stable organization, a winning organization, and to raise my kids in Toronto. I love the city and I love the people. To this day, we still go back and visit every summer. We got friends and roots over there. And at the end of the day, I'm blessed. I wouldn't have had it any other way."

Raptors Moment

May 27, 2016: Raptors vs. Cavs in the Eastern Conference Finals

The Raptors faced LeBron James and the Cleveland Cavaliers in three straight postseasons between 2016 and 2018. They lost all three matchups and were swept twice. James and the Cavs were simply a thorn in the team's side: the one player and the one squad that Toronto could never get past.

That story has been told time and again, and few today, in Canada and across the NBA, can forget the moniker given to the city in 2018 by Toronto's own Mark Jones, brother to Raptors radio analyst Paul Jones, who renamed his hometown "LeBronto." It's worth keeping in mind, though, that Toronto was hardly alone during those years of woe. Between 2006 and 2018, seemingly *nobody* in the NBA could beat LeBron: not the Pacers, Hawks, Pistons, Celtics, 76ers, Bulls, Knicks, Bobcats, or Nets. Whether LeBronto was a fair moniker or not can be debated, but there's no denying that LeBranta, PhiLeBrondelphia, and L'Indiana also fit the bill.

Here's the other thing that is easy to miss when lasered in on Toronto's struggles: The Raptors hit a plateau, but they also went on an incomparable run both before and after, piling up victories and making the playoffs year after year. The Raptors were one of the most consistent—and best—teams of the mid to late 2010s and did the hardest thing to do in the entire NBA in 2019: They won the championship, putting them in an annual club of one (a list that does *not* include a whole third of the league).

So it's worth looking back at the 2016 Eastern Conference Finals against the Cavs as an important milestone in team history. The Raptors had gone 56-26, a franchise-best record at the time, and the city and team were riding high after the 2016 All-Star Game in Toronto—the first and only time that the NBA's premier talent showcase had been held outside the US.

First the Raptors closed out the Pacers. Then they took down the Heat. Both seven-game series were tooth-and-nail scrums that offered a glimpse of the new Raptors. This was a team defined by growth, maturity, and tenacity—and one that the league had to take seriously, during both the regular season *and* the playoffs.

An exhausted Raptors team then dropped the first two games of the Conference Finals to the Cavs in Cleveland against LeBron, Kevin Love, Kyrie Irving, and a solid cast of players. The team nonetheless rallied back, picking up two wins at home in the ACC, only to lose game five back in Cleveland. Down 3–2 and going into game six, home at the ACC, the Raptors had their backs against the wall. It was the team's last chance to even things up, pushing everything to a third straight seven-game series. If only.

The Cavs took the lead just a few minutes into the game and never gave it up. Despite a 35-point game from Kyle Lowry and 20 points from DeMar DeRozan, the Raptors could never even up the score. Already by the fourth quarter, the fans had begun to rise, cheering the team. But the applause was not for some miraculous come-from-behind win. It was, instead, a gesture of gratitude and appreciation for how far the Raptors had come, not simply during the prior two seasons, but over the years: It was the deepest the team had ever gone in the postseason. Those roars only grew louder as Dwane Casey checked out Lowry, DeRozan, Patrick Patterson, and Terrence Ross with a little less than three minutes left in the game.

The Cavs would advance to their second consecutive Finals, a series they would also win, against the Warriors. But before all that, James took a moment to recognize something he had never seen. "Do you hear this?" James asked ESPN's Doris Burke during his postgame interview on the ACC hardwood, gesturing to the still-cheering Toronto crowd. "Unbelievable respect and much respect to these fans, to this country—this is unbelievable. I've never been a part of something like this in my thirteen-year career."

James reiterated his awe later that evening on the dais. "It's an unbelievable atmosphere," he told the swarm of reporters. "These fans, they mean a lot to their team. They were unbelievable all season long, and they definitely showed that toward the end of the game, all the way throughout."

It was a heartbreaking loss for the Raptors and the fans alike, but it also came with a silver lining. For Eric, who has seen or covered almost every major event in team history, game six against Cleveland was one of the most memorable moments for the franchise. The electric atmosphere. The never-ending fourth-quarter ovation. And then James recognizing the crowd, the city, the country, and the organization. It was further validation for the Raptors and their fan base—and something, finally, like league-wide recognition for what the team had become.

26

CJ Miles (2017–2019)

CJ Miles knew it was going to be a great season. It was the summer of 2017, and the twelve-year vet had just signed with the Raptors. He was in town for his team physical and was finally catching a glimpse of Toronto as a resident of the city. He had visited plenty of times before in his decade-plus in the NBA. But it was only during his experiences as a Pacer a year earlier, in a seven-game first-round playoff series against the Raptors, that he came to recognize the special connection between the fans and the team. "I knew what it was like," Miles told us. "But I didn't know their fan base was so big until we played them in the playoffs and they came to Indiana. It's not that close! That was the most eye-opening experience."

Now, touching down in Toronto, he was getting his first dose of that home-team love. "I hadn't been in Toronto an hour yet." Miles laughs recalling those first moments as a Raptor. "Ten seconds after I stepped out of the Uber, somebody was yelling my name: 'CJ!' I hadn't put a jersey on yet. I hadn't done the press conference yet."

He couldn't believe the reception. "I'd been in the league for over a decade already and it had never happened like that. I'm not a person they see all the time," he said with a shrug, admitting that the life of the role player is often about fading into the background—right until they're needed. He liked what that first shout-out portended. "That means they heard the news. That means they're on it. That means they're attached and they're paying attention to what's going on."

It was symptomatic of the fan base. Die-hards who weren't afraid to stand outside during a Canadian winter to cheer on their team. Devotees willing to drive the eight hours to Indiana to root for their guys. Hoops addicts who treated every new player like family the day—or even first ten minutes after—they arrived. That devotion came from a place of not blind faith but clear-eyed optimism. The fans were hungry to win—and with good reason. "It was the energy of the city, because they knew where the team was headed. They were knocking on that door. It might not have happened the way they thought it was going to happen, but they knew what was coming."

From Miles's vantage point, all signs pointed in the right direction. It was a skilled team that had consistently won year after year, built around a dedicated organization, with top-tier coaching and canny management not afraid to take risks. Personally, too, things were looking up for Miles, with his wife, Lauren, pregnant with their first child. It was going to be his year, both individually *and* collectively.

Then things started to go off the rails.

Raised in Dallas, Miles had made his offseason home near San Antonio. His parents, Calvin Sr. and Lanis, were driving with his younger sister, Andrea, to CJ and Lauren's house for a baby shower. Along the way, his parents got into a multi-car accident with a tractor trailer. "It was a *really* bad accident. My sister took a pretty good hit in the back seat and had some back and neck stuff. My mom was banged up a little bit, but mostly just terrified. My dad got the worst thing with his wrist, because he tried to hold on to the steering wheel. There was a drop-off off the road, and he was trying to make sure that the car didn't go over. My dad had to be put in a helicopter."

Luckily his family members survived the crash. "My parents are still both with us, together, getting on each other's nerves." Miles can laugh today, but at the time it was just one more strain to add to a growing list. He was about to join a new team, with a real chance to win, and he wanted to contribute to that success. His imminent fatherhood was also taking a toll. "While this is going on, Lauren's belly is getting bigger. I'm about to be responsible for a human. That weighs more than anything. I love my job, I love to play basketball, and I love the fans. But I was about to have my first kid—that's my first thought."

After his arrival in British Columbia for Raptors camp, the pressure started to manifest itself in surprising ways, including a massive oral abscess. "I thought I had something going on, maybe a wisdom tooth. I kid you not, I didn't feel anything. Then, during camp, I woke up one morning with a golf ball on the side of my face. I looked in the mirror, praying that it was going to go away."

The abscess eventually required two surgeries. "I had the first one when they scraped it out so I could scrimmage at camp." A second surgery soon followed—"They had to slice open my mouth and basically dig it out"—which led to stitches and a bracket that he had to play with for weeks. "The doctors think it was literally from the stress of everything that had happened—being worried about my wife, my kid, my dad. They told me that it could have killed me." At the same time, Miles was grateful for the intervention. "Honestly, I'm glad. If it had been smaller, I might not have said anything."

Things were finally getting back on track. Later in November, Lauren gave birth in Toronto to a healthy girl, Ava Reneé Miles. But Miles's preseason training had been interrupted again and again, and physically he just wasn't ready for the 2017–18 campaign. "I got there not in the shape that I wanted. It was a punch in the gut right before what I felt was about to be one of the biggest seasons of my career. I kept feeling like I was *never* going to get my feet on the ground."

Early on, though, everything seemed all right. In the team's first contest, a win at home against the Bulls, Miles played even better than his billing. In 20 minutes off the bench, he grabbed 5 rebounds and scored 22 points on efficient shooting. Maybe CJ Miles, newly rechristened CJ Kilometers, was going to work out just fine in Toronto, despite the behind-the-scenes tumult.

But the strain eventually affected his play. Miles was not allowing his spots and shots to come to him. Instead he was pushing for looks and opportunities, something formerly unknown to the patient bench player. "That was the first year that I did not surrender to the game. I was going to *force* it. I had never had to do that because I'm a basketball player: I would be on the floor and the game would tell me what to do, and I decided I was going to tell the game, so I shot badly." Those consequences were part of a vicious cycle. "At that point in my career, I had played so much basketball. There was no reason for me to have that type of anxiety going into the game. Why did I feel like I had something to prove? During the year, I would have these really good stretches and then something would happen."

As a role player, Miles knew how to adapt. To do what was asked of him. To play new roles. To fill gaps. It was that mentality that allowed him to regroup that season. "I started dealing with it in sections: 'All right, the last three, four, or five games, where are we at? What are the shots we missed? How are we shooting it?'"

Slowly but surely, Miles returned to his old self, playing in 70 games that season and averaging 19 minutes off the bench and 10 points per game. His bits-and-pieces system had worked. "That's what led me to be ready for the playoffs that year, just arcing at the right time, right before the season ended."

Miles came into the NBA alongside a raft of players straight out of high school, including Lou Williams and Amir Johnson, who also found themselves on the Raptors before Miles's time. The NBA beckoned the eighteen-year-old prodigy, but it was hard to imagine this game he loved as a career. "I was very good at being in the moment when I was a kid. I was so into playing that, as long as I could play basketball, everything else was easy. I was a hooper. That was it. If I wasn't sleeping or eating, then I was playing, even breaking into my high school gym, just to keep shooting."

When he was growing up, Miles's parents had often protected him and his siblings from financial hardships, so any NBA dreams he had involved feats on the court, not showing off luxury cars and fifteen-bathroom mansions. "My parents never let the financial woes bleed over into life. I didn't carry that concern into the decision to go to the NBA. I never played and was like, *Ooh, this is going to get me a Ferrari.* Those two things never went together for me—I just wasn't materialistic—until I got in the league and I was playing with guys who had Ferraris."

In 2005, Miles passed on an offer to play at the University of Texas and was drafted 34th overall by the Jazz. Suddenly the wide-eyed kid from Texas was working *as an NBA player*, and time was flying past. "It was a whirlwind after that. You get drafted. Next thing it's Summer League. I was the youngest guy on my team for three years, even after the draft. Next thing, I'm five years in."

Miles would spend the first seven years of his career in Salt Lake City, mostly coming off the bench, except during his fourth season, when he started and played in 72 games. Along the way, he would develop into a reliable small wing, someone who could be depended on to play 20 minutes, bag 10 points, play some defense, and generally spread the floor. Finding his spot was critical, both to his success and the team's. When players fail to recognize their specific role, Miles explains, "the whole ship's gonna sink. Even if you have to relinquish some opportunities, some guys can't. They can only see themselves as alpha all the time. You got to be prepared to *not* get recognized for the role you play." His less vaunted status suited him just fine. "I'm the first *second* option," he says with a laugh.

Along the way, he simply learned to do what his team—and, in fact, every team—needed. "I'm an observant person. I learned how to be who I was—just somebody who tried to see the game in its totality." In Utah, it was all about deferring to the team's headline talent. "You learn to play with two All-Star guys, Deron Williams and Carlos Boozer, and older guys, like Andrei Kirilenko. I noticed the way I was seen through the eyes of my coaches and the front office, and the effect that I had."

That malleability was also his ticket to court time. "I wasn't a shooter when I came in the league. I was an athletic scorer and a ball-handling wing, and I played point guard a lot until I got to the NBA. Then you start looking around. It's simple: Do you want to be in the NBA or do you want to fight for Deron Williams's position, the number three pick? Do you want to fight for Andrei Kirilenko's position? If you provide a service, and if your team wins, then you'll play. The rest of the stuff will take care of itself."

After seven seasons in Utah, Miles decamped to Cleveland for the 2012–13 season. Two years later, Miles left for Indiana, where he played for three seasons on a stacked Pacers team, again cultivating his complementary role. "I was with Paul George, George Hill, David West, and Roy Hibbert, on a team that was already number one in the East. They don't need me to come in and take the steering wheel. They need somebody to help throw the water out the boat. I needed to figure out where my spot was." That's exactly what happened during his second season in Indiana, in 2015–16, when he was asked to play up in the lineup. "They're like, 'Yo, we want you to try to play small forward,' after you spent a whole year training to be a two." He did as he was asked.

Again and again throughout his career, Miles saw the same thing: If you're not the face of the team, then your job is to identify gaps and fill them, no matter how thanklessly. "If I dropped you off in some strange village and you just tried to run it on day one, they'd kill you," he says. "There are customs. You don't know anything. There are guys who've been there for four, six, eight, nine years; there's that guy that makes forty-five million that's been an All-Star six times."

Keeping a level head also meant filtering out the noise, especially the misguided faux-confidence of one's entourage. "Everybody thinks their son, their brother, or their friend is special. They'll look at their guy blindly and be like, 'You could *definitely* take LeBron's spot.' I don't care how bad he's playing right now. It's not changing. We all know it's about opportunity most of the time, not a lack of talent. Understanding who you are and what you really want from this. I want to play. I want to help my team. That was my one goal." That self-sacrifice would then lead to opportunities. "Some nights, this guy's down or this guy doesn't got it. Then it's your day, and I always made sure I was prepared for that."

Miles embraced his role, something that kept him in the league for 17 seasons. "When I got asked to do all those different things, it got to a point where I learned to get excited about it. Because it was something else I had to learn." In turn, he attempted to mentor players who were struggling to identify their place on a team. "I remember having conversations with a young guy. I said that he should be watching P. J. Tucker and he took offense. PJ has played for a long time, made a lot of money, and won a lot of games," Miles said with a pause. "And this kid's not in the league no more."

In his first decade-plus in the NBA, Miles was never once traded. As master of his own destiny, he chose where he wanted to land. In 2017, the Raptors made the most sense as his next destination. "Toronto was a good team and we knew the talent we were dealing with. I was just turning thirty, I'd been in the league twelve years, and I was not going to play forever. I wanted to spend the latter part of my career winning."

Miles quickly found his role with the Raptors, becoming the old head to a second-unit of hungry, homegrown talents, including Fred VanVleet, Delon Wright, Pascal Siakam, Jakob Poeltl, and Norman Powell. The group was soon known as the "Bench Mob" for its efficient scoring and tenacious defense. "Everybody saw us the same way because we all wanted the same thing. We all wanted to play. We all wanted to win."

The Bench Mob was integral to the Raptors' success. The team went a franchise-best 59-23 en route to the playoffs for the fifth straight time. After disposing of the Washington Wizards, during which Miles shot an efficient .425/.387/.909 off the bench, the Raptors once again faced LeBron James and the Cavaliers. The series ended the same way as the past two postseasons, with the Raptors' title run derailed by the Cavs.

The loss rubbed Miles the wrong way—just one more disappointment in a season of frustrations. He wasn't going to let it happen again in his second year with the team. "At training camp I was confident and ready. I was in the best shape of my life. I was hell-bent on the second season being the season that the first season should have been. But the second year didn't start off well and I was exhausted mentally and spiritually from a year and a half of just fighting and fighting. The team was right there—they could win a championship—before I arrived, and they saw me as a piece of the puzzle to get across the finish line. That year, though, it just didn't work out. I was struggling."

By the 2019 trade deadline, the Raptors were 39-16. Masai Ujiri decided to gamble again, doubling down on the bet he had made in the 2018 offseason, when he had exchanged the face of the team, DeMar DeRozan, and Jakob Poeltl for Kawhi Leonard and Danny Green. That move had paid off. That same day, on February 7, 2019, the Raptors sent Miles, along with Jonas Valančiūnas and Delon Wright, to the Grizzlies for Marc Gasol. It was the first time Miles had ever been traded in his nearly 14-year career.

The trade, from his view, entailed a cruel irony: They were shipping out one veteran leader for another. "It was really, I think, one of those things that was about Marc's mind more than it was about his playing. JV was, obviously, really good. It was more about what Marc would add: another set of eyes from someone who has been some places and done some things."

Miles also understood his role in the trade. Sure, the NBA is a business—or so goes the cliché—but another cliché was equally true: Teams are in it to win it. It's hard to quibble today about Ujiri's final move in that season. "When I got traded, there was a little sting, but I understood it. They were trying to win a championship. It also let me know that my eye was right, because I really felt that team was going to win the championship that year."

The strain, the challenges, the trade: None of it in the end affected Miles's love of the team, his teammates, the organization, the fans, or the city. "It really was a good group of guys, man. I wish I could be a fly on the wall every time guys from that group run into each other. Just to witness the warmth, the good memories." That camaraderie was essential to the team's success in Miles's view. It permitted them to push past mistakes and to correct errors on court. "That team was very special, just super high-character guys, and everybody dealt with our differences like brothers. We had our days where we didn't like each other, but that let me know that you cared about what was going on. And how it was received let you know if a guy was being honest. Then it's not an argument. That's just trying to figure it out."

What the strain, the challenges, and the trade did provide, however, was an opportunity for personal growth. "This is another reason why my time in Toronto was so valued to me as a man. That year taught me a lot about myself. Not just for my daughter, Ava, but for what it taught me: who I was as a man. I don't know if I'd have gotten through that season two years before. That's what Toronto meant to me. Toronto made sure I was straight."

Years later, he can't help but think back to that first day in Toronto and that fan calling out to him on the street. "It's just love, man.

From the day I got there, they embraced me as a player and as a person. They treated me like I was Canadian, and they still do. People talk to me like I was there for five years. That's cool, because it lets me know that I gave something that was worth talking about. We exchanged inspirations, because they did a lot for me too. That is one of the greatest years of my life. Toronto is tattooed on my heart."

27

Danny Green (2018–2019)

Life in the San Antonio system had been good to Danny Green, though early on in his career, the three-and-D wing had struggled to find a steady spot on an NBA roster. A four-year player out of the University of North Carolina, Green had closed his Tar Heels career on a high note, winning the NCAA men's basketball championship. Just a few months later, in the summer of 2009, he was drafted 46th overall by Cleveland. But Green played only 20 games off the bench for the Cavs that season, spending a solid chunk of his time bouncing between Cleveland and the team's G League affiliate, the Erie BayHawks.

Then, just a week before the start of the next season, Green was waived. He eventually found a home in San Antonio, only to spend another year shuttling between the Spurs and another G League squad. There simply weren't a lot of spare minutes on the floor with a roster featuring Tim Duncan, Manu Ginóbili, and Tony Parker. The Spurs nonetheless liked what they saw in the young wing, eventually signing him for the remainder of the year.

In his third season, in 2011–12, Green broke out, starting 38 of 66 games. He even garnered votes for Most Improved Player while logging significant minutes as a starter in the team's run to the Conference Finals. From then on, Green was a staple of the Spurs' starting lineup, a versatile wing who could spread the floor and guard multiple positions, even helping the Spurs to claim the 2014 championship against LeBron James's Heat.

By the close of the 2017–18 season, San Antonio was in good but less certain shape. On paper, the team had finished strong, an impressive 47-35. But the West was stacked, and the Spurs finished only seventh in the conference, before being unceremoniously bounced in the first round by the Curry–Durant Warriors.

Even more troubling were the team's ongoing issues with their young star, Kawhi Leonard. He managed to play in only 9 games that season, hampered by a difficult-to-diagnose quadriceps injury. As the season wore on, Kawhi's absence from the team was increasingly felt, and his reticence left much of the NBA in the dark—even his teammates. "I just remember that whole year not knowing what was happening," Green told us. "If he was going to stay; if they're going to move him."

Green had his doubts that the Spurs would move on from Leonard, given his on-court impact and his stated desire to land in only a few spots. "I don't think people realize how valuable he really was," Green reflects now. "He won Finals MVP. He was an up-and-coming star. He's one of the best two-way players in the game, in the history of the game, and was probably the best two-way player at the time in the league. I didn't think a deal was gonna happen."

As the rumors swirled, Kawhi's name kept getting tossed around, all the way into the summer of 2018. "Everybody wanted him, but it was naive of me," Green said. "I thought they were gonna do a one-for-one for him or for a couple people in return and some picks." With summer upon him, Green was already looking ahead to his next season in San Antonio. "I guess I'm not going anywhere," he remembers thinking at the time, "because they would have wanted to trade me by now." Moreover, Green had been kept in the loop. "The Spurs always had told me if something was happening, 'We might have to put you in this deal.'"

Then came the surprise, on July 18, 2018. "One of my homies

texted me, 'I think you were in a trade.'" Shortly after came the call from Gregg Popovich, confirming that he had been moved with Leonard. "Pops was emotional. He wasn't happy about it, and he just told me, 'This is the part of the business that we hate. It sucks, but we made a trade.'"

"I was shocked," Green remembers. But then, almost as quickly, he looked to the future. "I was like, 'Damn, where am I going?'" Pop broke the news that Green was now a Raptor. (In exchange, Toronto had sent their own star, DeMar DeRozan, with Jakob Poeltl and a first-round draft pick.) For Green, it was the right answer. "Every player that you talk to loves Toronto and the energy there." Even still, it was a "bittersweet moment," he recalls. "I'm saying goodbye to home, but I'm welcoming a new place where I love visiting."

Toronto also had more to offer than just a good vibe and a raucous crowd. The Raptors had finished first in the Eastern Conference in 2018, going a dominant 59-23. "These guys were a top team in the East last year," Green remembers thinking. "They got some good players. We got a shot to do some special things."

He knew, moreover, that he could play an important role in the team's success. "Back then, I automatically assumed I was going to play. 'I'm not sure if I'm gonna start, but I know I'm gonna play, and I'm gonna be impactful regardless.'" Even still, doubts crept in. "'What if it doesn't work out?' I've only played in the Spurs system. 'Am I able to perform at the same level?' Are people gonna say, 'Oh, he's just role-playing in San Antonio's system?' Or: 'Are me and Kawhi able to win without Pop or outside of San Antonio?'"

Luckily, he had the summer to prepare. Green went back to the drawing board, honing his shot and working on his conditioning before arriving for training camp. Almost immediately, he saw the Raptors' promise. As the season progressed, it only looked better and better. "I wouldn't say there was an aha moment. But there were moments where it was like, 'Okay, we're making good strides. We have the potential.'"

Potential was one thing. But Green also knew from his experiences in San Antonio that it took more than just a bunch of promise and a raft of talent to survive an 82-game season and an arduous run to the Finals. "There's always a little bit of luck that comes into play with every championship team." He, and Kawhi, had seen firsthand that luck was often a euphemism for health. "We were playing well, but we needed to stay healthy. But to stay one hundred percent healthy throughout the whole playoffs? That takes some luck too."

Soon his earlier doubts about contributing vanished. Green was slotted into the starting lineup, a spot he never relinquished during his 80 games that season. But he was surprised to find out his role had changed. Green was still expected to D-up the league's premium wings, spread the floor, and hit corner threes—all things he did that season with casual aplomb, shooting a career-best 45.5 percent from beyond the arc. The surprise was something else. He was also, now, a seasoned vet. "It was very different in San Antonio, because me and Kawhi were the younger guys. We weren't the guys giving advice. During the season, we were listening to Timmy, Tony, Manu, Boris Diaw, all those guys."

In Toronto, both Leonard and Green had been promoted to mentors and leaders. "Now, *we* gotta teach these younger guys, keep them levelheaded, or get them to understand how to focus on the bigger picture. At that point, me and Kawhi had been through so many regular seasons. We knew we were playing for April, May, and June."

The Raptors already knew the heartbreak of playoff losses. During LeBron's second run in Cleveland, the Cavs knocked the Raptors out of the playoffs repeatedly. Green saw an all-too-familiar pattern playing out. He had gone to the playoffs all seven of the years he spent with San Antonio, but the team had only won one championship. It wasn't enough for the Raptors to show up during the regular season. "We're beating Bron or Giannis, but it doesn't mean in the playoffs that it won't be different. Toronto beat LeBron a bunch of times in the regular season when he was in Cleveland, but in the playoffs, they just couldn't figure it out."

With his new leadership role, Green came to appreciate how much he had learned under his own vets and coaches. "Now I see why Timmy, Tony, Manu, and Pop did things in certain ways. It's like, 'All right, we got to keep steady. Don't be satisfied. Don't be fat and happy, even if we win a series. That doesn't mean anything.' I was able to lead in Toronto because I went through so many battles and playoff series with those guys in San Antonio."

Green's experience came in handy, not least when the Raptors found themselves down two games to Giannis Antetokounmpo and the Bucks in the 2019 Eastern Conference Finals. Leonard, as usual, was unfazed. "He didn't waver or get worried," Green remembers, as he watched the often taciturn star pep a deflated Raptors squad up. "It's part of the season. Any game a whole series can turn around. 'Don't get discouraged. Don't be concerned.'" Leonard's quiet confidence also carried weight with his teammates. "He didn't speak often, but when Kawhi speaks, people listen. 'Stay positive and embrace this feeling. Good, bad, ugly.' Throughout the whole season, we tried to tell them that."

The Raptors eventually rallied against the Bucks, pulling out three wins to put them at home for a decisive sixth game. But staying focused meant keeping even those critical victories in context. In an interview with Zach Lowe years later, Nick Nurse recounted how he had tried to calm the Raptors after their game-five win. Nurse began to explain to the team that he had been in a similar situation in the 2011 D-League Finals with the Iowa Energy. "In the D-League?" Leonard asked, interrupting his coach. "I'm done listening to this story." Nurse can laugh about it now, but at the time it was testament to just how much high-level playoff experience both Leonard and Green had brought to Toronto. When they talked about playoff battles, the cast of characters was more *NBA Jam* than D-League grit-and-grind: LeBron's Heatles, Chris Paul and Blake Griffin's Lob-City

Clippers, Kevin Durant and Russell Westbrook's run-and-gun Thunder, Curry and Durant's Super-Death-Lineup Warriors. They had not only battled year after year in the playoffs; they had gone head-to-head with generational superstars.

Now Green, Leonard, and the Raptors were facing one of the era's greatest dynasties in the Finals, though the Warriors entered the series without Durant, who was nursing a right calf strain. The Raptors took the first game at home, 118–109, despite a 34-point barrage from Curry. And they did it through a team effort. Leonard dropped 23; Kyle Lowry dished 9 assists; Marc Gasol hit 20 points; Pascal Siakam offered a clinic in efficiency, scoring 32 points and hitting 14 of his 17 shots; even Fred VanVleet came off the bench to score 15. For Green, too, it was a redemption series. He had struggled in the first two rounds against the Magic and the 76ers, before going ice cold against the Bucks. "Life of a shooter," he says with a shrug today. How good it felt, then, to hit the Raptors' first bucket against the Warriors, a deep three that led to an efficient 11-point game for Green.

The second game at Scotiabank Arena went less to plan. Despite a 34-point and 14-rebound performance by Leonard, Toronto shot poorly from the floor, losing 109–104. Heading to Oracle Arena against the defending champs, the Raptors were exploring terra incognita. Nurse tried to steady his guys, telling them in the locker room after the loss that the Raptors only needed to win one of the two games in Oakland. "Fuck that," Leonard responded. "Let's get them both." For Green, Leonard's nonchalant confidence echoed lessons that had been drilled into them as Spurs. Whenever they had fallen behind in a series, Coach Pop said the same thing. "The mentality in San Antonio was 'We're not stealing anything; we're going in to take two.' The first time that I can recall Pop saying this, we were playing Miami." If it worked for the Spurs and against the LeBron–Wade–Bosh Heat, then Pop's advice might also work for Raptors. Just as Leonard commanded, Toronto went into Oakland and decisively took both games, 123–109 and 105–92.

In the end—as every Raptors fan well knows—Toronto won the Finals in six games. After almost twenty-five years of building and rebuilding, of trades and draft picks, of struggle, sweat, and tears, the Raptors, finally, were NBA champions. Even for Green and Leonard, who collected Finals MVP, it was special. "Every time you get in that moment, you think, *I'm going to cherish this one, because I may not ever experience it again.*"

There was only one thing left to do: celebrate. And celebrate they did—along with the whole city of Toronto and all of Canada. Never had the Raptors' motto of "We the North" resonated more powerfully.

On June 17, Toronto was transformed into one giant party, with upwards of two million fans taking part. At 10 a.m., open-air double-decker buses carrying the team and the Larry O'Brien Trophy made their snail's crawl across the city. They were supposed to finish some two and a half hours later at Nathan Phillips Square for a rally. If only. With millions lining the streets, the procession crept through the city, going hours over schedule. "I wasn't expecting it to be that long," Green recalls with a laugh. "I don't think anybody else did either, because we were in the sun for a while. It got warm, people were drinking. Marc ended up drinking more than he expected! By the time we got to the stage, guys were fried. It was an exhausting celebration—standing up, spraying champagne. It was a workout, but it was a lot of fun. That was probably the best celebration I had that whole summer." Toronto's mayor, John Tory, even declared June 17 "We the North Day" to commemorate the championship and the unity it had inspired among Canadians.

Green kept the party going, savoring every moment. "We went to Winnipeg and Halifax and Ottawa and Vancouver. We had a hell of a summer." He also knew how hard it was just to make the Finals, let alone win. He recalls thinking, *I might never experience this again, and this might be the best time of my life.* "I took it for granted being in the Finals two times before. The best one we had was in Toronto.

I thought, *I'm gonna take full advantage and celebrate this to the end.*" Little did Green know that he would be raising the Larry O'Brien Trophy the following season. Just a few weeks after the parade, Green signed as a free agent with the Lakers, who would go on to win the 2020 championship. From LA he went to the Thunder and on to the 76ers, Grizzlies, and Cavs, and back to Philadelphia, before retiring during the 2024 offseason.

For Green, his time with the Raptors remains a gem in his decorated career. "One of the best years of my life. Basketball-wise, probably the best year of my career. Looking back, I wouldn't have it any other way. The city left an unbelievable mark on me. The people were friendly and warm. The organization was very open. It was a family thing. That team will never be forgotten." Unsurprisingly, he is still grateful for that one season as a Raptor. "Whenever and wherever fans see me, they show so much love. Whenever you win one there, it's mutual on both sides. It's always a city that I see as a home."

28

Norman Powell (2015–2021)

During his almost six-year run as a Raptor, Norman Powell was a human highlight machine. Whether coming off the bench or starting at a moment's notice, Powell was often good for a show. Just ask Raptors fans, who can still reel off his signature moments today.

Think of his game-four heroics during the opening round of the 2017 playoffs. After Toronto had gone down 2–1 to Milwaukee, Powell was inserted into the starting lineup. There he rose to the occasion, dropping 25 points on 8-of-11 shooting and going a perfect 4-of-4 from three, en route to a Raptors win and a six-game series victory.

Powell extended his solid play in his third season in 2017–18. Alongside CJ Miles, Fred VanVleet, Delon Wright, Pascal Siakam, and Jakob Poeltl, Powell was a fluid member of the Bench Mob, an interchangeable wrecking crew that helped push the Raptors to a 59–23 finish.

Others will point to his key role during the Raptors' run to the championship in 2019. Throughout the playoffs, and especially against the Magic, Sixers, and Bucks, Powell led the team from the bench—becoming the team's go-to safety valve—offering timely scoring and relentless energy on defense.

The next postseason it was more of the same, when Powell put on a 23-point shooting expo off the bench in a 38-minute, game-six double-overtime win against the Celtics. He capped off the show in the final moments of the game, first driving to the rim for an and-one layup before hitting two free throws to seal the win with only five seconds left.

What almost all Raptors fans will recall, however, is the emergence of "Playoff Norm" years earlier, during his rookie campaign in 2015–16. Throughout the season, Powell had shuttled between the Raptors and Raptors 905, the team's G League affiliate, often only getting an opportunity to play when injuries took out DeMarre Carroll or Terrence Ross. Despite the inconsistent court time, Powell appeared in 49 games that season, starting 24 of them.

By the playoffs he was a confident first-year player, willing to take on any role asked of him, but he remained an unknown quantity. Any lingering doubts about the rookie evaporated in Toronto's opening-round series against Indiana, when Powell came off the bench, proving a clutch scorer and physical defender particularly against Paul George. That, in any case, is what Jonas Valančiūnas remembers. "Norm was *huge* in that series," Valančiūnas told us. "He's built tough—ain't no soft kid—so he could bring that physicality to PG."

That dirty-work attitude is also what Powell remembers from the series rather than the points he scored. As he told us, "I knew I could hang with him, so I wasn't going to shy away. I said, '*I'm* guarding Paul George. Don't worry about it.' 'PG, I'm guarding you and picking you up ninety-four feet. You're going to feel my presence.'"

Those Indiana games cemented his reputation as a clutch postseason performer and even earned him a new nickname: Playoff Norm. But Powell's rise as a key bench player, a versatile starter, a tenacious defender, and a staple of the Raptors' rotation was hardly guaranteed before his rookie season started.

A year earlier, in fact, scout after scout had expressed their skepticism about Powell. "The knock on me was that I was a four-year college player; I couldn't shoot and I didn't have the ability to score," Powell recalled—an unbelievable report for a player today with a 40 percent career three-point average, per-game scoring that has routinely hovered in the high teens and low twenties, and a career-best 21.8 points per game for the 2024–25 season.

No matter what scouts said about him as a college player, Powell knew his game would translate to the pros. "Once you open up the floor and allow more movement with guys actually having to rotate, rather than a big man sitting in the paint, I had the versatility and craftiness to score." Only one question, in fact, remained: whether NBA front offices were willing to take a risk on the four-year guard out of UCLA.

As a senior at UCLA, Powell had led the Bruins in scoring and was named first-team All-Pac-12, helping to lead the squad to a Sweet 16 finish in the NCAA tournament. Even still, by the time draft night rolled around in 2015, scouts still didn't know where to slot him. *Sports Illustrated* had Powell going early in the second round. Other mock boards pegged him as a late second-round pick. Some even left him off their big boards altogether.

Powell, though, was optimistic about his NBA future. "Honestly, I was pretty confident," he recalled thinking. "There was a lot of buzz from talking to people around the league. I thought that I was going to go mid to late first round or early second round."

He had good reason to be confident. Powell had worked out with almost twenty teams, proving himself again and again in head-to-head competition against hallowed lottery picks. "I thought I did enough in those pre-draft workouts," he said, nodding to his future NBA home. "Toronto was the best workout I had—I killed it—and I knew Toronto had the twentieth pick."

No surprise then that spirits were high at the Fox Sports Grill in downtown San Diego, Powell's hometown, where he had assembled almost ninety family members, friends, coaches, and teammates for his draft party. But the mood slowly shifted as Powell's name went uncalled well into the first round. Even the Raptors passed on him with the 20th pick, opting instead for Delon Wright.

No worries, Powell recalled thinking, knowing he had smashed workout after workout. But as the draft chugged along, he grew more and more tense. "When my name didn't go in the first round, I was upset," Powell said. "And then my name didn't go in the first forty. I was not even really focused by then on who was on the board next. I was literally getting ready to walk out of my draft party. It just didn't make sense to me."

Powell tried to call his agent at the time, Todd Ramasar, to find out what was happening. "I was more embarrassed for myself," Powell remembers thinking. "You hear these horror stories about guys being promised something or guys being a sure thing, and then their name doesn't get called. I was like, *I do not want to be one of those players.* It was frustrating. I'm supercompetitive, and I felt like I was the second-best shooting guard on the board."

Then, as he waited on the phone, the 46th pick was called. "My high school coach told me that I got drafted. It happened in slow motion. I remember literally crying. Then I saw Milwaukee, but I didn't work out for Milwaukee, so I was confused." In no time, the truth came out: Powell had been rerouted to Toronto alongside a 2017 first-round pick (which would become OG Anunoby) for Greivis Vázquez.

Suddenly, everything made sense. Even better: It felt like destiny—at least according to Powell, and not only because of his strong workout weeks earlier. "That's when I got excited. It was an aha moment. It's like, 'Man, you've done everything that you need to and you've spoken it into existence.' I knew the feeling that I had when I first got to Toronto to work out and I was standing in Jurassic

Park. Now I'm speaking in hindsight, but when I was there, I knew it was exactly where I was supposed to be. I sit back now and think about how my life has gone, and there were so many tie-ins to Toronto without me really knowing it. There's a picture of me as a kid in a Raptors jersey from the Boys and Girls Club, and I was a Drake fan when he was on *Degrassi* and I was in high school. I was like, *It's Toronto and everything's making sense.*"

Powell was also excited to be moving to Canada, though he understands why so many of his fellow players, at least historically, didn't know what to make of the country to the north. "It's just the US ego," he explained to us. "We have a negative perspective as soon as things are different. It doesn't matter what it is—Canada, Mexico, Europe. If things are done differently, if the rules are different, if the laws are different, it's just not what we're used to. So from a player standpoint, we don't know nothing about Canada as a country—how it's run and how the people are. We're in a brand-new place, and it's foreign to us—bagged milk, things are spelled differently. We don't know anything and we don't know anybody."

For Powell, the "uncharted territory" of Canada was actually a benefit, a chance to reinvent himself as an NBA player in front of a new home crowd. But it was hardly an adventure without its challenges. "Those first couple days in Toronto, I didn't know where to go," he said. "I didn't even know where to eat. I was looking for something familiar. There was a Little Caesars across the street from my place. I was eating very American food in Toronto, 'cause I didn't know anything and I was nervous to venture out. I didn't want to get lost."

The surprises kept coming. "The financial side was real early on," he remembers. "I thought, *Oh man, I'll be making some money.* But I was a second-round pick, in Toronto and living in Cali, so I was getting taxed on both ends. I signed my contract and my first paycheck was literally less than what I got for my Pell Grant check when I was at college."

What to eat—and what he could afford—aside, Powell was thrilled to be a Raptor. "It was different, but I loved it," he recalled in an interview in 2023. "I loved being in Canada, not only Toronto, but being able to experience all of Canada—going to Vancouver, Edmonton, Montreal, Quebec. The people there were amazing and super supportive. I had a feeling that this is where I needed to be."

Still, as a second-round pick on a stacked roster, he had to put in real work to carve out a place for himself. "I knew the grind. You're starting from the floor again, so you're not going to be given anything. Delon was the twentieth pick, so he was their guy. They're probably going to feature him more, they're going to promote him, and he's going to get more opportunities. I had a checklist of what I was going to do to make sure that they saw me as a steal and that I should have been drafted higher. I was going to do whatever it took, whether it was practice, Summer League, or training camp, to show them that I'm better than Delon, that I'm better than T. Ross, and that I'm better than James Johnson."

That competitive edge had grown out of his own experiences and philosophy, something he calls "Understand the Grind," which later became the name of Powell's youth basketball camp and clothing line. "It started back in college," he explained. "One of my best friends, Terrance Morgan, came up with the slogan. Him and my boy Kevin Smith were like, 'Man, a lot of people don't understand the grind. They don't understand what it actually takes to be successful: the sacrifice and the commitment.' That was our mantra and something that we went back to whenever we were faced with difficult times."

It was a philosophy that served him well, giving him the confidence to take on elite talent—and even his hero, Dwyane Wade. "I thought, I'm here to take names, even guys like D-Wade. You're my favorite player and I modeled my game after you, but this is where I make my mark. I'm going to go at you. I'm gonna make sure that I'm not afraid of you."

He eventually got to test that theory in the second round of the 2016 playoffs, when the Raptors faced the Heat. "It's funny, because I later talked to D-Wade about that series, and he remembers when I checked into the game and was guarding him in the playoffs. He said, 'I was going to lick my chops with this rookie.' Then the first possession he tried to post me up and I bodied him and fouled him. He was like, *What the hell is wrong with this kid?*" It was all part of the birth of Playoff Norm, just one more signature moment in his rookie postseason. "I thought it was so cool," he laughs today.

Moreover, his competitive spirit was welcomed in the Raptors locker room, even if it meant teammates were competing against each other for minutes. "It wasn't a jealousy thing," Powell recalls. "It was more like, 'How do we all become successful?' It was more like pushing each other to get on the floor, pushing each other to reach our potential, and pushing each other to be great. It was just, 'Let's have the most fun we can have with this and make sure all of us are on top of what we need to do to be successful.'"

Unsurprisingly, though, it was sometimes uncomfortable to compete against guys who had become friends and even mentors. "As a rookie, I started getting playing time here and there, and then they said, 'We're starting you,' and I started playing over James Johnson. I felt really awkward," Powell admits today. "James was my first vet, my big brother, my mentor, and they're playing me over him in the small-forward spot. I went to him and was like, 'I'm so sorry. I didn't know that they were gonna start me.' He said, 'Man, I'll never be mad at you for doing what you're supposed to do. That's not your fault at all. That's on the coaches. There's enough out here for everybody, so I want you to continue to go out and do what you do. This is your opportunity and time to show who you are.'"

Johnson's advice was a learning moment for Powell, a chance to see how mutual competition made everyone better on the team. "That aspect of 'we're friends but I'm going at you when we're on the court' made it easier for me to understand that it's a business, but you also want your friends to have success."

In the summer of 2017, the Raptors extended Powell's three-year rookie contract. The four-year, $42 million deal was a massive payday for the second-round pick, who had never been guaranteed a place in the league, let alone a critical role on a winning team.

In total, Powell would spend almost six seasons in Toronto. It was just enough time to add one more highlight to his Raptors sizzle reel in a career-high 43-point game against the Pistons in March 2021. It proved a final memory for fans: the image of Powell showing out once more in a newer version of that same Raptors jersey he had worn as a child. Just a week after his performance against Detroit, Powell was traded to Portland in exchange for Gary Trent Jr. and Rodney Hood. He finished out the season with the Trail Blazers, who signed him to a five-year, $90 million contract in the offseason. The next year he was sent to the Clippers just before the 2022 trade deadline.

At the time of the trade to the Trail Blazers, the Raptors were mapping out a fresh trajectory. The team was in the midst of its first losing campaign in eight years. Toronto had entered a new era and was pivoting to the future. Even still, the trade hit Powell hard, something he related in an interview in 2023. "I didn't wanna leave Toronto, if I'm being dead serious," he admitted. "I wanted to stay. I always felt that the team that we had, the youth that we had, that core that we had, I thought we had something special."

Even still, Toronto will always be an essential part of his Hollywood-ready journey. "If you look at my story—my career from high school to college to the NBA—I wasn't supposed to be starting. Here comes this forty-sixth pick, four-year player, not getting any playing time, going to the D-League, having to showcase his stuff down there playing spare minutes," he said, shaking his head. Toronto, instead, was more serendipity than simple grind. "Timing is everything," he told us. "You got to have the right coaching, you got to have the right player, you got to have the right mindset. And I think the timing for me—coming to the Raptors and being with some of those other guys and with the coaching staff—it was perfect. That I ended up in Toronto was the icing on the cake."

29

Garrett Temple (2023–)

As an undrafted four-year player out of Louisiana State University, Garrett Temple knew what it meant to get knocked down and get back up. Take his first year in the NBA, in 2009–10, when he signed a seemingly never-ending succession of ten-day contracts. First it was with the Rockets for 9 games. Then the Kings for 5 contests. And finally the Spurs for 13 more. That last stint stuck—at least initially. Temple even started the final four games of the season, subbing in for George Hill and Tony Parker, and logged time during the playoffs.

Even still, by the start of his second year in the league, the twenty-four-year-old shooting guard had hit a wall. During Summer League, while still a Spur, Temple had dislocated his ankle. It was a nagging injury, and by the start of the season he had not yet bounced back. Three games in, while averaging just 0.7 points per contest, he got cut. "I didn't play well," Temple admitted to us. "Gregg Popovich is looking at me crying as he's cutting me two weeks into the regular season. But I knew it. I *should* be cut."

Once again, Temple was out of the NBA, bounced down to the G League and the Rio Grande Valley Vipers. His body was suffering. His game was suffering. And, on top of it all, he had just found out that his father, Collis Temple Jr., had been diagnosed with cancer. It was another blow. But the Temple family—and not just Garrett—had always known what it meant to struggle against the odds and yet succeed.

In 1955, his grandfather, Collis B. Temple, had applied to the master's program in agriculture at LSU only to have his application rejected. At the time, the university did not accept Black students. The civil rights lawyer, and later associate justice of the US Supreme Court, Thurgood Marshall, even tried to recruit Collis for a class-action suit, but the state legislature, fearing a fight (and perhaps anticipating a loss), decided to cover Collis's costs to attend Michigan State University, where he earned an advanced degree in agricultural economics (only in 1964 was LSU finally desegregated after a series of back-and-forths in the courts). Collis later returned to Louisiana, where he became an educator and administrator. Back home he married Garrett's future grandmother, Shirley, who had studied biology at the Tuskegee Institute.

Garrett's father picked up the torch where his own father had left off. A basketball and football star, Collis Jr. was one of the best athletes in Louisiana in the late 1960s. The state governor, John J. McKeithen, even recruited him to become the first Black basketball player at LSU and the first Black college athlete to compete in a big-four sport at the school. He was eventually named captain as the only Black player on the team during his stint in Baton Rouge, between 1971 and 1974. After graduating, he was selected 94th overall by the Phoenix Suns in the sixth round of the NBA Draft, before playing a single professional season with the San Antonio Spurs of the American Basketball Association.

Now, in the fall of 2010, Garrett was battling a bunk ankle in the G League after catching a few brief glimpses of the big time. But as he told us, considering the true challenges that his father, grandfather, and entire family had faced in Louisiana, fighting for a spot in the NBA was actually a pretty good deal. "I'm a very positive guy," he explained. “My family’s history and how I was raised has a lot to do with how I act today and my values.”

One of those values was simple: Keep grinding. And so he did. In the G League he was traded from the Vipers to the Erie BayHawks. He then earned a ten-day contract with Milwaukee, suiting up 9 games for the Bucks before going back down to the BayHawks. Then it was another call-up to the NBA, this time with Charlotte, where he played in 12 contests. Another season, another year burning through fountain pens on short-lived contracts.

In the summer following his second season, the 2011 NBA lockout started, lasting five long months. Temple decided to head to Italy, where he played for Novipiù Casale Monferrato on a one-year contract. When the lockout finally ended, Temple was eager to continue his NBA journey. But it was another tough lesson for the shooting guard. “That’s when I found out,” he explained, discovering another of the league’s unwritten rules: “Out of sight; out of mind.” Not sure what to do, Temple turned to his father. “My dad said, ‘You think you belong in the NBA?’ I said, ‘Hell yeah.’ He said, ‘You keep going then.’”

By his own account, Temple was never destined for the NBA. Sure, he was a highly ranked high school player in Louisiana, but he never featured at the top of anyone’s big board. He was simply a small backcourt player known more for facilitating and his dogged defense than the kinds of gaudy scoring numbers that perk up the ears of college and NBA scouts.

When he decided to attend LSU, he had big shoes to fill. “The LSU Tigers mean a lot to my dad and my family, with my dad being the first Black player and then my older brother, Collis III, playing there too. A lot of people really thought I went there just because I was a Temple, not necessarily because I was a good enough basketball player.”

Being a supposed legacy admission at LSU was just more wood on the fire of his ambition. Going into his second year in Baton Rouge, Temple knew exactly what he needed to do to prove his worth. "The assistant coaches, Butch Pierre and John Treloar, told me, 'You need to be the best defender on our team and shut down the best wing or guard that we play.' This was how I was going to make my mark, and that set me on a course to say, 'This is my niche.'" Temple proved a dynamo on the defensive end, eventually making the starting lineup as a freshman en route to a Final Four appearance in the 2006 NCAA tournament.

Having a role and understanding his place in the food chain actually made life easier for Temple. As he told us, "2006 set me on a path. A lot of players, if they're really good, then they grow up never understanding how to be *not* the best player on the team. I had some great mentors who explained to me, 'Don't try to be anybody you're not. Do what you're supposed to do.' I played the same role in 2006 as I played on most of the teams in the NBA. That's one thing about the NBA. You have to have those guys behind the guys—the glue guys—who are more times than not grinders. They've never been highly touted, they've never been heralded, and they're okay with being under the radar, because that's what they've been their whole life. It's even more of a chip on their shoulder, which is a great thing for a player."

Early on at LSU, Temple never thought about his NBA future. "Life postcollege was on my mind, but it didn't consume me. I wasn't playing to go to the NBA. At the end of the day, it's not 1985 or 1990, when defense wins championships. You needed to put points on the board." In any case, he knew who he was. "When I left LSU," he says beaming, "I had some of the most minutes played in the history of the school. I always wanted to graduate. Nobody, not once, came in my ear and said, 'You could get drafted.' I'm glad they didn't, because I wouldn't have been ready."

Temple finally wrapped up his senior season in Baton Rouge in

2009. Strangely enough, it was his defensive chops that accidentally got Temple one step closer to the NBA. "A lot of teams brought me in to defend guys from that draft class during workouts, like Steph Curry, Ty Lawson, Danny Green, and DeMar DeRozan." Soon Temple was the go-to defender to test out future All-Star guards and championship wings. Doing so made it crystal clear to teams whether these skilled college players could handle the physicality of the NBA. It also crystallized something for Temple. "After I had had eighteen workouts, I thought, *Maybe I* can *play in the NBA*."

Just as he had anticipated, though, Temple went undrafted. Even still, the guy called in to defend top guards in pre-draft workouts was soon being called in to guard those same guys in games. "I played in Summer League and with the Rockets at training camp, in preseason games, and in the G League. I gained a lot of confidence in my shot and got called up to the Rockets in February 2010 on two ten-day contracts. From then on, it was just a matter of finding a way to stick. I didn't have a family to worry about. I wasn't trying to make crazy money. It was cool: I was just playing out of my suitcase."

After the 2011 lockout ended, Temple eventually made it back from Italy. Once again it was the usual NBA roller coaster to start the 2012–13 season. First it was the Thunder for Summer League in Orlando, then the Cavaliers for Summer League in Las Vegas. Finally Miami signed Temple in September. Then, in late October, just days before the season started, he got a call from Heat coach Erik Spoelstra. "Spo cut me but said, 'We're going to try to figure out a way to get you back.'" Just days after being waived, Temple was back in the G League with the BayHawks. Just four days after that, he was traded to the Reno Bighorns.

In mid-December, he got a call from the Wizards, who wanted to work him out. The Bighorns had just played a double-overtime game in LA and were at Los Angeles International Airport boarding a flight back to Reno. By the time his plane touched down in Nevada, the Wizards had booked him a flight back to LA that would put him on a red-eye to DC. When he finally got to Washington for his workout, he found out there was actually competition for the spot. It was none other than Chris Quinn, an undrafted four-year player out of Notre Dame (who is today an assistant coach with the Heat). "It's the same guy who took my spot with the Spurs," Temple recalls with a laugh. "The Spurs also brought Chris in three days before San Antonio cut me. So I saw the writing on the wall." It was history repeating itself, Temple thought. He did the workout in Washington, but expected that, once again, he was going to be left flapping in the wind.

Temple headed back home to Louisiana for a holiday break with his family. Then an early Christmas present arrived. "I get a call on December twenty-third from the Wizards at ten o'clock at night: 'We'd love to sign you to a nonguaranteed deal.' That's a good thing. But the morning of the twenty-fourth, my agent, John Hamilton, calls me and he says, 'We talked to Miami and they also want to bring you back.' So at this point I have to decide."

It was no easy decision. The LeBron-led Heat were coming off a Finals win (and on their way to repeating), but the roster was stacked. The Wizards, conversely, were 3-22, with room at guard thanks to an injury to John Wall. As Temple weighed his options, Coach Spoelstra reached back out to him. "G, I'm gonna talk to you like a friend," Temple recalls the Miami coach saying. "I wanted you from the start. You have a chance to come back. Worst-case scenario, you go to DC. They've already cut two NBA-level point guards this season. Maybe you're just another guy that gets cut. But if you come to Miami, and you get cut here, at least people are thinking, *Miami brought him in. He* must *be something.* You're not gonna play in Miami; we got Mario Chalmers and Norris Cole ahead of you. But if there's an injury to one of them, you're playing deep into the playoffs." It was a tough call, but Temple knew what he had to do, telling Coach Spo, "I just gotta bet on myself. I have never actually had a chance to play. I'm going to DC."

On Christmas Day of 2012, Temple signed as a free agent with the Wizards, who re-signed him in the summer. "I signed a *one-year* guaranteed contract," Temple marvels, "and I was *ecstatic*, bro!" The Wizards then re-signed him on a multiyear deal in 2014. Hardly did it spell the end of his days moving from one team to another, but it gave Temple a taste of stability. It had also become clear around the league that he was the kind of even-keeled glue guy who could stabilize a locker room. From Washington he signed with the Kings in 2016, before being traded to the Grizzlies during the 2018 offseason. Before the 2019 trade deadline, he was sent to the Clippers and signed as a free agent with the Nets in the offseason.

The following year he signed as a free agent with the Bulls, who sent him in a sign-and-trade back home to Louisiana to play in New Orleans. When he was waived by the Pelicans in the 2023 offseason, he once again had a tough decision to make: whether to hunt for another team and contract, or call it a career, back home in Louisiana. Temple wasn't ready to call it quits, though, and signed a one-year deal with the Raptors in the summer of 2023.

Fifteen years. Twelve NBA teams. "I'm for sure a journeyman," Temple says, not flinching at the word. "I don't take it as a negative. At the end of the day, somebody wants you. I'm fine with the term. I'll tell you one thing: it's not easy to stay in the league for five years or ten years or fifteen years, whether it's with one team or with twenty."

Just to be in the NBA: *That's* the dream, Temple asserts. "I'm getting chills and goose bumps thinking about it. When I was in Miami working out one summer, Juwan Howard was in his seventeenth year, so they called him 'Seventeen.' He was walking in the gym, and I called out, 'What's up, Seventeen?' He said, 'Another day in paradise. You can't have a bad day in the NBA. We're living a dream in a fantasy world.'"

That's the gratefulness that Temple has always cultivated. "I credit my dad and my brother Elliott and my whole family for keeping it all in perspective," Temple reflects. "Who would have thought I'd be in the NBA this many years? There *are* no bad days. I've had two or three days where I'm ungrateful or something like that, which we all can be, but then I remind myself: *Wow. Can y'all believe we do this for a living? We play* basketball *for a living.* You got to pinch yourself sometimes."

It's that levelheadedness that has made Temple a quiet leader in the NBA. Since 2017, he has served as vice president of the National Basketball Players Association. His cool-headed reputation is just one of the products, he admits, of having bounced around the pros. "I got to see so many things by being on so many different teams. I've been able to take things with me. That has been very powerful."

His current stint with the Raptors is a good example of the type of veteran leader Temple has become. It was always a team that he had admired from afar. "We played against each other a lot when I was in Washington. They had a great home-court advantage for three reasons. First, it's a great city to go out in when you're in your mid-twenties." He laughs. "You only get to come once or twice a season, and a lot of times when we played in Toronto, it was at twelve o'clock on a Sunday. So Saturday, you're going out. And then you're playing, and you're like, 'Oh God, we're down by twenty-five after the first half?' That happened a lot. Second, the fans are amazing. I remember the 2015 playoffs, when I played against y'all on Washington. The atmosphere was crazy. I can also remember the fans outside the arena in 2019 during the championship game. And third, the Raptors were really big and defensively played so hard. They made you uncomfortable."

When Toronto became an option in 2023, it was not on the court, at least initially, that Darko Rajaković wanted to put him.

"Interestingly enough, I was offered a coaching job first by Darko. I had definitely never thought about coaching before."

Temple asked for some time to take in what Rajaković was saying. "I knew New Orleans wasn't going to bring me back, and they were looking for a trade partner for me. I had seen Darko before and shook his hand on the sidelines when he was an assistant coach with Memphis, but we had never had a conversation. Then I talked to some other guys and Masai Ujiri, who said, 'We want you in the organization.' He was basically saying, 'I hope you don't find a team, because we want you to come here,'" Temple laughs.

Ultimately, Temple wasn't ready to hang them up yet, and the Raptors were more than happy to sign the veteran guard. His leadership was what they wanted, on and off the court. Temple also felt he had more to offer, particularly as a mentor, if he could stay in uniform. "I really believe that I can still impart so much more from the player side. I've talked to a lot of guys that have transitioned to coaching and the one thing that they say, 'Play as long as you can, because once you become a coach, you have the exact same knowledge, but there is a difference between a player hearing it from you as a player versus that same player hearing it from you as a coach.'"

In Toronto, in any case, Temple has already assumed coachlike duties. "I love to play for a coach that thinks of me as a coach. They understand my value. That was the reason why I ended up coming to Toronto." His wife, Kára McCullough, also agreed, excited about the new opportunity. "My wife is an army brat, so she was happy. She was like, 'I'd *love* to be in Toronto.'" After Temple's one-year deal with the Raptors expired, the team was also eager to bring him back and re-signed him in the summer of 2024.

Life in Toronto and in Canada has lived up to both Kára's and his expectations. "My wife and I love it for our family, for ourselves, and for our kids. The multiculturalism is something that I love, especially raising kids here and for them to be able to see different cultures. And the fans—the fans just *love* this game and their Raptors, and they're across the country. One of the best things about this city is that it feels like a community."

Since arriving, Temple has also slid into his unofficial coaching role, playing the canny vet to a core of young players. "Garrett's one of the most selfless dudes out there and I really trust him," Gradey Dick told us. "My two older brothers helped to raise me with my parents, so it was tough when I first got to Toronto. It's a different role with Garrett, because he's a mixture of a brother and a dad. He's at the age now where I could basically be his son," Dick joked.

Temple has also proven a mentor to the Raptors' young star Scottie Barnes. As Barnes told the media at the end of Temple's first season in Toronto, "Sitting next to Garrett Temple, picking his mind, and watching the way he handles things as a leader—how he gets out there on the floor and plays so hard and so passionately—just seeing the type of vet he is and how he just doesn't take things for granted helps me."

Temple, in turn, is happy to play both coach and mentor, knowing what these young players might mean for the future. "The organization has done a great job of getting guys around the same age to complement each other on the team. With that core group going forward, I definitely think that it's sooner than the NBA believes that Toronto can be back in contention in the East."

30

RJ Barrett (2023–)

Growing up, RJ Barrett got to watch a pro, day in, day out—somebody who could model the work ethic and commitment that a life at the highest level in sports demanded. That pro was his own father, Rowan Barrett. Born in Toronto in 1972, the combination shooting guard–small forward played at West Hill Collegiate Institute in his hometown before attending St. John's University in New York City between 1992 and 1996.

Though undrafted, Rowan carved out a decade-long career overseas, with stops in Spain, Argentina, Venezuela, Cyprus, Greece, France, Italy, and Israel, where he led the Israel Basketball Premier League in scoring in 2002, averaging 25.5 points per game. During all those years abroad, he always kept a close connection to Canada, returning each summer to the Greater Toronto Area to spend time with his family, especially after his son, Rowan Jr.—or RJ, as he is known today across the NBA—was born in Toronto in 2000.

Rowan's connection to Canada was in fact a constant in a career defined by change. He even had several stints playing for the Canadian Men's National Team, including in the 1998 FIBA world championship, the 2000 Summer Olympic Games, and the 2002 FIBA world championship. For RJ, his father's connections to Team Canada helped to forge a bond with a country he often only saw during holidays. It was also something for RJ to strive for. "At my home in Canada, my dad had his Olympic jersey framed on the wall," Barrett told us, "so I'm walking by that every day. It was just one of those motivations from early on."

It was during the Barrett family's time in Italy, between 2005 and 2006, that Rowan began to model the life of a pro for his five-year-old son. "We lived right across the street from the arena," Barrett recalled. "I remember watching my dad go to work every day. I had a little basketball and I would dribble around and pretend that I was dunking all the time." Watching his dad hoop also inspired him. "It is one of my first memories: There was one game when my dad hit a crazy shot—a fading three from the corner—to tie it and send it to overtime. I remember jumping up and down on the chairs in the arena. That's definitely where the love for basketball started."

Still, Barrett's father, having moved his family again and again across Europe, the Middle East, and South America, was hesitant to have his son embark on that same path. "He actually didn't want me to play when I was younger, because he understood how hard it was. I had to push my dad to coach me." His mother, Kesha Barrett (née Duhaney), herself a successful college athlete as a sprinter and long jumper at St. John's, where she met Rowan, became RJ's advocate. "I remember my mom actually telling him, 'It's a crime if you don't teach your son! He *wants* to play; he *wants* to learn. You got to teach him!' She tricked him into coaching me," Barrett says warmly today.

Eventually, Rowan would retire. It was a jarring transition, the decision being made quickly one summer, while the family was back in Mississauga, a suburb of Toronto, where they had bought a home and spent the offseason. "My dad was thirty-six and I was eight. My dad was actually supposed to go back to Europe and play again, but he came home and said, 'You know what? I'm just going to retire.' We had no plan. That's when I started to live in Canada."

The sudden move proved a stroke of luck for his son, one that would coincide with his growing love for the Raptors. "I didn't really start paying attention to the NBA until I came back to Canada. Then I would watch *every* Raptors game. I loved DeMar DeRozan. It's amazing now to be in the league playing against DeMar. Every time I see him, I show him love. I tell him how much he meant to me."

Thanks to his father's connections to professional basketball—and some stints on the media side of the NBA—Barrett caught a glimpse of DeRozan before anyone knew the star he would become. "I met DeMar his rookie year," Barrett recalled. "Chris Bosh was still with the team and my dad and I were at the old practice facility in Scotiabank Arena. I was like, 'Dad, who's that?' He said, 'He's a rookie, DeMar DeRozan. You see how he's coming back in at night and working hard? Watch, that kid's gonna be good.'"

For the most part, Barrett followed DeRozan and the Raptors from his parents' home in Mississauga. But the experience in Scotiabank Arena also offered a true taste of the action—of what could be, if only Barrett's stars aligned. "One time my dad said, 'I'm going to take you to one game this year. Which game do you want to go to?' I'm a LeBron guy, so I said, obviously, Cleveland. I was fourteen or fifteen, right when LeBron went back to Cleveland. So I also got to see Tristan Thompson again—and Tristan is like my big brother—and I met Kyrie Irving and LeBron. The atmosphere was just amazing." There was only one problem. "I remember that every game I went to was close and the Raptors lost," Barrett recalls, laughing about it. "I felt like I was their bad-luck charm."

Being the son of a former pro had its benefits. There was the God-given skill, size, and talent, of course. But there was also the closeness to the NBA. For Barrett, in fact, it's not Steve Nash, two-time NBA MVP. Instead it's "My Uncle Steve." "He invited me to the playoffs one time when the Suns were playing the Lakers, so I got to meet Kobe. I was ten years old at the time. One time he played the Raptors when he had Shaq on his team. I got to catch up with him and meet Shaq after the game."

That proximity to the pros inspired Barrett, pushing him toward his own hoop dreams. "I had a lot of opportunities to meet players and I was around the NBA for sure. But I had my own life and I was trying to make it on my own." Those dreams were also something that his parents continued to support. "I saw my parents and how hard they worked. They went to work all day to come home, drop their stuff off, and take me to practice. I practiced all over the Greater Toronto Area and they would drive me everywhere. I remember being with my mom, sometimes on twelve- or fourteen-hour car rides down to the States for games. Just seeing the kind of investment that they made in me, I felt like I had to make it."

By the time he turned fifteen, however, he had also reached a ceiling in his development at St. Marcellinus Secondary School in Mississauga. The ever-ambitious Barrett knew he had to make good on his promise, doing the hard thing that his father had done again and again: moving countries. "I wanted to leave to go to the US to study and play. My parents didn't want me to go. I forced them. I literally said, 'I'm not getting better here in Canada.' At the time, basketball was different. Now you can go to the league from Canada. There's so much more opportunity. Back then, we all had to go to the States if we wanted to get noticed."

Barrett eventually ended up at Montverde Academy in Florida, a prep school known for its basketball program, though the experience was hardly all roses. "I hated every second of it," Barrett admits today. "It was a boarding school and I hated the rules." Only later did he come to understand how the school's rigorous schedule and demanding workload taught him the discipline needed as a college and NBA player. "They were teaching you tools for life."

Barrett excelled at Montverde, and even kept ties to the Canadian junior team, which he led to the country's first-ever men's youth championship at the FIBA U19 World Cup in Egypt in 2017.

For his leadership and play, the seventeen-year-old was named tournament MVP.

By the time he was considering college programs in 2018, Barrett was the number-one-overall recruit—not just from Canada, but also in the US, ahead of his future teammates at Duke: Cam Reddish, Zion Williamson, and Tre Jones. The team's coach, Mike Krzyzewski, had also proved a key mentor, encouraging Barrett's professional success and personal growth. Even still, after only a year in Durham, Barrett declared for the draft.

At the time, the Raptors were playing in the Finals. "My boys and I were in LA watching the games, going crazy, screaming, cheering. We took real pride in the Raptors. I went to Oracle to watch one of the games with my agent, when Danny Green went crazy." That was game three, when Green hit 6 of his 10 three-point attempts. "I wish I would've gone to Jurassic Park for one of those games in Toronto. If I knew back then, I would have been there, but I was a kid, just training in LA. I regret that."

Eventually he was picked third overall by the Knicks. It was just one more change, but one he was in part prepared for thanks to his time at Montverde and Duke. "The transition was always going to be hard," Barrett recalled. "I'm nineteen, but I have a bunch of thirty-year-olds on my team—old heads like Taj Gibson, Marcus Morris, and Wayne Ellington. I had no clue what was going on. I played at Duke, so playing in MSG wasn't a crazy adjustment for me, fan-wise. But getting used to the league was harder. You have eighty-two games. You have to go to the gym every single day. You're sometimes playing four games in a week. The amount of work that it takes to be ready for every single NBA game, it's way more than anything any high school or college player has done leading up to that."

Luckily, Barrett was ready for the challenge. "I've basically been on my own since fifteen, so I had to grow up a lot faster than most people." Barrett played consistent minutes almost exclusively as a starter during his time in New York. Performing at MSG was of course cool. But it was the games against the Raptors, and especially games back in Toronto, that got Barrett truly excited. Unfortunately for him, due to both injuries and the 2020 coronavirus pandemic, Barrett had few chances to play against the Raptors in his hometown. His first game at Scotiabank Arena, just a month into his rookie season, did not go entirely to plan. "I was way too excited," he recalled with a laugh. "I couldn't even focus on the game. I hadn't really played in Canada—maybe four games total from the time I was fifteen. I was loving it, just playing there where I grew up as a fan. Scotiabank is home for me. But I played terribly. I had sixteen points and shot five-for-seventeen. But I didn't care. It was so much fun. I was like, 'Man, I had sixteen points *in Toronto*. Everybody saw me do that!'"

With each matchup against the Raptors, Barrett felt more and more comfortable. By his fourth season, he was finally ready to perform at an All-Star level against his boyhood squad. "I had a crazy run," he recalls, still glowing with pride. "I had thirty, thirty-two, and thirty against them." Those would be three of his five highest-scoring games that season. One of those games also included a moment he still relishes today. The Raptors were at MSG for a game on Martin Luther King Jr. Day in January 2023. Toronto was leading New York 110–108 with only 6.6 seconds left and with his future teammate Scottie Barnes on the line. He missed his second free throw, which Barrett gobbled up, pushing the floor and driving all the way to the rim for a monster left-handed dunk over Barnes to tie the game. "I say it all the time, any chance that I can, but I punched it on Scottie," Barrett laughs. "He's such a great defender and he blocks so many shots, so to be able to dunk on him, I had to let him know."

His fifth season in New York would be his last. He suspected a trade was coming, but the details were hazy at best. "There had been rumblings of OG Anunoby getting traded to the Knicks, but they didn't know who for. I knew Immanuel Quickley and I were going to get traded. But I didn't know we were going to get traded together." When the news finally broke on December 29, 2023, Barrett was stunned. "First, I was conflicted. I'm like, *You guys are trading me and that hurts.* But then I'm like, *I'm going home.* I was so excited. It was a big blessing." The details of the trade finally emerged: Both Barrett and Quickley were headed to Toronto in exchange for Anunoby, Precious Achiuwa, and Malachi Flynn. "Quick asked, 'You going back home?' I said, 'Yeah, you coming with me?'" Quickley, too, was excited for the change of scenery. Then Barrett's phone started blowing up as word got out. "My boys saw the tweet. They're like, 'My guy's coming home! Let's go!'"

That homecoming started the next day. Barrett packed two suitcases and got on a flight to Toronto for his physical and first practice with the team. When he arrived, five Raptors jerseys were laid out on the hotel bed waiting for him. "It was surreal," Barrett recalled. "Just me being from Canada, and that red, white, and black. I'm used to wearing those colors for the national team. I felt at home."

He didn't have to wait long to put on those familiar colors. On January 1, just a day later, the Raptors were hosting Cleveland and reality struck. "When we ran out, just to look at the crowd, I thought, *I'm playing for the Raptors. This is the team I've cheered for as long as I can remember. And I'm here.*" The fans reciprocated. "I didn't know whether the crowd was going to accept me or not. They traded OG, who was a big staple for the Raptors for years, so I didn't know how I was going to be received. Then hearing the crowd, it was just a lot of love. It felt great."

Even still, for all the personal success and growing chemistry on court, that first year in Toronto was not without its challenges—some of which were life-changing, including the death of Barrett's younger brother, Nathan, another rising basketball star who had followed Barrett to Montverde Academy. "That was the worst time of my life," Barrett reflects today, still shaken by the loss. "I was playing the best basketball that I'd played since I'd been in the league. I was like, 'How does this make sense?' But the Raptors organization is exactly where I needed to be at the time. I got traded to Toronto and my brother had already returned to Toronto and checked into the hospital."

Barrett's entire family was blindsided by Nathan's sudden illness. "He just went to go get a checkup, to check a rash or something. He didn't even know he was that sick."

The team also stepped in to support one of their newest players, both during Nathan's illness and after he passed away on March 12, just a few months after Barrett had joined the team. "I told the Raptors organization what was going on early. I would sleep in the hospital, and sometimes, with the traffic, I was late to practice at the beginning, but they didn't fine me or scold me. Sometimes I had to be excused from my media responsibilities, because he would have an emergency, and I would leave right after the game. One time we were in Denver and were supposed to go to Detroit. Immediately the Raptors got me on a plane to Toronto to go see Nathan, before he passed. The whole team was at the funeral. My family and I are very close, but the Raptors, they really saved me. I enjoyed going to work every day. I was having so much fun with my teammates, and I was playing good basketball and trying to build connections with coaches. Everyone from top to bottom in the organization has been amazing, and I'll forever be grateful for how they held it down for me during that time."

During his stay in the hospital, Nathan, too, became a rock of support for his brother. "I still have all of our text messages and I specifically love the texts from him when he was in the hospital. He didn't act like he was sick. He was like, 'Yeah, man, I'm good. You have a good game, bro. I'm really proud of you. I can't wait to come watch the game in person.' He couldn't even speak sometimes, so he would send me pictures of him watching the game on his laptop. He never got to come to a game in person, but he definitely watched all of them before he passed."

Nathan is still a part of Barrett, quite literally, and quietly features in his routine before each game. "I got his initials, 'NTB Forever,' tattooed on my wrist. Right below his initials are my mom's and my dad's. So I have my family with me. Before every game, I do this little thing. I probably look so stupid doing it," he admits with a laugh. "I lock in, which I've been doing since high school, and I hit my leg three times. But now I'll kiss my wrist before every game. That kind of brings Nathan into the game with me. I definitely have him with me all the time."

Those family connections are still supporting him today as Barrett looks ahead to the Raptors' future. The next step is as clear as day: making the playoffs—and then maybe even winning another championship. "You have to think that way because that's the goal," he explained. "Think that way and talk about it all the time. With this city and having the whole country behind us, they deserve it. I look forward to getting the Raptors back to that championship pedigree."

ACKNOWLEDGMENTS

This book would not have been possible without many, many people, and above all the players, who sat down for hours upon hours of interviews, sometimes repeatedly, over many months during 2024, and who answered late-night and last-minute questions by text, phone, and email about their lives, their families, their careers, and their time with the Toronto Raptors. This book, quite literally, would not exist without them.

Behind the scenes, too, dozens of people made *We the Raptors* possible. Eric would like to thank in particular Annie Cho (Alumni Relations), Phil Summers (Senior Manager, Communications), and Jennifer Quinn (Vice President, Communications) of the Toronto Raptors. Their assistance in facilitating contacts and tracking down phone numbers for past and present players was instrumental from start to finish. Roven Yau, Jim LaBumbard (Washington Wizards Vice President, Basketball Communications & Outreach), and Alisha Smith (Client Relations Manager, BDA Sports Management) were also integral in the process of contacting and interviewing players.

Eric is also grateful for all his colleagues. Dan Toman (Director, Sports Products & Audio at Sportsnet) supported this book from the beginning. Mark Boffo, JR Manatad, and Austin Maki—all producers at Sportsnet 590 the FAN—shared contact lists, offered assistance in research, and helped to arrange interviews time and time again.

Finally, Eric's broadcast partners deserve honorable mention. Paul Jones, Jack Armstrong, and Matt Devlin were all invaluable as historians, storytellers, and mentors throughout this whole process. Special mention goes out to Alvin Williams, former Raptor and Eric's current colleague, who sat for multiple conversations with us and who went above and beyond to help coordinate other interviews with former players.

We both also want to thank the team that helped to pull *We the Raptors* together. Carolyn Forde and Evan Brown at Transatlantic Agency were integral in shaping our ideas for this book, both offering feedback and shepherding us through this entire process. Jim Gifford, our editor at Simon & Schuster, has been equally important. He was a pleasure to work with throughout and improved every sentence that we wrote.

Last but not least, we would like to thank our families for their support—and patience and understanding—especially in the final months of drafting, editing, and rewriting this book, when putting the final touches on the manuscript meant sometimes late nights, disrupted family vacations, and missed dinners and events. Again, without Shannon, Jackson, Huey, Charity, and Lola, this book doesn't get written. Thank you.